A Rediscovered Frontier

A Rediscovered Frontier

Land Use and Resource Issues in the New West

PHILIP L. JACKSON AND ROBERT KUHLKEN

ROWMAN & LITTLEFIELD PUBLISHERS, INC.
Lanham • Boulder • New York • Toronto • Oxford

ROWMAN & LITTLEFIELD PUBLISHERS, INC.
Published in the United States of America
by Rowman & Littlefield Publishers, Inc.
A wholly owned subsidary of The Rowman & Littlefield Publishing Group, Inc.
4501 Forbes Boulevard, Suite 200, Lanham, Maryland 20706
www.rowmanlittlefield.com

PO Box 317
Oxford
OX2 9RU, UK

British Library Cataloguing in Publication Information Available

Library of Congress Cataloging-in-Publication Data

Jackson, Philip L. (Philip Lloyd), 1946-
 A rediscovered frontier : land use and resource issues in the new West / Philip L. Jackson
and Robert Kuhlken.
  p. cm.
 Includes bibliographical references and index.
 ISBN 0-7425-2616-X (cloth : alk. paper) — ISBN 0-7425-2617-8 (pbk. : alk. paper)
 1. Land use—West (U.S.) 2. Land use, Rural—West (U.S.) 3. Cities and towns—West
(U.S.)—Growth. 4. Real estate development—West (U.S.) 5. Natural resources—West
(U.S.)—Management. 6. Land use—West (U.S.)—Planning. 7. Public lands—West
(U.S.)—Planning. I. Kuhlken, Robert, 1953- II. Title. HD209.J33 2005
 333.73'13'0978—dc22

2005013696

Printed in the United States of America

∞™ The paper used in this publication meets the minimum requirements of American
National Standard for Information Sciences—Permanence of Paper for Printed Library
Materials, ANSI/NISO Z39.48-1992.

Contents

Introduction

This book describes the changing geography of contemporary land use in the western United States. The American West on the whole is experiencing rapid population growth, but with wide variation and disparity in both the pace of development and the provision of infrastructure required to support different levels of land use intensity. The region has been rediscovered as a settlement frontier, which presents both opportunities and challenges to local government planning efforts and for state and federal land management policies. Accelerated development in certain favored areas creates a need to respond with innovative growth management programs, while much of the neglected hinterland searches for stability as former natural resource-based communities attempt a transition toward greater economic diversity. This situation has not only created disproportionate and often unrealistic expectations for the future, but has affected attitudinal biases toward land use as well.

Perhaps because the West offers such a wide variety of natural landscapes, contemporary occupancy and settlement patterns reflect much more than the pragmatic location and site attributes that were so important during the late nineteenth and early twentieth centuries. Technological advances in communications and transportation, combined with a continuing trend toward footloose economic development opportunities free from the constraints of urban support requirements, have given rise to landscape transformations that are truly revolutionary in their scope and significance. Furthermore, recent increases in expendable personal wealth and the rising demographics of retirement have resulted in amenity and lifestyle relocation choices that have had profound impacts on land use in even the most out-of-the-way places in many western states. These new communities and their inhabitants often harbor very different views toward land

and natural resources than their more rooted neighbors. Local governments and utility service providers are often unable to keep pace with the need to direct and/or support these new growth patterns. Land use planning agencies also may be politically and professionally incapable of dealing with these different types of development. And, while much of the rural West seeks to maintain a way of life based on mining, agriculture, forestry, or grazing, these traditional commodity procurement practices increasingly are coming under attack as harmful to the environment and unhealthy to society. Likewise, local economic dependence on surrounding federal lands has now taken a different direction as new public input to management plans demands that ecological concerns, recreational opportunities, and scenic resources take priority over timber, forage, or minerals.

Such conflicts and contrasting viewpoints are inevitable in a growth frontier, and these issues make land use planning in the western United States an uneven proposition. In the face of a modern-day land rush, some places with scenic amenities and desirable locational attributes have responded with open arms to accommodate the new influx with infrastructure expansion and permissive zoning. Other places have instituted emergency braking efforts using heavy-handed growth management strategies and development moratoria. Conversely, some areas as yet remain relatively undiscovered or have been dealt the fate of being unattractive locations within the new settlement regime. Consequently, they may suffer from extremely slow growth or decline, with associated threats to community health and welfare.

The dilemma of land and resource planning in the American West represents a balancing act between responding to rapidly changing social needs and aspirations on one hand, and the maintenance and respect for long-standing community ideals, lifeways, and cultural ecologies on the other. As geographers, we attempt to chart these transformations to the western landscape, to provide insight into evolving land use trends, and to portray a renewed vision concerning the realities of planning in what has been called the "New West." In this book we look at archetypal development patterns and survey a number of trends that seem to dominate recent land use transitions. We examine places where phenomenal and unexpected growth has occurred and provide examples of areas that should have seen it coming. Based on such a synthesis we become better positioned to make a number of predictions regarding areas in the western states that seem ripe for the picking by developers and other agents of change. We also take note of the various responses to development pressure undertaken by local governments and land use planning agencies. We highlight numerous cases that serve as examples of what might be done, and perhaps what not to do. Change is inevitable, of course, but the rapidity of rural land use change in the American West has caught many people off guard. It is our hope that this book will communicate a regional perspective of development issues for professionals involved in managing land use and natural resources, as well as a timely synopsis for all people interested in the future of western landscapes and rural communities.

The need for such a book becomes evident when taking stock of existing titles now available. While several scholars have looked at the rapid growth of western cities (Abbott 1993; Nash 1991), others take note of land use change and development along urban edges with the usual diatribes against sprawl. There is certainly no shortage of books tackling the topic of public land management in the West, but very few look at private land planning and local growth management. For those western communities dependent on public land resources, economic development specialists point to amenity values as being fully capable of taking over when natural resource–based economies have completed their ultimate bust cycle (Power 1996; Howe, McMahon, and Propst 1997). Rural sociologists have also investigated human–environment relations from the social side of that equation, and several have conducted research in this arena for more than a decade (Field and Burch 1988). Increasing numbers of historians are likewise paying closer attention to the process of rural change in the West, and have been able to link many of these changes to inherent functions of the larger economic system (Limerick 1988; W. Robbins 1994; White 1995; Rothman 1998; Goble and Hirt 1999).

Derived from academic traditions of landscape architecture and ecological design theory, the newly formulated field of "landscape ecology" has tried to provide a catalyst for any number of prescriptive volumes that seek to encourage holistic frameworks for action, but that too often seem unaware of the political and geographic limitations of local government agencies (Van Der Ryn and Cowan 1995; Nassauer 1997; Lyle 1999; Bissonette and Storch 2002). The so-called sustainable communities movement has also spawned numerous manuals and edited volumes (Audirac 1997; Corbett and Corbett 1999). In addition, "conservation planning" offers some direction for professionals to consider when fashioning tools that shape land development in an environmentally friendly fashion (Groves 2003). Yet save for a scattering of older texts (Lassey 1977; Getzels and Thurow 1979), little attention has been given to the specific needs and everyday problems of local planning at the scale of the county or small town, especially in the western states. In recent years, a few publications have begun to point out the actual landscape changes taking place in the rural West (Marston 1989; Ringholz and Muscolino 1996; Decker 1998), and we will be able to merge that kind of awareness with practical ideas of what might be done by local communities to manage such change.

This book is intended for the general interest audience of people who care about western environments or care to know what is happening to them. It is equally intended for use as a university-level text or reader for courses in planning, geography, landscape studies, and landscape ecology, or in American studies, anthropology, and sociology. In that respect, it is intended to serve equally well as a primary or supplementary text. Finally, and perhaps most importantly, this book serves as a sourcebook of scenarios, ideas, and examples for professionals in the field of land use planning and environmental management. The capability for dealing with change in the New West does not depend on political integration that may never happen but is already in the hands of numerous local governments at the county and municipal level. Decisions that are now being made on a daily basis likewise cannot wait for the implementation of "ecosystem-based models of integrated sustainable development." This book addresses the dynamic realities of land use in the West today: social, economic, political, and above all, geographical. As such, it should prove to be an extremely useful primer for students, planning professionals, and all who wish to understand contemporary transformations in the western landscape.

This book offers a geographer's view of contemporary changes and developments—in the context of locational attributes and newly appreciated amenities that have stimulated a reappraisal of the livability of rural and small-town settings in the eleven western states. In chapter 1 we review the regional concept—what is meant by the term "New West"— and portray its salient features. Chapter 2 outlines changing development characteristics and describes prototypical land use patterns that may now be found throughout the region. Chapter 3, by far the book's longest and most detailed, examines the spatial circumstances of rural and small-town growth patterns, by means of a regional land use digest that sweeps across the entire West, and provides examples of the kinds of development that could potentially occur elsewhere in areas having similar geographic situations.

Our discussion of population growth and development issues, along with resultant landscape impacts and the need to anticipate change, leads us in chapter 4 to review the regional status of institutional land use planning. Chapter 5 then takes a closer look at Oregon's highly regarded statewide planning approach to managing growth and reviews the recent electoral challenges to that program. We conclude that there is no common, regionwide approach to land use planning in the West, but that there exist common attributes and features that characterize efforts to shape community. Thus, in the final chapter, these features are distilled to describe a forward-looking, rational model that focuses on local control and management of an information-driven, cooperative approach to comprehensive planning.

This project has developed from our concern that citizens, representatives of local governments, and university and college students interested in land use and resource issues should be aware of the contemporary, rapidly occurring changes in land use across the West. Our intent is to encourage informed and active citizen interest and civic engagement in the affairs of local government, and to continue to develop cooperative processes that respond to the rights and aspirations of landowners, guided by the broader goals and safeguards of the community interest.

REFERENCES

Abbot, Carl. *The Metropolitan Frontier: Cities in the Modern American West.* Tucson: University of Arizona Press, 1993.

Abbott, Carl, Deborah Howe, and Sy Adler, eds. *Planning the Oregon Way: A Twenty Year Evaluation.* Corvallis: Oregon State University Press, 1994.

Athearn, Robert. *The Mythic West in Twentieth-Century America.* Lawrence: University Press of Kansas, 1986.

Audirac, Ivonne, ed. *Rural Sustainable Development in America.* New York: John Wiley & Sons, 1997.

Baden, John A., and Donald Snow, eds. *The Next West: Public Lands, Community, and Economy in the American West.* Washington, D.C.: Island Press, 1997.

Beyers, W. B., and P. B. Nelson. Contemporary Development Forces in the Nonmetropolitan West: New Insights from Rapidly Growing Communities. *Journal of Rural Studies* 16 (2000):459–474.

Bissonette, John A., and Ilse Storch. *Landscape Ecology and Resource Management: Linking Theory with Practice.* Washington, D.C.: Island Press, 2002.

Cawley, R. McGreggor. *Federal Land, Western Anger: The Sagebrush Rebellion and Environmental Politics.* Lawrence: University Press of Kansas, 1993.

Cloke, Paul J., and Chris C. Park. *Rural Resource Management.* New York: St. Martin's Press, 1985.

Comer, Krista. *Landscapes of the New West: Gender and Geography in Contemporary Women's Writing.* Chapel Hill: University of North Carolina Press, 1999.

Corbett, Michael, and Judy Corbett. *Designing Sustainable Communities: Learning from Village Homes.* Washington, D.C.: Island Press, 1999.

Decker, Peter. *Old Fences, New Neighbors.* Tucson: University of Arizona Press, 1998.

Diamond, Henry L., and Patrick F. Noonan. *Land Use in America.* Washington, D.C.: Island Press, 1996.

Echeverria, John, and Raymond Booth Eby, eds. *Let the People Judge: Wise Use and the Private Property Rights Movement.* Washington, D.C.: Island Press, 1995.

Einsweiler, Robert, and Deborah Howe. Managing "the Land Between": A Rural Development Paradigm. In *Planning the Oregon Way: A Twenty Year Evaluation,* edited by Carl Abbott, Deborah Howe, and Sy Adler, pp. 245–273. Corvallis: Oregon State University Press, 1994.

Fabry, Judith. Agricultural Science and Technology in the West. In *The Rural West since World War II,* edited by R. Hurt, pp. 169–189. Lawrence: University Press of Kansas, 1998.

Field, Donald R., and William R. Burch Jr. *Rural Sociology and the Environment.* New York: Greenwood Press, 1988.

Friedberger, Mark. Cattle Raising and Dairying in the Western States. In *The Rural West since World War II,* edited by R. Hurt, pp. 190–212. Lawrence: University Press of Kansas, 1998.

Getzels, Judith, and Charles Thurow, eds. *Rural and Small Town Planning.* Chicago: American Planning Association, 1979.

Goble, Dale D., and Paul W. Hirt, eds. *Northwest Lands, Northwest Peoples: Readings in Environmental History.* Seattle: University of Washington Press, 1999.

Golany, Gideon. *Desert Planning: International Lessons.* London: Architectural Press, 1982.

Gressley, Gene M., ed. *Old West/New West.* Norman: University of Oklahoma Press, 1997.

Groves, Craig R. *Drafting a Conservation Blueprint: A Practitioner's Guide to Planning for Biodiversity.* Washington, D.C.: Island Press, 2003.

Hart, John Fraser. *The Rural Landscape.* Baltimore, Md.: Johns Hopkins University Press, 1998.

Herbers, John. *The New Heartland: America's Flight from the Suburbs and How It Is Changing Our Future.* New York: Times Books, 1978.

Hess, Karl Jr. *Visions upon the Land: Man and Nature on the Western Range.* Washington, D.C.: Island Press, 1992.

Hess, Karl Jr., and John A. Baden, eds. *Writers on the Range: Western Writers Exploring the Changing Face of the American West.* Boulder: University Press of Colorado, 1998.

Hibbard, Michael. Land Use Planning and the Future of Oregon's Timber Towns. In *Planning the Oregon Way: A Twenty Year Evaluation,* edited by Carl Abbott, Deborah Howe, and Sy Adler, pp. 189–201. Corvallis: Oregon State University Press, 1994.

Holthaus, Gary et al., eds. *A Society to Match the Scenery: Personal Visions of the Future of the American West.* Boulder: University Press of Colorado, 1991.

Howe, Jim, Ed McMahon, and Luther Propst. *Balancing Nature and Commerce in Gateway Communities.* Washington, D.C.: Island Press, 1997.

Hurt, R. Douglas, ed. *The Rural West since World War II.* Lawrence: University Press of Kansas, 1998.

Ilbery, Brian, ed. *The Geography of Rural Change.* Harlow, U.K.: Longman, 1998.

Jacobs, Harvey, ed. *Who Owns America?: Social Conflict over Property Rights.* Madison: University of Wisconsin Press, 1998.

Jobes, Patrick C. *Moving Nearer to Heaven: The Illusions and Disillusions of Migrants to Scenic Rural Places.* Westport, Conn.: Praeger, 2000.

Kelly, Eric, and Barbara Becker. *Community Planning: An Introduction to the Comprehensive Plan.* Washington, D.C.: Island Press, 2000.

Kittredge, William. *Who Owns the West?* San Francisco: Mercury House, 1996.

Knapp, Gerrit, and Arthur Nelson. *The Regulated Landscape: Lessons on State Land Use Planning from Oregon.* Cambridge: Lincoln Institute of Land Policy, 1992.

Lassey, William R. *Planning in Rural Environments.* New York: McGraw-Hill, 1977.

Lewis, Pierce. The Urban Invasion of Rural America: The Emergence of the Galactic City. In *The American Countryside: Rural People and Places,* edited by Emery Castle, pp. 39–62. Lawrence: University Press of Kansas, 1995.

Limerick, Patricia Nelson. *The Legacy of Conquest: The Unbroken Past of the American West.* New York: W.W. Norton & Company, 1988.

Logan, Michael. *Fighting Sprawl and City Hall: Resistance to Urban Growth in the Southwest.* Tucson: University of Arizona Press, 1995.

Lyle, John Tillman. *Design for Human Ecosystems: Landscape, Land Use, and Natural Resources.* Washington, D.C.: Island Press, 1999.

Marston, Ed, ed. *Reopening the Western Frontier.* Washington, D.C.: Island Press, 1989.

Mazmanian, Daniel, and Daniel Kraft. *Toward Sustainable Communities: Transitions and Transformations in Environmental Policy.* Cambridge: MIT Press, 1999.

Nash, Gerald. *Creating the West: Historical Interpretations, 1890–1990.* Albuquerque: University of New Mexico Press, 1991.

Nash, Gerald D., and Richard W. Etulain, eds. *Researching Western History: Topics in the Twentieth Century.* Albuquerque: University of New Mexico Press, 1997.

Nassauer, Joan Iverson. *Placing Nature: Culture and Landscape Ecology.* Washington, D.C.: Island Press, 1997.

Nelson, Paula. Rural Life and Social Change in the Modern West. In *The Rural West since World War II,* edited by R. Hurt, pp. 38–57. Lawrence: University Press of Kansas, 1998.

Olson, Richard K., and Thomas A. Lyson, eds. *Under the Blade: The Conversion of Agricultural Landscapes.* Boulder, Colo.: Westview Press, 1999.

Pease, James. Oregon Rural Land Use: Policy and Practices. In *Planning the Oregon Way: A Twenty Year Evaluation,* edited by Carl Abbott, Deborah Howe, and Sy Adler, pp. 163–188. Corvallis: Oregon State University Press, 1994.

Power, Thomas Michael. *Lost Landscapes and Failed Economies: The Search for a Value of Place.* Washington, D.C.: Island Press, 1996.

Raphael, Ray. *Edges: Human Ecology of the Backcountry.* Lincoln: University of Nebraska Press, 1973.

Rasker, Ray. *A New Home on the Range: Economic Realities in the Columbia River Basin.* Washington, D.C.: The Wilderness Society, 1995.

Richardson, Jean. *Partnerships in Communities: Reweaving the Fabric of Rural America.* Washington, D.C.: Island Press, 1999.

Riebsame, William, ed. *Atlas of the New West: Portrait of a Changing Region.* New York: W.W. Norton & Company, 1997.

Riebsame, William. Subdividing the Rockies: Ranchland Conversion in the New West. In *Under the Blade: The Conversion of Agricultural Landscapes,* edited by R. K. Olson and T. A. Lyson, pp. 398–409. Boulder, Colo.: Westview Press, 1999.

Ringholz, Raye, and K. C. Muscolino. *Little Town Blues: Voices from the Changing West.* Salt Lake City, Utah: Peregrine Smith Books, 1992.

———. *Paradise Paved: The Challenge of Growth in the New West.* Salt Lake City: University of Utah Press, 1996.

Robbins, Jim. *Last Refuge: The Environmental Showdown in Yellowstone and the American West.* New York: William Morrow and Co., 1993.

Robbins, William G. *Colony and Empire: The Capitalist Transformation of the American West.* Lawrence: University Press of Kansas, 1994.

Robinson, Guy M. *Conflict and Change in the Countryside: Rural Society, Economy and Planning in the Developed World.* London: Belhaven Press, 1990.

Rohse, Mitch. *Land-use Planning in Oregon.* Corvallis: Oregon State University Press, 1987.

Rothman, Hal, ed. *Reopening the American West.* Tucson: University of Arizona Press, 1998.

Rudzitis, Gundars. *Wilderness and the Changing American West.* New York: John Wiley & Sons, 1996.

Salamon, Sonya. Cultural Dimensions of Land Tenure in the United States. In *Who Owns America?: Social Conflict over Property Rights,* edited by Harvey Jacobs, pp. 159–181. Madison: University of Wisconsin Press, 1998.

Sherow, James. Environmentalism and Agriculture in the American West. In *The Rural West since World War II,* edited by R. Hurt, pp. 58–75. Lawrence: University Press of Kansas, 1998.

Starrs, Paul. Conflict and Change on the Landscapes of the Arid American West. In *The American Countryside: Rural People and Places,* edited by Emery Castle, pp. 271–285. Lawrence: University Press of Kansas, 1995.

Stroud, Hubert. *The Promise of Paradise: Recreational and Retirement Communities in the United States since 1950.* Baltimore: Johns Hopkins University Press, 1995.

Tricart, Jean, and Conrad KiewietdeJonge. *Ecogeography and Rural Management: A Contribution to the International Geosphere-Biosphere Programme.* New York: John Wiley & Sons, 1992.

Van Der Ryn, Sim, and Stuart Cowan. *Ecological Design.* Washington, D.C.: Island Press, 1995.

White, Richard. *Land Use, Environment, and Social Change: The Shaping of Island County, Washington.* Seattle: University of Washington Press, 1980.

———. *The Organic Machine.* New York: Hill and Wang, 1995.

Wilkinson, Charles F. *The American West: A Narrative Bibliography and a Study in Regionalism.* Boulder: University Press of Colorado, 1989.

———. *Crossing the Next Meridian: Land, Water, and the Future of the West.* Washington, D.C.: Island Press, 1992.

———. *The Eagle Bird: Mapping a New West.* New York: Vintage Books, 1993.

Wunder, John, ed. *Working the Range: Essays on the History of Western Land Management and the Environment.* Westport, Conn.: Greenwood Press, 1985.

1

Land Use and Resource Issues in the New West

The New West is a geographic term that delineates a dynamic region undergoing rapid transformation. This catchy phrase has been used before, in any number of contexts, and our use of the conceptual idiom is in many ways merely its latest iteration (Riebsame, Gosnell, and Theobald 1997; Limerick 2000). In the rural areas of the West, primary economic activity historically formed the basis of a peripheral region's dependent relationship with core areas of urban wealth and power. Once considered a vast and rugged realm of natural resources ripe for the taking, public perception now views the place much differently. This transition has been anything but subtle. Mining, logging, farming, and ranching, though still quite active in many places, have for the most part become anachronistic activities that have largely given way to a new amenity-driven landscape. In the scheme of New West development, outdoor recreational pursuits and tourism have replaced the more traditional extractive enterprises. Moreover, changing economic and technological conditions favoring footloose entrepreneurism combined with the initial wave of baby boom retirements have now targeted the outback of the western United States and declared it a desirable place to live. Sometimes it seems as if the more remote the location the better. Where resource appraisals once focused on strictly utilitarian goals of converting raw materials into marketable commodities, we now witness a commodification of scenery and a selling of "the view." And these days, it is no longer enough simply to visit the scenic vistas of the West. People wish to move here, or at least own a piece of it. Consequently, we are in the midst of a rediscovery of the rural West as a settlement frontier, following the predictable dictates of a different set of geographic attributes that have once again attracted people to the land.

1

Contemporary changes in settlement patterns, cultural attitudes, economic status, and land and resource use in the less populated regions of the western United States are everywhere apparent. In the popular imagination it continues to be perceived as a region unlike any other. Legacies derived from past boosterism have created images of the pioneer in a virgin land that are not easily erased, and public perception of the region as a "land of promise" lingers still (H. Smith 1950; Billington 1981). The mythic West has always been endowed with a rich diversity of majestic, rugged landscapes, sparsely populated by individuals and families who shared a common interest in deriving livelihood and economic opportunity from the natural resources of the land. Here, living close to nature was strictly for the purpose of economic survival. Although such a traditional resource economy remains an enduring feature of many parts of the region, today we are able to chart the expansion of a new development frontier where the landscape is viewed more as a place to live rather than a place to make a living.

The postmodern rural West at the beginning of the twenty-first century evinces rapid population growth, speculative real estate markets, and a frenzied rush to develop a facsimile of suburban America with little regard for the region's unique natural, historical, and cultural values. This perspective is superbly described both textually and cartographically in the *Atlas of the New West* (Riebsame et al. 1997, 12), which examines:

> a region's transformation into something resembling the rest of the country: a land-scape of shopping malls, cookie-cutter subdivisions, ranchette estates and golf courses—an archetypal case of an American region yanked from its historical and myth-based sense of place into hyper-development and plugged-in modernity . . . conventional American society in an unconventional place.

THE NEW WEST: A REDISCOVERY OF RURAL AMERICA

Land use and resource utilization are concepts that involve people, time, and place. The New West can never be the same place as the Old West, despite mythic trappings of a former material culture that persist as currently lucrative style trends (Flood 1992; Ewald 2000). Historical changes in society, economy, institutions, and technology have dramatically altered both perception and realization of land and resource use. Shifting locational attributes not only promote new affinities for the land, but embrace enhanced geographic and economic accessibility as well. Collective perceptions favoring rural geographies have changed, and transportation improvements and technological advances in telecommunications now enable settlement in areas previously considered too remote. The rural West has become reachable, and in general terms, more livable, enticing those who, for instance, might wish to establish a comfortable "homestead" overlooking a TPC-class golf course with a snow-capped mountain range in the background.

Settlement and stability in the New West results from 150 years' accumulation of infrastructural investment by local, state, and federal government for the purpose of enhancing comparative advantages of rural locations. Here was a territory insulated by mountain barriers and great distances between major population centers, characterized by extreme seasonal climates and drought, and plagued by recurring cycles of economic boom and bust tied to fluctuating markets for natural resource products (Wyckoff and Dilsaver 1995). Limitations imposed by aridity and isolation resulted in settlement of the region as a nodal network of urban oases, a pattern that largely continues to this day (Nash 1973; Reps 1981; Abbott 1995). The rural West historically has been a fluctuating frontier zone, often with different areas at different times manifesting rapid population expansion followed by equally rapid decline. The story of human occupation and use of this region is one of great drama and poignancy and involves an ever more closely entwined political ecology that goes well beyond simple notions of conquest (Worster 1992; Nugent 1999). Despite popular misconceptions that the frontier closed a long time ago, the history of settlement in the West is an unbroken process that continues to this day (Limerick 1987).

The factors of distance and isolation largely have been overcome by national and international access via air, water, rail, and highway transportation systems and by electronic communications. The daunting climates have been technologically conditioned, and a significant number of seasonal residents with financial means are able to simply avoid the extremes of heat or cold by moving to their other seasonal home. Drought has not been overcome, but massive surface water storage reservoirs and distribution systems support arid land agriculture and domestic uses alike. In many locations deep aquifer groundwater increasingly supports new land development. Where surface water supplies are already fully appropriated or simply not available, crop irrigation allocations along with residential, commercial, and industrial development have come to depend on groundwater and the electric power required to pump it (Wilkinson 1992). The extraction of local minerals, the harvest of timber and croplands, and the grazing of range lands remain significant and observable economic endeavors, but today, the regional economy is greatly enhanced by a stronger, more stable financial base tied to national and international trade, to value-added agricultural processing, and most important, to new residents and businesses with external sources of income (Jackson and Kimerling 2003).

This postmodern settlement activity differs significantly from the land use and resource development aspirations and lifestyle concepts of earlier eras. Most notably, active migration into the New West is no longer dependent on traditional agriculture or resource extraction activities. The region's scenic landscapes, outdoor recreation opportunities, and the warm winter season climates of the desert Southwest are the contemporary factors that drive up demand for residential property and the concurrent expansion of commercial and service-sector land uses. These new arrivals are generally more affluent and financially capable of supporting the local expansion of commercial, educational, health, and financial services more often found in urban settings. The overall result is a housing boom, a dramatic increase in economic activity, and a consequent demand for greater development of land and water resources. Economic reverberations include land purchases, service improvements, residential and commercial construction, and heightened entrepreneurial opportunities—unavoidably altering the character of small communities and the use of adjacent rural lands as the often frantic build-out continues.

The newest land rush to the West has been given free rein. The question becomes: Can this land rush be rationally managed by people who have come to live in the New West—those who aspire to maintain livable communities, and those who cherish the region's historical and cultural heritage, and who enjoy the land's unique natural qualities? Can it be possible to reap the benefits of economic growth and at the same time conserve farm, forest, range, and other resource lands for their natural intrinsic values? Should rural communities anticipate the land use effects of growth or simply react to their consequences?

Available land, its location, the uses to which it may be put, and the character of the local decision-making process are fundamental considerations in the new land rush (Platt 2004). Real estate values across the West have increased with rising demand, and developable land in select geographic locations has attained unprecedented market value. Landowners seeking to maximize the value of their holdings and enhance their development options understandably have strong interests in protecting personal property rights. They have every right to expect that local institutional land planning procedures, decision processes, regulations, and controls will conform to state laws, and that they are reasonable, fair, and equitably applied. The community interest in land use, as interpreted by representative local government, has an equally important obligation to seek broad consensus on land use and future development patterns as these will invariably affect aspects of public safety, efficiency, environmental quality, and livability. Rapid growth and the financial windfalls it brings about inevitably result in legal, institutional, economic, and social disagreements between personal property rights advocates and those who support community-wide land use regulation and decision making. The regulation of private property to protect and conserve important timber, crop, and range resource lands, watersheds, or unique scenic features necessarily diminishes the potential economic value of some parcels while enhancing the values of others.

Government institutions and local land use planning and management programs are evolving across the region to better address these contentious issues by proposing legally responsible, factually based, rational approaches to community development. During the 1970s and 1980s, state and federal planning and management programs proposed to deal comprehensively with land and resource issues on a regional scale. The geographic scale, organizational structures, and the scope of the issues proved to be important contributions to resource planning. Breaking with tradition, local governments have assumed (perhaps reassumed), an influential role in regional issues by establishing their own regional associations for collaborative resource management, forming public–private partnerships and designing strategies for negotiated consensus building (Platt 2004). The role of representative local government institutions for promoting orderly growth and resolving important community land use disputes should prove equally as valuable in the New West as it did in the Old West.

PATTERNS OF GROWTH AND DECLINE IN THE NEW WEST

Land and resource development the New West is spatially uneven, characterized by rapid growth in some areas and decline in others. Historically, the high mountains, vast intermountain basins, and arid regions of the West have been the home of relatively few people. A scattering of small towns developed in response to resource utilization needs. Overwhelmingly, larger towns and cities, and eventually metropolitan centers, came to dominate the population distribution pattern. It is therefore remarkable that remote, out-of-the-way places that stagnated for decades have suddenly become desirable. While the pattern of growth in the West continues to be characteristically urban, new development corridors are emerging, and small towns in amenity-rich environments are expanding. Preferred rural locations include small towns in close proximity to existing seasonal resort communities, distinctive coastal villages, destination ski and golf resorts, and towns that feature an Old West heritage. These places are viewed as prime for commercial and residential redevelopment, the construction of additional large-lot subdivisions, and the marketing of high value small acreage residential parcels. New stand-alone destination resorts and seasonal condominium complexes continue to emerge near well-known gateway communities. In the most desirable locations, the supply of private land may be limited by federal property boundaries, but one of the distinct advantages of buying even a small parcel of land in the New West is the access it provides to vast nearby tracts of land (and water) that you don't have to own to enjoy.

The New West retains the bulk of the nation's public lands and many of America's natural landscape treasures. National parks, monuments, forests, recreation lands, and wilderness areas represent more than 45% of the land area of the region. The federal government owns 86% of Nevada, 66% of Utah, 63% of Idaho, and 52% of Oregon, and more than 25% of the other Western states (Bureau of Land Management [BLM] 2002; Natural Resources Conservation Service [NRCS]

2000). The natural allure of majestic snow-covered mountain ranges, red sandstone cliffs, verdant timbered valleys, and wild rivers, mostly managed by the federal government in the public interest, has created an unprecedented demand to develop the limited amount of private land in the immediate vicinity of scenic and recreation lands.

Because of significant geographic distances from major urban populations, these public lands were once considered remote and isolated. Formerly used mostly by local livestock grazers, and a relative few sportsmen and outdoor recreation enthusiasts, the West's public lands are now much more accessible via the interstate highway system and an extensive network of upgraded federal, state, and county highways. National brand accommodations are available at convenient locations in nearly every small town along the way to major public land destinations. Today the public lands, and especially the "Crown Jewel" national parks, attract thousands, even millions of tourists and recreational visitors each year. Some of the visitors are so enchanted with the scenic beauty, wide open spaces, clean air, and low-stress environments of nearby communities that they want to *move* there either as permanent or part-time residents. Greater personal wealth has allowed more people than ever before to realize their dreams of living within minutes, not days, of the West's national scenic treasures.

What happens to small community character when a growing portion of seasonal visitors decide to stay? What happens to the timber, range, and farmland when new golf courses and associated housing subdivisions are developed to accommodate the new residents? Once the water transfers are made and redistributed and farmland is partitioned into high-value lots, is it even conceivable that these resources could ever again be reconsolidated for intrinsic resource uses?

Local initiatives are presently under way across the West to develop cooperative planning and management oversight for the development of private and public lands. Traditional organizations such as local Soil and Water Conservation Districts and other farm and ranch organizations have been joined by newly organized regional land use associations formed from participating local governments. Their purpose is to develop credible, citizen-backed mandates for local governments to form agreements for the purpose of establishing priorities, policies, and regulations with which to review large-scale land use and resource development proposals. Individual property owners are assured of the right to take advantage of reasonable use and development opportunities, and local citizens have the right to review potential impacts of proposed projects (McKinney and Harmon 2004).

It has been said that in a dynamic society land use change is inevitable. The results of change may be desirable, undesirable, and even degrading or damaging to the long-term sustainability of land and water resources. The changes may also result in safety or health hazards, reduction in property values, or excessive costs of community services. Debate among individuals and groups about the impacts of land use change most often involves perceptions and value judgments, but some of these changes may result in irreversible changes to the physical natural environment or worse, direct health and safety hazards (Lounsbury, Sommers, and Fernald 1981). In such cases, it is only reasonable and socially responsible to evaluate the potential impacts, to consider the consequences of land and resource use, and where deemed necessary by factual information and community support, institute practical public regulation and land use controls through community planning.

Unanticipated rapid growth, which results in dramatic rural land use conversion, presents the greatest challenge to maintaining community character. The nature and type of land use controls and planning structures in place may allow for growth to be reasonably and rationally accommodated, and in some cases restricted, by locally important social, economic, and environmental concerns. Without land use planning, problems are likely to escalate with the sheer number and wider distribution of recently arrived migrants to the area. These problems can be exacerbated by differences in values, attitudes, and perceptions of the new inhabitants, and with new land developments unsuited to the natural characteristics of the landscape.

A TRANSITION FROM THE OLD WEST TO THE NEW WEST

The basic land use patterns of the American West were established by the late nineteenth and early twentieth centuries. Once indigenous peoples were forcibly removed from their traditional territories and placed on reservations, the region was deemed open to Euro-American occupation. To facilitate rapid disposal of the public domain, federal laws promoted settlement by granting fee simple title to lands after a claimant "proved up" by living on the site for five years. Official homestead acreages were quickly increased as the expanding frontier encountered conditions of greater aridity, from 40 acres, to 160 acres, on up to 320 acres in the desert regions. Pioneering farmers sought out water sources, identified the best agricultural soils, and installed cooperative irrigation schemes where necessary to enhance crop productivity on drylands. The federal government later initiated large-scale irrigation projects developed and managed by the Bureau of Reclamation.

But farming was not the only imprint on the land. Prospectors located ore deposits, and large corporations followed to fully exploit mineral resources. Towns associated with mining flourished as long as the lode held. Eventually, many of these isolated settlements in the mountains would revive with recreation activities, especially the development of the ski industry (Rothman 1998). In the vast expanses of the West that nobody else wanted, cattlemen built fortunes by freely grazing unclaimed rangelands still in public ownership. And gyppo loggers and corporate interest alike harvested timber and other wood products from the great western forests. Railroad companies capitalized on a lucrative loophole utilizing federal land grants to help defray line construction costs, by claiming and attempting to sell every other section of land for twelve miles on either side of their chosen route. Intervening public lands have in many locations come under the control of federal land management agencies such as the BLM or Forest Service, but the checkerboard pattern of public and private ownership is still in place, and it effectively hinders proper stewardship.

Railroads outlined the initial routes of commerce, but by the late twentieth century, a federally funded interstate highway system along with a network of state and local highways established highly efficient surface access. Air transport became a standard mode of conveyance not only to and from large urban hubs, but likewise for medium-sized cities and recreation destinations across the West. Transmission grids distributed power from the hydroelectric dams in the Pacific Northwest and the Colorado River projects to urban and rural America alike. Pipelines transferred natural gas and petroleum products, and industry, manufacturing, and related employment flourished in the cities that grew at the nexus of commercial, agricultural, and raw materials flows.

In the traditional Old West, rural and urban were distinct geographic terms, representing a functional dichotomy that was recognized and well understood. Recently, however, specialized urban land use categories have become manifest in many of the small communities and rural lands of the West. This has blurred the distinction between what is rural and what is considered urban. Accelerated technological developments, demographic and social changes, migration and relocation, greater accumulation and liquidity of personal wealth, and changes in personal values and attitudes have materially altered the patterns of land use across the rural western United States, thereby helping to establish a new geography for the region (Kotkin 2000).

In the New West of the early twenty-first century, entrepreneurs have recognized the importance of "place" not only as a land development attribute but as a marketing tool as well. Place names and their association with the qualities and character of the West have assumed marketing value for consumer products, home sites, and destination resorts. Recreational products produced in Bend or Hood River, Oregon; Hurricane, Utah; Cody, Wyoming; and Big Timber, Montana, carry an unspoken seal of approval—made by outdoors people for outdoors people. Developers of destination resorts and high-value residential subdivisions, not to mention makers of sport utility vehicles, choose to bank their investments on popularly known place names like Sedona or Scottsdale, Taos or Santa Fe, Durango or Aspen. In each case, real estate speculators have made geographically influenced financial decisions to convert formerly rural lands to urban uses based on legendary attraction, the romantic or the rugged image of the landscapes of western America. Never mind that the dream of isolation and rugged living is often lost in the reality of high-density condominium villages, "trophy" housing subdivisions, manicured golf fairways, restaurants featuring international cuisine, and the myriad of associated services that are required to meet the needs of urban clients.

Overcoming geographic distances and rural isolation has been one of the greatest challenges in the settlement of the region. Historically, remoteness from national markets and major population centers was a limiting factor to the growth of population and intensive land development in the rural West. Technological and engineering advances in electronic communications and in air and surface transportation have significantly contributed to reducing isolation and improving accessibility. The routes of the interstate highway system channel both people and commerce and have contributed significantly to patterns of new development. Most readily observable are the localized linear patterns of residential and commercial real estate development that connect nearby communities to the highway interchanges. Travel-related services, shopping malls, regional warehousing, and storage and distribution centers readily obtain access to the high-speed routes and high–traffic volume locations advantageous to their businesses. Regional accessibility is a paramount locational factor for high–traffic volume enterprises such as manufacturer's outlet malls, automobile dealerships, and national big box retailers such as Costco and Wal-Mart super centers. True to the old locational advantages inherent in clustering, the success of one enterprise attracts another, often leading to new localized corridors of development. Enhanced locational advantage along the routes of the interstate highways is certainly a significant geographic factor that has contributed to the development of growth corridors. But improvements to secondary federal and state highways and the upgrading of regional airports have likewise greatly enhanced access to some of the West's high-quality amenity areas.

Decisions made in the private land sector determine the patterns of land use change, but ever greater societal concern over loss of prime crop land, residential encroachment into natural landscapes and wildlife habitat, the allocation and consumption of water supplies, and waste disposal issues have prompted increasingly bitter and litigious land use conflicts in small towns and rural communities. While private land use and ownership rights in the West have a strong constituency, a new and growing trend of public planning, regulation, and control over local private land use and land management practices is presently underway.

There is no national land use planning model to guide local land management decisions, and there are no standardized state requirements. Although federal laws related to environmental and housing issues must be followed to receive federal capital improvement grants, no federal land planners oversee local private development projects. State governments have traditionally delegated planning, zoning, and community development authority to local governments—a democratic tradition based on the principle of local self-determination.

Small communities and rural county governments are at a distinct land use management disadvantage, however, when beset by rapid population growth, increasingly complex citizen lifestyles, the views and demands of special interest groups, and the financial and legal pressures associated with large-scale development proposals. Political and legal issues often force local governments to make land use decisions based on current economic demands and short-term population growth forecasts without adequate information, or suitable comprehensive long-range plans in place. The alternative consequences may be unanticipated changes in local community character, or at worst, loss of local control to outside economic influences.

Presently, there is no text that attempts to bring together common issues, themes, and management approaches relevant to the land use changes occurring in small communities and rural lands in this region of the western United States. In this book we offer our observations of the present changes and challenges to community character in the rural western United States, and we provide a review of both established and contemporary models, principles, procedures, and practices relevant to the issues of land planning and resource management encountered here. To better understand the nature of land use in the New West, we identify and compare traditional location attributes with contemporary factors that have influenced both community growth and decline. Beyond the geography of land use change, our intent is that this book be of practical use to interested citizens, local elected officials, planning professionals, and college and university students who seek a broader understanding of contemporary land use and management issues confronting the rural West.

As previously discussed, contemporary growth and decline in the rural West is influenced in large part by innovations in high-technology, private land investments, and government resource policy and infrastructure improvements. Traditional societal motivations have changed as well, driven by a new set of contemporary land and resource perceptions, attitudes, and beliefs. In combination, these factors have had profound impacts on local land markets, and have adversely affected the ability of local governments to provide timely, reasoned responses to land development proposals. Consequently, in some areas of the West, the rapid growth of a new affluent population and the heightened demand for land conversion and new building has produced unanticipated changes in community character. The snow belt–to–sun belt migration and the urban California exodus to the rural West has resulted in incremental opportunity-driven development. Profit-taking in the local land market has in some cases taken precedence over the long-term planned community-vision approach to local decision making.

For many small communities and rural counties, land use planning is primarily accomplished by local zoning ordinance and building permit inspection. The enactment of a comprehensive development plan greatly improves the ability to rationally guide growth, but it requires local leadership, community participation, and significant investments of time and money in professional and information resources. For the local elected official, the process of land use planning is sometimes likened to a political minefield, but it is the purpose of local government service to provide the institutional leadership necessary to ensure the rights of landowners while accomplishing responsible and reasonable community interest objectives. Many resources exist to help local officials assume a more proactive stance on determining the future of their communities. State land grant universities, through their education extension programs, offer assistance for developing community meetings and workshops and encouraging citizen leadership and participation in rural and local government affairs. Associations of city and county governments provide legal and legislative assistance for planning and management issues. Professional assistance is offered by the International City Management Association as well as state chapters of the American Planning Association and land use and environmental law specialists of State Bar Associations.

Land use planners and land use attorneys are the highly trained, credentialed, and accredited professionals that assume primary responsibility for the legal and procedural aspects of community development. Their expertise is essential to understanding local state and federal legal requirements and for effectuating local policy. However, their role varies from advisory to discretionary depending on local government policies and on the prevailing political culture (Smutny 1998). In most areas of the rural West, the University Extension Services, operating from the land grant universities, are especially well-known and locally accepted sources for developing local leadership training programs. The Extension Community Development Programs in Oregon, Idaho, Utah, and Colorado offer innovative leadership development programs that increasingly focus on cooperative approaches to the resolution of land and resource conflicts in rural, developing areas.

Research by J. M. Shumway and James Davis (1996) shows that the dynamics of growth and development in the New West are becoming better understood. Nonetheless, as management policies are developed to guide it, "planning for this growth increasingly takes place in a potentially explosive political climate" (Smutny 1998, 318). The "Wise Use" movement, along with similar loosely organized groups, promotes an agenda of minimal government interference and advocates strongly for property rights supremacy (McCarthy 1998). Such organizations generally oppose local planning and growth management on the grounds that these programs unduly restrict free enterprise (Echeverria and Eby 1995). It is perhaps ironic that the Wise Use group, itself an "outside" advocacy group, opposes "model land ordinances" as examples of outside influence (Jacobs 1998). Analytical planning criteria based on environmental protection or preservation are the most suspect and most feared (Miller 1993). While small communities of the New West might learn from the mistakes and success stories of land use planning undertaken elsewhere, they must carefully fashion regulatory tools and other methods to fit their own individual circumstances. Studies indicate that the wholesale adoption of urban planning techniques is often not well suited to the particular tasks of rural planning due to the character and types of new growth and the need for establishing a stable economic base for the community

(Lapping, Daniels, and Keller 1989). The "model" growth management ordinance and the "one-size-fits-all" approach may be inappropriate when applied to a diverse set of priorities faced by small communities and rural county governments.

Our own research confirms that rapid population and economic growth, and the land use change it fosters, is uneven across the West. Moreover, we find that this variability accounts for many of the differences observed in the stated purposes, decision structures, and management techniques currently utilized in rural land use planning. The degree to which state and local governments have responded to land use and population changes with enabling legislation requisite for institutional planning is also uneven. The resulting landscape of regulation, rather than being inconsistent, as some have charged, perhaps simply differs from state to state. Legal provisions authorizing community land use planning presently exist in all western states, and some states require it, but there is no regionwide agreement on the role, purpose, and methods for achieving community development goals. In some parts of the West, land use planning by any government entity, at whatever scale or level, is viewed as an unwarranted intervention into what should function as a laissez-faire real estate market, representing an infringement of property rights.

Planning, however, is an essential, fundamental activity in nearly every endeavor of personal and societal behavior. For those areas presently experiencing rapid, seemingly uncontrollable growth and development, the introduction of a concerted land use planning effort is welcomed by most people as a rational, responsible approach to achieving a livable community. Likewise, rural communities seeking to reverse economic decline must promote a sound development strategy that logically connects their private investment solicitations and government grant applications with a distinctive community vision. Such economic development efforts are rendered even more potent when formulated within the context of a general or comprehensive plan for implementing strategies that address transportation, capital improvements and infrastructure, and future land use (Kelly and Becker 2000).

Individualism, often prefaced by the term "rugged," is a cherished legendary quality particularly associated with the West. Land rights, and in some cases water rights, are legally protected as personal property in part to prevent unreasonable confiscation by government or conflicting ownership claims. Equally admired in the settlement and development history of this region, however, is the attribute of cooperation. The spirit of cooperation was fundamental to establishing the foundation for contemporary growth and prosperity on the western frontier. Prime examples of cooperation to reduce isolation and to improve economic and personal well-being include the development of water resources for town water supplies and for irrigating arid lands, agreements on carrying capacity allotments for managing public grazing on the public domain, and the establishment of farm commodity and marketing cooperatives as well as rural transportation and utility infrastructures. Private land rights are protected by state and federal constitutions to prevent a "tyranny by the majority" over an individual property owner. But the private landowner is an integral part of the community system and as such has an obligation to take part in the cooperative effort to support order, function, safety, education, and well being.

In our view, comprehensive land use planning represents one of the cooperative strengths of citizens acting through their local representative governments to develop a set of community priorities and common goals that can be translated into patterns on the land. Planning in a contemporary democracy requires the cooperation of individuals and a complex of special interests and constituency groups. Collective decisions are difficult to make, but local representative government provides structures and procedures to identify land use priorities, and to develop community goals and policies to guide decisions. The officially adopted comprehensive plan provides a consensus view for overall community development, articulates a set of procedures and policies for consistent decisions, and constructs capital development strategies and schedules with a view to deriving the greatest infrastructure efficiencies for local tax dollars.

Communities operating with outdated information cannot adequately anticipate land use changes, nor estimate the scope of public investments needed to accommodate new growth. Communities operating with land use plans based on incorrect growth assumptions or insupportable policy guidelines cannot effectively respond to a large volume of incremental decisions related to the timing and location of land conversions and community infrastructure requests. Updating these government functions requires local support, financing, and planning. The fact is, without the initial influx of growth and improvements to the local tax base, financing for information systems and city planning is dependent largely on outside grant support. Even the implementation of a revised comprehensive plan that includes "growth management" or "smart growth" policies may come as a belated reaction to a fast-growth situation rather than in anticipation of it

Who Is Interested in the Land Use Changes Occurring in the New West?

There is a tendency for people to be most concerned about practical land use issues in their immediate vicinity. Development can bring both positive and negative consequences. Managing growth for community safety to prevent the loss of life and property is a primary function of local government. Development regulations that restrict land use in areas of known hazard risk are considered by most people to be a vitally important function of community planning.

The conversion of agriculture or timber land to high-density residential housing, warehousing, manufacturing, or shopping centers will likely increase local property values, but the changes will directly affect the levels of congestion, traffic, and noise and decrease the general well-being of nearby neighbors. Scenic amenities, rural solitude, and traditional lifestyles may be adversely affected by land use changes. Some people will react positively to the changes if they perceive that the changes will lead to increased local employment or enhanced commercial services or a greater tax base for funding of local schools. But if local tax rates are to be significantly increased to pay for infrastructure improvements largely bene-fiting the new migrants, or if scenic amenities will be degraded or water resources diminished, or potential wildfire risk increased, there will likely be a strongly neg-ative local reaction.

Local concern is most often expressed regarding the availability of affordable and low-cost housing in fast-growth communities. The construction of high-priced homes commands the market for buildable lots. Since a greater profit mar-gin can be realized from high-value residential construction, there is little economic incentive to utilize land for affordable housing. However, if there is a community priority to do so, affordable residential construction opportunities can be improved through cooperative agreements among financial institutions, real estate groups, and local government. Financial incentives, density incentives, reduced development charges, and other strategies should be explored in the community interest.

Beyond local, practical considerations, there is also a "long distance" interest in land use, resource, and environmental issues in the New West. America's urban populations have long maintained a commitment to conservation, preservation, and wilderness issues. National environmental advocacy organizations, which represent the remote interests, have frequently entered land use debates on public land issues and presently advocate for individuals in local private land use cases as well. This participation by "outside" groups is both puzzling and aggravating to local residents, and even well-meaning intervention may draw local resentment, perceived as interference in local affairs.

So who is responsible for making land use decisions in the New West? Nearly half of the land area of the eleven western states is under federal management, and many economists, geographers, and sociologists suggest that it is the attraction of the West's public lands that presently drives rural growth and land use change. Many fast-growth communities are located adjacent to the "Crown Jewel" na-tional parks, and the prime ski areas situated on national forest lands in the Rock-ies, the Cascades, and the Sierras. Nearly all of these outdoor recreation facilities are found on public lands and are regulated by and operated under concession permits granted by a federal agency. The Bureau of Land Management is respon-sible for land use decisions on more than 161 million acres, an area roughly the size of California and Oregon combined, and the Forest Service manages approx-imately 141 million acres. There are twenty-six national parks and 12.1 million acres of wilderness under the jurisdiction of the Department of Interior (NRCS 2000). The intent of public policy on these lands ranges from conservation to preservation. And while recreational use is permitted under the "multiple-use" principle of the U.S. Forest Service, environmental impacts from recreation, forest practices, and mining are highly regulated. The use of land and water, minerals, timber, grazing, and wildlife habitat and access to sensitive environments are controlled by federal law.

The pattern of federal lands in the West is not contiguous, nor discrete. Topography often distinguishes the federal holdings. National Forests occupy the timbered uplands and mountains, and except for the most arid lowlands, the valleys and plains are generally in private ownership. This geographic juxtaposition of ownership and control is a continuing source of contention among those agencies that regulate resources and the traditional economic activities that derive a livelihood from them. Land required for new development is situated in areas that have traditionally supported agriculture, mining, and logging. And while the key resources in the economy of the New West continue to be derived from the federal lands, the nature of resource use is different. Natural scenic forested landscapes and access to outdoor recreation opportunities and free-flowing streams and rivers are key to contemporary land development.

Prevailing nineteenth-century federal land policy encouraged settlement for agrarian and resource use purposes. The pattern of private land holdings logically developed in the most accessible, climatically favored, and easily irrigated lowland areas. The mountainous highlands could only support seasonal use for livestock grazing, timber harvest, and mining activity, and therefore offered limited homestead potential. Today, each western state has a varying amount of federal land, with the mix of federal–private ownership dependent on landform limitations and the evolution of federal policy regarding priorities for settlement, conservation, and preservation. Additional patterns reflect those lands withdrawn from general settlement to establish sovereign lands for indigenous people and for military training and national research endeavors. The map of federal land holdings in the West shows patterns most strikingly related to landform types and positions. Federal land holdings dominate mountain ranges with extensive tracts of high montane forests and equally vast expanses of the most arid of desert landscapes.

The relative amount of federal landownership in the West is unusually large when compared to ownership patterns east of the Rockies. Still, more than 55% of the West is in private ownership. An adequate supply of private land exists for traditional land uses, and for providing residential sites for small town growth in the rural West. However, the new growth patterns and land market forces are not traditional and require new issues to be discussed as cooperative management and planning arrangements between federal and local land use agencies.

Gateway communities to the national parks, national monuments, and national forests generally show the greatest demand for available private lands (Howe, McMahon, and Propst 1997). Booming land sales, construction, and rapid population growth and employment characterize many gateway communities such as Mammoth, California; Bend, Oregon; Livingston, Montana; Cody and Jackson, Wyoming; Park City, Utah; and Boulder City, Nevada. These residential communities and many others have become geographically important for the growth of regional commercial and medical services, vacation accommodations, entertainment attractions, and residential developments. New business ventures energize the economies of local rural communities, promoting a strong demand in the private land market for available, buildable land. However, in some cases rapid growth has encouraged the marketing of lands marginally suited to intensive development, and many communities are nearing the limits to build-out as they approach federal property boundaries, impending water shortages, extreme slope hazards, and road access and sewage disposal limitations.

THE EVOLUTION OF FEDERAL LAND POLICY
AND THE SUPPLY OF PRIVATE LANDS IN THE WEST

"The federal government shall not be the landlord of the public domain" is a generalized statement characterizing the young republic's land policy and is often attributed to Alexander Hamilton, the first secretary of state and treasury secretary. In this view, public domain lands should be sold, both to serve the social purposes of commerce, ownership, and enterprise and to provide a source of revenue for the federal government (Motheral 1958). This basic policy perspective served to influence a populist federal land policy that in the West continued into the early twentieth century. With the exception of the forest and range conservation reserves associated with Theodore Roosevelt's administration, 1903–1909, the U.S. government encouraged the settlement of the West based on securing economic opportunity through resource development with a myriad of land policy compromises deriving from Hamilton's federalist enterprise perspectives and Jefferson's populist-agrarian ideal (Motheral 1958). Land and resource policies following the American Civil War encouraged the wholesale transfer of public domain lands to private ownership by providing a range of incentives that included homesteads that came to be owned outright for a modest transfer fee or by "proving up" and a residence period. Further incentives included low-cost rangeland leases, mineral claims, timber sales and claims, and government investments and subsidies to develop irrigation water, transportation systems, and electric power. The progressive intent of the federal policies was to make land available for individual and family enterprise, to reduce economic risk, to overcome geographic isolation, and, through reclamation projects, to enhance the land's productivity.

Federal land use decisions today are largely governed by land management policies that seek to promote sustainable resource use, to protect significant cultural and historical sites, and to safeguard critical habitat including the protection and preservation of plant and animal species potentially endangered by human impacts. The Taylor Grazing Act of 1934 required the federal government to assume management responsibility for unreserved pubic lands until their eventual transfer to private ownership. Under this Act, the U.S. Grazing Service was first given the task of organizing land allotments and scheduling livestock rotations among local grazers to conserve soil and water resources. After the extended drought of the 1930s and the social and environmental catastrophe of the dust bowl era, the U.S. Bureau of Land Management was formed in 1946 to assume a broad range of local area resource use coordination and conservation responsibilities pending the eventual disposal to state governments or directly to private individuals.

After a good deal of resource inventory and analysis during the 1950s and 1960s, however, the U.S. Congress, with information supplied by the BLM, concluded that a good deal of the remaining unreserved public lands in the West were marginally suited to traditional agricultural settlement. The arguments for federal management were primarily based on economic conclusions that individuals could not use these lands intensively enough to justify owning them (Bennett 1958). The bulk of these lands were too rocky, too high, too dry, or too isolated to effectively benefit from reclamation investments and consequently presented unwarranted economic risks to private landownership. Marginal lands that had been homesteaded prior to the great drought of the 1930s proved to be particularly ill suited to sustained production, and much of the land claimed had been abandoned. Under the Bankhead-Jones Farm Tenant Act of 1937 and various Agricultural Adjustment Acts, the federal government repurchased thousands of acres of private land in the arid west to compensate landowners on the brink of economic failure (Bennett 1958). The Bankhead-Jones Act offered reasonable compensation to farmers and ranchers most financially hard hit by the persistent drought, providing an alternative to tax foreclosure or land abandonment. The specter of farmland abandonment presented potentially severe consequences to the conservation of soil, water, wildlife, and rangeland resources.

In most cases, local governments did not have the financial resources to effectively manage these lands. Initially, the Grazing Service, later the U.S. Soil Conservation Service, and finally in 1946 the Bureau of Land Management, was given management authority to permit limited resource use on these and other large tracts of unclaimed lands with an obligation to contribute a portion of all grazing, timber, and energy revenues to local government institutions in lieu of private property taxes. While official federal policy maintained the original intent to promote private landownership, the congressional act to buy back former public domain lands provided compelling evidence to many observers outside the West that the remaining marginal lands could not sustain settlement and, in the future, should be managed for conservation in the national interest.

Ironically, the federal government has most recently authorized the sale of federal lands surrounding the nation's fastest growing metropolitan area, Las Vegas, Nevada, to allow for the nearly unbridled growth of a city in one of the West's most arid places. The BLM's "Excess Lands Program" designed in the mid-1980s as a relief-valve response to the "Sagebrush Rebellion" proposed the limited sale of selected federal lands under a rigorous set of rules and regulations. Little of this land was actually sold for traditional purposes at the time, largely due to the fact that the BLM was not giving the land away but rather accepting land sales bids based on prevailing market values. There is little about Las Vegas that can be described as "traditional," including any intention of deriving a living from the land by grazing or crop production. However, with land values escalating daily in the Nevada desert surrounding Las Vegas, BLM land, even at prevailing sky-high market prices, is a relative speculative bargain. While serious questions have been raised about the advisability of further large-scale residential and commercial development due to limited water supply and high infrastructure costs, land development continues unabated.

In 1976, federal legislation was passed that dramatically changed the course of prevailing national policy toward the eventual privatization of public domain lands. Entitled the Federal Land Policy and Management Act (FLPMA), the basic tenet of this legislation was that the public lands of the West would not transfer directly to private ownership or to local governments, but would remain in federal ownership to be managed for the benefit of the entire nation under a multiple-use, sustainable resource doctrine. Further, strict regulations would enforce a federal mandate to inventory, analyze, plan, and manage public lands for ecological sustainability. The effect of the legislation had a major impact on traditional land use practices related to livestock grazing, the use of recreation lands, watersheds and surface water resources, energy development, wildlife habitats, and historic and anthropological resource sites. Importantly, three key features would dominate a new decision-making structure: the "public interest" would be defined from a consensus of diverse views and broad public input rather than the sole opinions of traditional local constituency boards. Second, the rationale for long-term land use management plans would give added weight to the purpose of ecological sustainability, rather than the use of resources to benefit the local economy. Finally, detailed land management plans would be based on scientific information rather than the experiences and informed opinions of traditional use groups.

There was an immediate adverse reaction by individuals and local governments to this new land policy. It came to be viewed as a "taking" of lands and resources traditionally used to support the economy of local communities (Platt 2004). Much to the advantage of private enterprise, economic risks of extraction as well as uncertain markets for timber, minerals, and livestock products had been somewhat buffered by the low access cost to public lands. Local government operating budgets and school funding had become dependent on revenues from in-lieu payments derived from the use of these lands. Open entry to all public lands, considered a traditional right of local citizens for hunting, fishing, and recreation, was restricted to protect habitat and to prevent erosion. Federal land management agencies and local governments represented differing views about how lands should be managed in the public interest, and these differences often escalated into personal confrontations as well as legal challenges.

FOUNDATIONS FOR RECENT CHANGE

The foundations for the growth of the New West were laid during and immediately after WWII. Large sums of federal money were transferred to the West to construct military facilities, but also to build and improve roads, airports, dams, hydroelectric and irrigation works, power transmission lines—in short, to create new jobs and economic opportunity. Much of the impetus, however, remained focused on the expansion of the traditional natural resources sector—in agriculture, mining, and timber. Another unintentioned consequence of the war effort was the firsthand geographic introduction of America's eastern population to the West. Thousands of GIs, both men and women, who were from other parts of the country, saw the interior West for the first time, and many of them would come to prefer the climates, the scenic landscapes, and the wide open spaces over the cold winters and crowded cities of the eastern United States. Many military personnel migrated to the West upon leaving the armed forces, and even greater numbers planned for eventual retirement in the sunny desert Southwest. Indeed, some of the "minimalist" land development schemes that irrevocably altered the arid landscapes of the West actually targeted men and women in the services.

The "National Defense Highway System" was initiated in the mid-1950s as a strategic response to the potential need for rapid mobilization in the cold war era. President Eisenhower had witnessed firsthand the important advantage the German autobahn offered for the rapid mobilization and deployment of troops, tanks, and material support. The existing federal highway system of low-speed, low-volume, two-lane highways and weight-limited bridges was completely inadequate to support mechanized defense strategies in the continental United States. While the rationale for federal funding of the ultraexpensive, limited-access, high-volume, high-speed highway system was defense, the automobile-driving, and especially the truck-driving, public would use the new system and repay the costs of construction with an increased federal fuel tax. Over time, the interstate system would expand the benefits of high-speed access to numerous routes across the rural West, becoming one of the principal location factors influencing patterns of new development.

By the early 1970s the West's natural resource-based economy seemed to be at its peak of development. The national consumption rush that resulted from the post-WWII economic expansion had stimulated a strong demand for mining, timber, energy, and agricultural products. International agricultural export policy encouraged the expansion of irrigated crop acreage throughout the West, and substantial portions of the high-speed, high-volume interstate highway system were either completed or under construction. The OPEC oil embargo of the late 1970s and early 1980s brought a renewed interest in exploration and development of energy resources on western lands, both public and private. Boom towns based on oil, natural gas, and coal such as Rock Springs and Gillette, Wyoming; Price, Utah; and Billings, Montana, attracted new growth and development. Construction of natural gas pipelines such as the Williston Basin and Columbia Pipeline Projects expanded employment opportunities across the West. A subsequent relaxation of OPEC production limits and the availability of cheaper foreign oil immediately reduced the demand for higher priced domestic oil. As a result, many smaller energy economy boom towns suffered population declines, increased poverty, falling property values, and the consequent loss of community tax revenues. The big cities, with their diversified economies and essential financial, government, educational, and medical facilities, remained stable and continued to expand services to surrounding communities and rural areas. These larger communities are most often found astride the federal interstate highway system, which serves not only the needs of regional commerce, but as an economic lifeline to national and international trade.

LAND USE CONFLICT

We end this chapter with a brief discussion of the various conflicts that may arise from new development across the rural areas and smaller towns of the West. These can be associated either with inappropriate development on a given physical site or with incompatible development that does not fit in with the existing land use pattern. Thus, we can have land use in conflict with the environment, and land use in conflict with other land uses. While space does not permit a more robust treatment of the topic, there are several aspects of land use conflict that people need to keep in mind. One is the idea that new development is often being permitted to occur in areas that should be understood as hazardous because of adverse environmental conditions that are unpredictable or occur only sporadically. Floodplains are an especially deceptive location in the more arid regions and typically provide what many might perceive as ideal level building sites in areas of otherwise rough terrain. Stream channels may appear insignificant, or in the case of ephemeral washes, virtually invisible. Yet bankful flows could appear at any time, and are often dependent on chance meteorological events elsewhere in the watershed. Floods may occur only occasionally, but can easily derive from a distant thunderstorm that may supply enough precipitation and overland flow to cause the stream to swell rapidly. But the lure of water and the amenities of lush riparian vegetation in an otherwise sparse landscape are translated into powerful economic forces not readily overcome. Even where local authorities know better, building permits are continually being issued for waterfront trophy homes along our western rivers and streams, and where tsunami flooding presents potential risks to beach zone development in highly attractive Pacific coastal communities.

Steep slopes represent another hazard that is unfortunately very difficult for planning officials to properly regulate. Despite the imminent threat of landslides and liquefied soils caused by persistent rains, people are so intent on purchasing real estate with a view that any warnings about slopes are likely to go unheeded. As the El Niño–triggered events in California during the winter of 2004–2005 amply demonstrated, building either on or directly below steep hillsides is an invitation to invariable disaster. Other soil-related development concerns include shrink-swell capacities and the likelihood for damage to foundations or underground utilities, particularly as the residential settlement frontier extends to ever higher elevations in mountainous environments. But of all the natural hazards that require greater awareness on the part of both the public and regulatory agencies in the West, wildfire is perhaps the most pervasive. As timbered areas are usually deemed most desirable, rural subdivisions can take hold of entire districts in rapid fashion. This actually *creates* the fire hazard, by allowing development to occur in a dispersed manner within an environment that often experiences dry conditions in the summer and fall. Seasonal home heating with wood stoves or fireplaces and cooking with outdoor barbecues are just several of the risky behaviors associated with residential land use in the forest. The desire for scenic landscaping around structures can deny the necessary creation of "defensible space." People and their activities provide all the spark that's needed for fuel-laden woods to burn.

An increasing concern throughout the West is the inevitable disruption that new development brings to the functioning of natural environments (Maestas, Knight, and Gilgert 2001). This can take the form of threats to biodiversity caused by altered habitats, along with more direct human–wildlife interactions that can result in injury and death for numerous species. Larger, relatively intact natural areas represent islands of habitat needed by many plants and animals that have declined elsewhere in the West, and are thus particularly prone to human infringement. Such is the alarm over rapid land use change in places like the Greater Yellowstone Ecosystem, or the fragile southwestern deserts (Hansen, Rasker, Maxwell, Rotella, Johnson, Parmenter, Lagner, Cohen, Lawrence, and Kraska 2002). In addition to natural hazards and ecological disturbance as constraints to development, we can likewise briefly take note of the potential incompatibility between various land uses and how this has played out in the rapidly changing landscapes of the region.

As we shall see in the chapters that follow, land use patterns in the New West are now experiencing a profound transformation. Sometimes the pace of this change can be unsettling to long-time residents of the region. When these changes arrive in a hurry, or in somewhat unexpected fashion, they can come up against established land use patterns in a way that may result in conflicts between different uses or dissension among neighbors. Not every land use conflict is as dramatic or as tragic as the case in a small town in Colorado during the summer of 2004 when a disgruntled property owner upset over a zoning decision went on a rampage with a large fortified bulldozer and destroyed many buildings in the central business district before taking his own life. But small towns across the West are feeling the strain of accommodating waves of fresh migrants with different values and expectations. The scale and density of new residential developments within these towns may seem out of place to long-time residents. In the commercial sector, family-operated shops now face increasing competition from larger establishments, often national "big box" chains able to both undercut pricing and offer greater variety. Businesses more likely to be found in urban settings are perceived as intruding upon the traditions and sensibilities of rural and small town folk.

In the rural areas, those engaged in traditional livelihoods that use the land a certain way or that result in performing necessary activities on the land may feel threatened by all these new residents moving in from out of state, or even from urban areas within the same state. Such potential threats might become actualized by neighbors not acting very neighborly, either through ignorance or perhaps through self-righteous indignation. A concentration of new residential units, at whatever density, in an area where traditional farming and ranching for the most part continues to operate is likely to create some conflicts. At best, new residents may not know about local farming and ranching traditions, and in their ignorance they can cause problems with their pets getting loose or fences and gates left open, or by disrupting seasonal livestock movement along the roadways. Worse, they may not wish to be good neighbors at all, and will complain about noise or dust, or nighttime field operations such as plowing or cutting and baling hay. Conversely, as a new development nears build-out, neighboring property owners who are barely getting by as ranchers or farmers may view the successful implementation of these subdivisions as a chance to sell out to a developer while the price is right. And so there ensues more of the same, as if following a set formula.

A revealing symptom of land use conflict in the New West has been the issuance and rapid dissemination across the region of a new "Code of the West"—a revised set of guidelines for ethical conduct for folks just moving to the countryside. Attributed initially to a former county commissioner from Larimer County, Colorado, the standard version of this document has diffused across several states, and has been officially issued by numerous counties in Utah, Oregon, Washington, and Montana, as well as Colorado. It offers sage advice about living in the rural areas of the western states, and outlines some common misconceptions and pitfalls to avoid (see the appendix).

In the next chapter, we examine some of the more common types of development and land use patterns that are currently emerging across the region. In many ways, it is new residential development that has become both symptom and vector of New West malaise. Large trophy homes now occupy the choicest building sites, especially those higher promontories that command a marketable view. Where there were no dwellings before, sprawling subdivisions have begun to gobble up the countryside at various densities. Associated with residential expansion are the new commercial and even industrial land uses that have become apparent in even the most remote sectors of the region. For a part of the country that historically has exhibited a traditional settlement pattern of urban oasis combined with a more or less strictly demarcated rural hinterland, this new suburban simulation can seem downright surreal.

REFERENCES

Abbott, Carl. *The Metropolitan Frontier: Cities in the Modern American West.* Tucson: University of Arizona Press, 1995.

Bennett, John B. The Heritage of Our Public Lands. In *Land: The 1958 Yearbook of Agriculture,* pp. 42–52. Washington D.C.: USDA, 1958.

Billington, Ray E. *Land of Savagery, Land of Promise: The European Image of the American Frontier in the Nineteenth Century.* Norman: University of Oklahoma Press, 1981.

Burchell, Robert W., and David Listokin. *Development Impact Assessment Handbook.* Washington, D.C.: Urban Land Institute, 1994.

Bureau of Land Management. Land Ownership Statistics, 2002. <www.id.blm.gov>. [accessed June 2004]

Cannon, Brian Q. *Remaking the Agrarian Dream: New Deal Rural Resettlement in the Mountain West.* Albuquerque: University of New Mexico Press, 1996.

Echeverria, John D., and Raymond B. Eby, eds. *Let the People Judge: Wise Use and the Private Property Rights Movement.* Washington, D.C.: Island Press, 1995.

Ewald, Chase R. *Cowboy Chic: Western Style Comes Home.* Salt Lake City, Utah: Gibbs Smith, 2000.

Flood, Elizabeth C. *Cowboy High Style: Thomas Molesworth to the New West.* Salt Lake City, Utah: Peregrine Smith Books, 1992.

Garnsey, Morris E. *America's New Frontier: The Mountain West.* New York: Alfred A. Knopf, 1950.

Hansen, Andrew J., Ray Rasker, Bruce Maxwell, Jay Rotella, Jerry Johnson, Andrea Parmenter, Ute Lagner, Warren Cohen, Rick Lawrence, and Matthew Kraska. Ecological Causes and Consequences of Demographic Change in the New West. *BioScience* 52 (2002):151–162.

Howe, Jim, Ed McMahon, and Luther Propst. *Balancing Nature and Commerce in Gateway Communities.* Washington, D.C.: Island Press, 1997.

Jacobs, Harvey M. The "Wisdom," But Uncertain Future, of the Wise Use Movement. In *Who Owns America? Social Conflict Over Property Rights,* edited by Harvey M. Jacobs, pp. 29–44. Madison: University of Wisconsin Press, 1998.

Jackson, Philip L., and A. Jon Kimerling, eds. *Atlas of the Pacific Northwest,* 9th ed. Corvallis: Oregon State University Press, 2003.

Kelly, Eric D., and Barbara Becker. *Community Planning: An Introduction to the Comprehensive Plan.* Washington, D.C.: Island Press, 2000.

Kotkin, Joel. *The New Geography: How the Digital Revolution is Reshaping the American Landscape.* New York: Random House, 2000.

Lapping, Mark B., Thomas L. Daniels, and John W. Keller. *Rural Planning and Development in the United States.* New York: Guilford Press, 1989.

Limerick, Patricia N. *The Legacy of Conquest: The Unbroken Past of the American West.* New York: W.W. Norton & Company, 1987.

———. *Something in the Soil: Legacies and Reckonings in the New West.* New York: W.W. Norton & Company, 2000.

Lounsbury, John F., Lawrence M. Sommers, and Edward A. Fernald. *Land Use: A Spatial Approach.* Dubuque, Ia.: Kendall Hunt, 1981.

Maestas, Jeremy D., Richard L. Knight, and Wendell C. Gilgert. Biodiversity and Land-use Change in the American Mountain West. *Geographical Review* 91 (2001):509–524.

McCarthy, James. Environmentalism, Wise Use, and the Nature of Accumulation in the Rural West. In *Remaking Reality: Nature at the Millenium,* edited by Bruce Braun and Noel Castree, pp. 126–149. London: Routledge Press, 1998.

McKinney, Matthew, and William Harmon. *The Western Confluence: a Guide to Governing Natural Resources.* Washington D.C. : Island Press, 2004.

Miller, Anita. All Is Not Quiet on the Western Front. *The Urban Lawyer* 25 (1993):827–840.

Motheral, Joe R. Land and Our Economic Development. In *Land: The 1958 Yearbook of Agriculture,* pp. 28–41. Washington, D.C.: USDA, 1958.

Nash, Gerald. *The American West in the Twentieth Century: A Short History of an Urban Oasis.* Albuquerque: University of New Mexico Press, 1973.

Natural Resources Conservation Service. *State of the Land.* Washington D.C.: USDA, 2000 (1997 revised).

Nugent, Walter. *Into the West: The Story of Its People.* New York: Alfred A. Knopf, 1999.

Platt, Rutherford. *Land Use and Society: Geography, Law and Public Policy,* rev. ed. Washington, D.C.: Island Press, 2004.

Reps, John W. *Cities of the American West: A History of Urban Frontier Planning.* Princeton: Princeton University Press, 1979.

———. *The Forgotten Frontier: Urban Planning in the American West Before 1890.* Columbia: University of Missouri Press, 1981.

Riebsame, William, Hannah Gosnell, and David M. Theobald, eds. *Atlas of the New West: Portrait of a Changing Region.* New York: W.W. Norton & Company, 1997.

Robbins, William G., and James C. Foster, eds. *Land in the American West: Private Claims and the Common Good.* Seattle: University of Washington Press, 2000.

Rothman, Hal K. *Devil's Bargains: Tourism in the Twentieth-Century American West.* Lawrence: University Press of Kansas, 1998.

Shumway, J. M., and James Davis. Non-Metropolitan Population Change in the Mountain West: 1970–1995. *Rural Sociology* 63, no. 3 (1996):513–529.

Smith, Henry N. *Virgin Land: The American West as Symbol and Myth.* Cambridge: Harvard University Press, 1950.

Smith, Michael D., and Richard S. Krannich. "Culture Clash" Revisited: Newcomer and Longer-Term Residents' Attitudes Toward Land Use, Development, and Environmental Issues in Rural Communities in the Rocky Mountain West. *Rural Sociology* 65 (2000):396–421.

Smutny, Gayla. Legislative Support for Growth Management in the Rocky Mountains: An Exploration of Attitudes in Idaho. *Journal of the American Planning Association* 64 (1998):311–323.

Wilkinson, Charles L. *Crossing the Next Meridian: Land, Water and the Future of the West.* Washington, D.C.: Island Press, 1992.

Worster, Donald. *Under Western Skies: Nature and History in the American West.* New York: Oxford University Press, 1992.

Wyckoff, William, and Lary M. Dilsaver, eds. *The Mountainous West: Explorations in Historical Geography.* Lincoln: University of Nebraska Press, 1995.

2

Development Patterns and Prototypes

The western states are in the midst of lasting and far-reaching changes, not only regarding public perceptions of what constitutes a natural resource, but also with respect to private land use patterns. Indeed, the very conceptualization of today's West as "New" has been brought about by a recognition of these regional landscape transformations. It should thus prove advantageous to understanding current trends if we look at typical patterns or prototypes of development occurring across the region and make an attempt to classify some of them by means of land use typology and intensity. This will help reveal the potential kinds of land use change a given area may anticipate, as well as call attention to the impacts associated with each type of development. We start with residential, which alone has several subcategories, and then proceed to look at new commercial and industrial growth patterns, followed in turn by agricultural and recreational land uses. In the sections that follow, we outline and describe some of the more characteristic forms of land use within each of these broad categories. Some development proposals and certain land uses are simply too difficult to classify or else exhibit characteristics of several categories, such as a combination of recreational and commercial. Others might be unusual or even offbeat, yet may involve very large parcels and have far-reaching impacts to surrounding properties. We shall see that in the New West, it is best to expect the unexpected.

Residential growth, almost in and of itself, is largely responsible for the widespread changes throughout what used to be rural landscapes in the eleven western states. Vacation homes, retirement, and footloose employment options have created a housing demand that is not necessarily accompanied by proportionate industrial or even commercial support. Certain retail businesses will indeed expand to serve the needs of new residents, however, much more so than the traditional

27

support system of job opportunities. Industries that do emerge are largely associ-ated with elements of regional identity or perhaps make use of locally available materials. Farming and especially ranching are historically dominant livelihoods that are both ubiquitous across the region and culturally symbolic of western landscapes (Starrs 1998). Recent changes in agricultural land use across the New West present unprecedented challenges for local communities caught between customary supportive roles and potential new economic directions. Some of the more visible alterations to the western countryside have been associated with recreational trends and leisure activities. These have occurred at many scales and intensities, but one particular form of recreational development—the destination resort—warrants special attention. Recreational use of land is not always concen-trated at one specific site, however, and the increasing popularity of trail rides, bus tours, rail excursions, and other linear and/or mobile pursuits of scenic amenities also represents a trend that will affect western landscapes and lifestyles in the coming years. Along those same lines, the emerging land use patterns across the West have in many cases been stimulated and spurred on by transportation im-provements to the region, particularly the completion of the federal interstate highway system. Thus, we close this chapter with a brief discussion of transporta-tion as a land use, especially the interstate highways that have acted as a catalyst for so much landscape change. We are able cartographically to identify a series of "growth corridors" along selected highway segments, most of which have experi-enced a dramatic increase in residential, commercial, industrial, and recreational land development.

RESIDENTIAL

Residential land use patterns across the region are changing fast. Indeed, the very landscape transformations that visually signal the emergence of the New West are essentially residential. The nearly insatiable demand for housing in scenic but re-mote areas where traditionally there has been little need for new dwellings has in-stigated and helped to shape land use change in several ways. First, any new residential development is likely to be a first-time conversion from resource lands. Thus, the appearance of what is being constructed is almost never "softened" by an existing mosaic of surrounding residential parcels, and so it tends to stick out, and cannot help but be incompatible on several levels. Second, although the sup-ply of private land is often limited in the mountainous and arid regions of the West, the parcels that *are* there have been used as ranches and farms for decades and are usually relatively large in size. Consequently, the scale of new projects tends to be much larger than in an urban or small town setting, resulting in de-velopments with either a very large number of lots, or else a fewer number of in-dividual lots that are very large in size. On the one hand you have a scattering of low-density ranchettes, and on the other, a great many new houses at a suburban density that may overwhelm local services and infrastructure. Some of these subdivisions may have thousands of individual lots surveyed out with minimal provision of utilities, and thus are not much more than modern versions of the retirement land schemes described in greater detail later in the chapter. In keeping with prevailing trends, however, the availability of larger acreages has also enabled the development of more extensive master-planned projects, which may take any number of forms. The best ones may try to fit in with the existing landscape, carefully siting homes to be as unobtrusive as possible, and perhaps keeping a majority of acreage as open space held in common. Increasingly, however, they seem to become yet one more supposedly exclusive subdivision of tract homes around a golf course.

The single-family home on an individual lot dominates the residential land use pattern of the rural American West, as it does for most of the nonurban United States. Whether that parcel is a stand-alone piece of rural property, or simply one among many similar-sized lots in a subdivision or planned unit development, the American dream of homeownership is alive and well out West, and effectively drives the real estate market. What most characterizes the emerging pattern of New West residential subdivision, however, is often the *size* of parcel. This, of course, is generally related to blanket conditions of national fiscal confidence, market trends, mortgage rates, and the ability of new homeowners to pay. The appearance of wide open spaces in the western states, however, seems to trigger the desire for developing larger lot sizes. Moreover, as many new arrivals to the region come from somewhere else, perhaps flush from the sale of a higher-priced house in an urban market, they may want to flaunt their ability to upsize. Ostentatious displays of "having arrived" often involve the homestead: "When Americans achieve wealth, typically the symbol of upward mobility is a bigger home on a larger lot" (Salamon 1998, 175). Nothing symbolizes the New West more than a mountain valley formerly used for livestock pasture and/or irrigated hay production, now punctuated with massive log homes perched upon the upper hillsides on parcels ranging anywhere between 10 and 160 acres. These newly divided pieces of land—now too small for commercial ranching—are being marketed as upscale equestrian estates or even weekend corporate retreats. A quick sampling of western river basins would show nearly identical landscape change: the North Fork Shoshone River west of Cody, Wyoming; the upper Yakima River west of Ellensburg, Washington; and the aptly but thereby unfortunately named Paradise Valley of the Yellowstone south of Livingston, Montana. The rural West is now a landscape of scenic and recreational amenity, and even the more remote portions of the region are being vigorously marketed as such. Yet no longer is the object simply to tour the national parks during a few weeks in summer and then go home. The overwhelming catalyst for land use change across the New West is the willingness by new migrants to establish residency. And where there is a ready market, the rules of supply and demand will always pertain.

These days, it seems the entire West is up for sale. But the market no longer focuses on traditional farms and ranches trading hands to other agricultural owner-operators, representing a transfer of ownership and title but effectively ensuring a continuation of the same land use. Real estate practice in the rural West is anything but business as usual. Rural lands are now being marketed for their amenity value. Numerous slick paper publications such as *Farm & Ranch* specialize in higher end properties that are deemed convertible from crop and livestock operations to recreational hideaways. In the past it was just *Arizona Highways*, but there now exists an entire stable of magazines titled after specific places—either states or cities across the New West, from Santa Fe to Spokane—featuring full-page advertisements for real estate holdings, many of which are former working ranches turned playgrounds. Leisure potential rules real estate, and a whole new lexicon has sprung up to entice would-be buyers. Where once the sale of a ranch might have depended on the security of grazing rights on nearby public lands, or a senior water right, these days it is much more common to proclaim that the spread is surrounded by public recreation lands or has superb hunting and fishing. In those areas known for exceptional big-game hunting or fly-fishing opportunities, that actually becomes the lead enticement in real estate promotions. Perceptions of water resources have likewise shifted, and priorities have turned from quantity to quality. Amount of acre-feet for irrigation has been replaced by length of river frontage, while "stock ponds" are not nearly as important as "stocked ponds." So often are properties declared as "one-of-a-kind" that one begins to wonder if every parcel for sale is all that unique. Catch phrases in many a sales pitch include "privacy," "year-round access," and "protected views." Not only is attractive scenery now a valuable component of the land itself, but scenic views *from* the property command a higher price, especially properties with sweeping vistas that the real estate agents like to call a "territorial view." Targeting vast wealth compounded elsewhere, underlying most offers is the implication that the property would make an ideal second home or vacation getaway. One of the more common terms used in high-end advertisements is "corporate retreat." It is astonishing overall to view a high-end real estate prospectus for property in an area of the West where not so long ago there was virtually no market. In many places asking prices for land have increased fivefold or more in just a few short years.

Residential development can assume many forms, even in the rural areas and small towns of the West. Based mainly on what we have witnessed during the course of fieldwork around the region (see next chapter), in this section we try to describe the housing patterns and densities that are most likely to be encountered. Of course, in terms of accommodating sheer numbers of people, the suburban edges of larger cities and metropolitan areas continue to show the greatest population increase, and therefore, the most dramatic landscape transformations. As geographer John Fraser Hart (1998, 326) once exclaimed, "The urban edge is the newest frontier of settlement. It is wild and chaotic, and it is changing feverishly, virtually overnight." Yet for many of those places, rather than growth being contained and managed, discontinuous and relatively low-density sprawl is being perpetuated as the predominant land use pattern. Even sophisticated planning programs in the smaller satellite jurisdictions surrounding large cities show little aptitude for channeling the pressures of imminent urbanization into more sustainable forms. One only has to look at the northern edge of Las Vegas, or the outer suburbs of Tucson and Albuquerque, to see how true that has become for the New West.

The main reason generally given for the lack of regulatory control is market demand. Conventional wisdom holds that this is what most people are buying, although most people if given the choice would probably not wish to live surrounded by tract houses and strip malls. It's as if the residents in these new housing belts somehow believe that they will always be on the perimeter, cherishing their views across open space to the tranquil rural landscape beyond, and would dare not envision a future when more of the same envelops them and spurts ever outward. This is the dilemma faced by planners in rapidly expanding suburban areas across the country, but it seems particularly tragic here in the West, where open space and scenic vistas are up for grabs, and inherently finite land and water resources can quickly become overallocated. Thus, although there are notable exceptions, such as Portland, most of the larger metropolitan areas of the West have apparently adopted the Los Angeles model of growth that has largely been shaped by acquiescence to the status quo (Fulton 2001; Ozawa 2004).

There are numerous scholarly accounts of the rise and development of suburban landscapes in the United States (Jackson 1985; Fishman 1987; Hayden 2003). Based on an earlier publication (1984) that has since been revised and expanded, Dolores Hayden (2002) provides a meaningful treatise on the ramifications of suburbanization as a decidedly male project, and the further implications for gender roles and relations. Despite the changing circumstances brought on by dual careers, increasing numbers of women in the workplace, and so-called nontraditional family units, the majority of standardized new housing stock being built on the outskirts of towns and cities has failed to keep pace with radically divergent societal realities, other than to add a bay or two to the garage. Indeed, it was not that long ago when an observer of the evolving residential landscape marveled at the necessity of the two-car garage (Jakle 1990). These days, three bays have become common in many areas, sometimes with an additional, taller doorway for the boat or recreational vehicle. Las Vegas historian Hal Rothman tells of houses that cannot be sold in that city because they do not have a three-bay garage.

Another internal change to house design and layout would be those currently fashionable entertainment rooms or home theaters, which can be viewed as indicative of declining participation in civic society, as suggested by Robert Putnam (2000) in his book *Bowling Alone*. Perhaps in the large-lot residential landscapes of the New West, where neighbors by and large are not even within shouting distance, the provision of private amusement facilities makes perfect sense. Nonetheless, the loss of community identity, and identification with community, is still apparent. Along these same lines, trend spotter Faith Popcorn (1991, 27) some time ago coined the term "cocooning" to describe the tendency that first came about during the 1970s for the household to turn inward upon itself, away from sociability and civic engagement:

> Everyone was looking for haven at home—drawing their shades, plumping their pillows, clutching their remotes. Hiding. It was a full-scale retreat into the last controllable (or sort of controllable) environment—your own home. Cocooning is about insulation and avoidance, peace and protection, coziness and control—a sort of hyper-nesting.

Such behavior consequently leads to the habitual establishment of an introverted lifestyle, a world in which gated subdivisions and home security alarms are but outwardly symbolic manifestations. Rather than a trend that has begun to play itself out, cocooning has actually intensified into a posture that can been identified as "burrowing," defined as "the ultimate expression of cocooning in which consumers dig in, ever deeper, with a bunker mentality" (Popcorn 1991, 192). In terms of land use, and especially residential components of the built environment, this pulling away from public space and social interaction is reflected in everything from the preferential market demand for housing parcels fronting on cul-de-sacs within subdivisions to the fortified appearance of entire developments, enclosed and segregated against a more diverse world at large.

The closing of ranks or cloistering of residential subdivisions is a significant trend in suburban-style development. Where this is allowed to happen, each new project attempts to reach for its own distinctive identity and physically separates itself from the rest of the area by limited-access points to collector streets or arterials, providing no interconnectivity. Increasingly there are walls enclosing the property, and gates across the entrance. A prominent sign or fancifully landscaped entryway intended to elevate status has become indispensable. Guidelines established by the Urban Land Institute have stressed the role of this particular aspect of residential development:

> Entrance gateways are very important for establishing the overall image and identity of the residential community or neighborhood. Gateways can also be important in providing security and privacy. Landscape materials requiring a high degree of maintenance may be appropriate for the entrance gateway, provided that the effect is compatible with the overall character of the project. (Bookout 1990, 245)

Creating community is avowedly the ultimate goal for developers of such projects, who are never merely building houses, they would claim, but rather homes in a neighborhood. Yet instead of creating community, following this template in fact obliterates its very possibility, as explained by Setha Low (2003, 71): "Community is a slippery term that can be used to market housing, stabilize resale values, and defend neighborhood boundaries, as well as bring people together. But gating does not necessarily create community; it only selects for a certain type of person and level of income."

The segregative nature of these quasi-neighborhoods is reinforced by institutional controls such as homeowners associations (HOAs) with their hefty annual dues, and the privately enforced covenants, conditions, and restrictions (CC&Rs) that accompany the transfer of fee simple title (McKenzie 1994). In a much more tangible, territorial context, many of these developments are indeed now gated, which may also entail a guardhouse and/or a private security patrol. William Fulton (2001, 339) elucidates the socioeconomic appeal of such design:

> As any real estate developer will tell you, the hottest idea in new suburbs these days is the gated community, the subdivision not merely surrounded by a wall but protected by a gate that residents control. Whether secured by a guardhouse or operated by remote control, the gate offers suburbanites a sense of security and exclusivity. Indeed the idea of a gate is so compelling that it is literally impossible to sell a suburban subdivision to homebuyers above a certain income category—upper-middle-class and up—if it comes without a gate.

Gated communities have been on the increase for more than a decade, and have actually become quite common in many of the West's suburban zones (Blakely and Snyder 1997). But these days they are also staking a claim to rural areas and are appearing even on the edge of small towns, ironically the very places that intrinsically hold the most appeal for people who have escaped from both cities and suburbs in search of some quaint unfettered location where they might feel more safe and more secure. The presence of a gate has become a selling point for new subdivisions that are showing up in the most unlikely and remote places, as depicted in Figure 2.1.

Suburbia, we now find, has invaded the wide open spaces of the West, and has superimposed its style and aesthetic sensibilities on what was once remote and rustic countryside. There is nothing more disconcerting to a modern pilgrim on a road trip across the western outback than to top a rise or round a curve and find a cul-de-sac full of split-level "ranch houses" dominating the scene (Fig. 2.1.). What once promised to be an adventure in discovering some unique sense of place within the region's more obscure locations has turned into an exercise in treading through tantamount terrain. In many cases, the internal street layout of these subdivisions also mimics their true suburban counterparts. There are often curvilinear streets, despite being situated on flat ground that does not require reconciling design to slope. Even in the most rural settings, rights-of-way are usually paved, perhaps lined with sidewalks, and typically include concrete curbs and gutters. There may be street signs and lightposts, maybe even a set of gang mailboxes.

FIGURE 2.1
Gated residential developments are now the rage even in some of the West's more remote locations, as indicated on this billboard outside Oatman, Arizona. *Photograph
by Robert Kuhlken.*

FIGURE 2.2
Once-rural countryside in the New West can instantly assume the look and feel of sub-
urbia, as shown by this residential subdivision outside of Prescott Valley, Arizona.
Photograph by Robert Kuhlken.

It *looks* like suburbia, but in fact is geographically neither subordinate nor in close proximity to any nearby urban area. Perhaps it reminds new homeowners of what they have left behind, and provides the comfort of maintaining a familiar facade in these otherwise strange surroundings.

In their more rudimentary form, many rural subdivisions of the New West are nowhere near as complex nor as symbolically charged. Landowners who might wish to capitalize on the residential development potential of a property they may have held for years typically do not hire a planning consultant or design a site plan beyond basic survey requirements. The most common way for a piece of land to be divided for the purpose of creating a series of homesites is to simply align the front boundaries of any number of proposed parcels along a right-of-way, and draw as many property lines as can reasonably fit, either by adhering to the minimum lot-size limitations of existing zoning regulations or by taking into consideration the marketability of elbow room. In any case, each side lot line would extend straight back to the rear lot line. Every lot, then, has its own individual driveway access off what is typically a secondary county road but in many cases might be a well-traveled state highway. While a few more dwellings here and there may not create substantial impacts, the cumulative effects of replicating this pattern along an increasingly busy road can only lead to more congestion, not to mention safety concerns and traffic hazards.

FIGURE 2.3
Many rural counties do not have the fiscal capability to take on additional right-of-way dedications and are not willing to assume responsibility for road maintenance. *Photograph by Robert Kuhlken.*

The safer alternative, of course, would be for new subdivisions to manifest internal street patterns that intersect with the main road, perhaps at several points to promote circulation alternatives, while other design elements could address the need for common open space and/or the clustering of homesites. Individual driveways would then front this internal right-of-way, which ought to be dedicated to the public but in many cases turns out not to be, given the additional costs of maintenance that rural counties may not wish to bear (Fig. 2.3).

For larger tracts of developable land, or for pieces of ground without lengthy highway frontage, the nearly ubiquitous residential settlement pattern that we have encountered in the New West is what we term the perpendicular cul-de-sac. The design is simple and requires little imagination to plan or to implement. A single road, paved or not, will extend at a right angle from a public right-of-way as far back as the size of the property will accommodate. These roads can be quite lengthy, but their basic form as a single access for an array of new homesites stays the same. The shape of the property—either too skinny or broad enough—will determine if the individual lots are arranged on both sides of the new roadway, or strung out in series along one side only. Again, the size of the lot is predicated by what is allowable by local zoning laws, if there are any, but also by the prevailing market indicating what people want and what they are currently buying in that particular area. It may be 10 or 20 acres of unimproved grazing land, or it might be 3- to 5-acre lots with irrigated pasture.

If the shape and composition of the property allows for squeezing in more lots at the end of the new road where a turnaround ought to be, then additional access may be provided by extending outward from that terminus, again typically at a right angle, effectively making the main access road terminate in a T-intersection. Sometimes labeled a hammerhead (Hall and Porterfield 2001, 102), we call this pattern the winged cul-de-sac, and it too has become fairly common across the New West. Both the perpendicular cul-de-sac and the winged cul-de-sac are designs that are easy to accomplish without development expertise or the assistance of a project engineer. All that is usually required is an official survey for filing the plat, once the proposed project has been approved. This is probably one reason they have turned up everywhere in the region. Once the number of lots in a project becomes unwieldy, or access to lots involves loop roads or a modified grid, property owners would do best to turn the development process over to professional site planners.

Whatever the shape of the street pattern, for smaller developments, and in some cases for the larger ones as well, basic utilities are usually provided to each lot, with electricity and telephone lines buried underground wherever feasible, which is preferable to overhead wires and poles. For rural subdivisions in general, sewage disposal is almost always relegated to individual septic tanks. This can become problematic in areas of heavy soils or poor drainage where too high a density of development has been permitted. For lot sizes of two acres or more, the provision of drinking water is likewise typically left up to the property owner, who must drill an individual well, although so-called community water systems consisting of several homes on a shared well are also common. Fire protection has become an increasing concern in rural areas that are seeing a rapid increase in residential development, especially along the so-called wildland-urban interface where native vegetation patterns can turn into a combustible natural hazard to new housing. Not only do individual wells preclude the availability of hydrants along a newly developed road, but many rural fire protection districts, usually staffed by a volunteer force, are becoming overwhelmed by the sheer number of new houses being constructed for which they must provide coverage. Roads ideally should be built to county standards and dedicated to the public. This has not occurred for a number of reasons. Sometimes the road is simply not wide enough, or the base material and thickness do not measure up to code. County governments already strapped for road maintenance outlays may not wish to accept additional mileage into their system. In that case, the roads may not only fail to meet initial construction standards, but may likewise not be maintained either.

FIGURE 2.4
Without proper roadway and drainage standards, access to new subdivisions can become problematic, as shown by this arroyo crossing near Silver City, New Mexico. *Photograph by Robert Kuhlken.*

Drainage is another consideration, for while many areas of the West look perpetually dry, when it does rain, runoff can funnel rapidly into and across roadways.

Larger residential subdivisions are usually handled by development corporations whose experience and scale of operation enables them to work out all of the details necessary for the successful implementation of the project. If market research ascertains demand for housing in a given area, the pressure is on to break ground, almost as if the first development is viewed as the victorious initiator that gets all the spoils. But likely as not, other residential tracts will swiftly follow, along with commercial retail space, and perhaps an office park or two. This is one sense of what we mean by "a rediscovered frontier," the development phenomenon that once a claim has been made in "virgin" territory, the word gets out rather quickly, and the landscape becomes something else entirely.

Special attention must be given to manufactured housing, since so many of our zoning codes continue to treat this type of dwelling differently. Following World War II, the nation's acute need for housing prompted not only massive suburban tract developments, but mass production of the dwelling unit itself. To protect property values within the more traditional on-site stick-built neighborhoods, local officials often segregated placement of mobile homes through restrictive zoning practices. Mobile home subdivisions (frequently delineated as "trailer parks" on U.S. Geological Survey [USGS] quadrangle maps) became a common element of many towns, not only in the West, but across the country (Hart, Rhodes, and Morgan 2002). The popularity of factory-built structures that were once known as mobile homes has not diminished. Indeed, they have become, under their new name, an affordable alternative to conventional on-site construction. This occurred as the baby boom generation was confronted with escalating home prices and climbing mortgage rates, as Dolores Hayden (2002, 75) has explained:

> Between 1970 and 2000, average prices for existing houses across the nation jumped from $28,700 to $177,000. Demand grew when thirty million baby-boom children of the post-World War II era came of home-buying age in the 1970s; an equivalent or greater number reached their thirties in the 1980s. As the price of houses turned into a steadily rising line on real estate agents' graphs, millions of these young Americans, most of them the product of the veterans' suburban tracts, wanted homes. At the bottom of the housing market, makers of mobile homes saw their chance. Changing the name of their product to "manufactured housing," they argued that they could make houses cheaply enough to "save the American dream."

In their contemporary, more spacious configurations, commonly known as double-wides or even triple-wides, manufactured houses can be virtually indistinguishable from their stick-built counterparts (Kuhlken 2000). And as their appearance has improved, so has their acceptance by communities. As the Urban Land Institute's *Residential Development Handbook* points out, "factory built housing historically has suffered a negative image, but that image is changing" (Bookout 1990, 167). Because costs for manufactured housing typically run about half that of conventional on-site construction, these units are becoming much more common in the New West, and can fill the need for affordable housing in many high-amenity locations where housing and land prices have jumped beyond reasonable levels. A case study of Flathead County, Montana, indicated a wide geographic distribution of older trailers (Hart, Rhodes, and Morgan 2002). Once relegated to "mobile home parks," today's factory-built house is more typically purchased for the purpose of placement on an individual rural property. Still, "many local zoning ordinances will not permit the installation of manufactured houses in standard, residentially zoned areas" (Bookout 1990, 170). Thus, to facilitate the capability for these homes to be sited anywhere stick-built structures are allowed, zoning regulations need to be trimmed of any lingering discrimination against manufactured housing.

At the other end of the housing spectrum, certain exclusive types of residential developments are also becoming more common than one might imagine, and a prime example is the airpark. Also known as a skypark, this is a residential neighborhood in which each dwelling, besides having an automobile approach, also has access to a runway for aircraft landings and takeoffs. The runway is integral to the development and is privately controlled and maintained, typically by the homeowners association. Each house in an airpark will usually have an airplane hangar in addition to its one- or two-car (sometimes more) garage bays, as shown by the example in Figure 2.5.

FIGURE 2.5
This otherwise conventional looking home in Drycreek Airpark south of Prineville, Oregon, exhibits the unusual configuration of an attached three-bay garage with an aircraft hangar. *Photograph by Robert Kuhlken.*

Because they also function as aircraft taxiways, streets and roads in such a development need to have carefully restricted traffic access, and for most of them, they are retained in private ownership and are not dedicated public rights-of-way.

A private airstrip is not an uncommon feature of rural western landscapes, for numerous ranches in the semiarid expanses of the intermountain region have maintained one since the early days of general aviation. What has not been so common, however, is the basically residential land use that now requires the accompaniment of aircraft-related infrastructure. Of course, there have always been a few vacation homes situated on prime real estate in the roadless backcountry that necessitated wealthy vacationers dropping in by air. But now there are permanently occupied or primary residences where the airplane has become the main mode of transport, as well as a primary source of recreation. Where there exists enough demand, a concentration of these lots will be built as an airpark, which allows the cost of developing and maintaining the runway to be divided among the owner-occupants of the homes. Sometimes, however, aircraft-accessible residential properties may be developed adjacent to publicly maintained general aviation facilities.

One of the first airparks in the country was built in 1941 and was located in Carmel Valley, California. Recognition of the advantages of such a development was delayed by the country's engagement in the war, but afterward, their popularity began to increase, for they allowed commuters who could afford this alternative form of transportation the capability to travel to jobs in nearby larger metropolitan areas while avoiding highway traffic congestion. That seemingly interminable hour-long automobile commute can now easily become a quick fifteen-minute flight; alternatively, the duration of the surface trip can be replaced with the same time in the air and effectively extend the feasible commuting distance four- or fivefold. Another famous airplane-supported subdivision was the Sierra Skypark near Fresno, constructed in 1960, which allowed for quick commutes to the urban entrails of the Bay area. Developments of aircraft-accessible homes have proliferated, and there are now well over 400 airparks nationwide; California alone has 30 residential subdivisions with a runway. An article in the *Los Angeles Times* recently highlighted the setting and lifestyle in Rosamond Skypark, where residents utilize aircraft for both work and leisure:

> Rosamond is on the edge of the Mojave Desert, in southern Kern County, and within easy commuting distance of Los Angeles—especially by air. The 60-home park, established in 1986, is surrounded for miles by tumbleweeds and Joshua trees—the area is nearly devoid of dining or entertainment venues. The Rosamond homes, built on half-acre lots, cost from $225,000 to $400,000 and come with garages and hangars. There is a monthly upkeep fee of $54 to maintain the runway and taxiways. The airstrip and other facilities are co-owned by residents—similar to the way common grounds in a condominium are owned. (Carpenter and Willman 2001)

An alternate facet of this kind of development is the increasing number of facilities being sited in relatively remote and otherwise basically inaccessible locations, such as Mogollon Airpark in northern Arizona or the Sunrise Sky Park in Melba, Idaho, along the Snake River southwest of Boise.

Planners who encounter applications to develop such a facility are faced with many additional concerns and regulatory checklists during the project review process. These include working with the Federal Aviation Administration (FAA) to ensure that flight safety standards can be met, and that there are no hazards to aircraft operations situated nearby or potential conflicts with existing airports. Landing approach areas often form a triangular overlay zone extending outward from either end of the runway, where potentially conflicting land uses must be carefully regulated. Besides safety, noise is another concern that must be addressed in the planning process. Despite such challenges, the airpark might be considered the quintessential high-end residential development in the New West, where long-distance commutes from remote locations favored for lifestyle domiciles almost demand such a solution.

By way of another example of residential land use at the higher end of the market, there is an increasing trend toward the creation of master-planned residential developments focused on a single-amenity feature. These could be quite large, and extensively spread out, requiring an inordinate amount of land area, or very dense, depending on the recreational facility involved. Most typically the recreational focus is a golf course, but in other areas such as lakeside or coastal settings, it may be a marina for recreational boating. In other regions such as southern California or parts of the intermountain West where riding of horses for leisure is a popular activity, it could be an equestrian-oriented subdivision, complete with a covered arena and/or perimeter riding trails surrounding an array of low-density dwellings and associated paddocks. In the mountainous West, integrated residential properties associated with a skiing facility are on the increase. An example here is Beaver Creek, Colorado, where a "2,132 acre ski-oriented community will contain 3,223 dwelling units ranging in density from one to 26 units per acre" (Bookout 1990, 188).

Because of the soaring popularity of the game, and the apparent chronic shortage of available links, golf course developments are by far the most common form of what has come to be called "themed recreational communities" (Bookout 1990, 182). Many of these projects verge on being resorts, which we examine in greater detail at the very end of this chapter. To differentiate here, resorts are where people tend to have second homes or timeshare condominiums for either a periodic or extended stay away from their primary residence for the purpose of rejuvenation and relaxation, and are most likely all-inclusive developments that encompass a wider range of recreational facilities and supportive land uses such as hotels and retail shopping districts. But there are many recreation-focused developments that are not vacation destinations at all, but contain the main residence, perhaps the *only* dwelling, for workers who regularly commute to jobs and who still wish to play while at home. These are commonly found on the outer edge of the commuting fields of larger metropolitan areas, but are on the increase around smaller towns as well. Likewise, within many of the more upscale retirement communities, which are not hampered by locational constraints associated with employment opportunities, golf courses and other recreational features such as tennis courts and swimming pools are almost expected, and we examine these at the end of this section.

Golf course developments by their very nature not only take up a large area of land but also have excessive water needs. A standard 18-hole course requires 120 acres of land, and "a water source capable of producing 1.5 million to 3.5 million gallons per week for irrigation" (Bookout 1990, 187). That is in addition to the aggregated acreage and total water usage of the associated housing parcels. Because a golf course also requires a huge capital investment up front for land acquisition, design, and construction, along with expensive maintenance outlays, housing and residential lot prices in these developments tend to be exclusionary. This is the only way that developers are able to recoup their initial investment and to manage the ongoing costs of upkeep.

Finally, scattered across the West are an ever-increasing number of housing developments and platted subdivisions specifically catering to people entering the golden years of retirement. This has been an accepted element of the western landscape for some time, ever since Del Webb initiated and then replicated the successful formula embodied in Sun City, Arizona, northwest of Phoenix. Yet the demand for this particular land use is now beginning to rise dramatically, as members of the baby boom generation finish out their careers and look for a final place to hang their hats. Retirees in large numbers now look forward to indulging in those activities they previously may have had little (or never enough) time for: fishing, hunting, golfing, gambling, and socializing with like-minded neighbors.

Not all retirement communities were as legitimate as those various incarnations of Sun City, however. During the post–World War II years, but beginning even earlier, many large-scale "developments"—in the arid West especially—were traced out as simple lines in the sand with no intention of ever "proving up," to use the old homestead terminology, but were simply money-making ruses. William Fulton (1991, 106) outlines the basic tale of greed, the land use ramifications of which are still being grappled with in many jurisdictions:

> One of the most colorful chapters in American history is the story of land speculation in the United States—and, especially, the story of the land swindlers who bought property, divided it, and sold it to gullible people who had never seen it. By the turn of the century . . . these shady characters turned to exotic "resort" areas like California and Florida, subdividing mountains and deserts and swamps into lots

that existed only on paper—and in the minds of small buyers who dreamed of re-tiring there.

Fortunately, attorneys general in many western states have cooperatively erected legal roadblocks to the continuation of most of these fraudulent schemes. But even when the transaction itself was entirely legal, the end result of learning that ownership involves a nearly worthless piece of property can come as quite a shock. When RK worked the counter at the planning office in rural Crook County, Ore-gon, older folks would often come in seeking directions to the five- or ten-acre parcel they had owned for years but had never set eyes on. In some cases, these were retired military personnel who had purchased the land through an adver-tisement in the *Stars and Stripes* newspaper. I had the unfortunate role of inform-ing these people that obtaining necessary infrastructure such as water, electricity, and in many cases, even legal access, was highly unlikely.

Geographer Bill Stroud (1995, 3) has studied the nation's recreational-retirement communities as "important elements of landscape change" and reck-ons that their successful and extensive establishment has been the result of several combinant factors: "the desire of millions of Americans to own land, promotional efforts by land developers, the amenities of a rural environment (pull factor), the desire to escape an urban environment (push factor), the availability of large tracts of relatively inexpensive land located near interstates or major highways, and the absence of government regulations." While Florida has been the leading target for these kinds of developments, the next three states with the highest num-ber of recreational subdivisions of 1,000 acres or more are Arizona, California, and Colorado. Moreover, there are some noteworthy geographic patterns. For ex-ample, Costilla County, in south-central Colorado, has fully one-fifth of its total land area parceled out as recreational-retirement subdivisions, while Arizona shows a concentration of these developments in Yavapai County and Mohave County (Stroud 1995, 7–10). But during the 1960s and 1970s, retirement-lot fever seemed to spread rapidly throughout the western states, particularly in the more remote areas, which have the locational advantage of only adding to the feeling of "getting away from it all."

Many of these developments were never really "developed" at all, but were speculative ventures bordering on bait and switch operations, as outlined by Stroud (1995, 13):

During the land acquisition phase, developers acquire large tracts of relatively inex-pensive land that meets their development requirements. The land must be easily fi-nanced, with little or no cash down, and zoned for subdivision. Ideally, it should also have scenic and developable terrain, soil with suitable load-bearing capabilities and adequate drainage, a potable water supply, and adequate utilities. After acquisition, the developer moves into the development phase, which combines the construction of on-site facilities and the implementation of an elaborate promotional campaign. A showcase core area and a road network (usually unpaved) are built, the latter to provide access to lots. The core area has an attractive entrance, paved roads, and large, well-constructed sales and administrative office buildings, which contrasts sharply with the remainder of the project.

Sometimes developers go to nowhere near even such minimal lengths, as attested by the numerous named subdivisions that consist merely of simple rectilinear survey lines on a map. Even in those areas that may now uphold certain regulatory standards for rural land development processes, and where authorities might view large-scale subdivisions especially with much more scrutiny, what's done is done, in terms of surveying and splitting up large pieces of land into numerous tiny lots, albeit only on paper. Despite often having inadequate access, little or no service infrastructure, and perhaps the impossibility of obtaining on-site drinking water, thousands of these recreational-retirement lots have been "grandfathered in" as approved parcels. Consequently, throughout the West, the seeds of discontent have already been sown, as more and more landowners over the past few years have started showing up at county offices with blueprints, plans, or a receipt for a manufactured home in hand, requesting a building permit or siting approval. Inactive developments, sometimes referred to as "platted lands," can become a serious problem for many counties that have little recourse to remedial procedures. Known as "sagebrush subdivisions" in eastern Oregon, they were partly responsible for the robust land use laws enacted more than thirty years ago in that state. They represent an ongoing concern in Arizona, where lands that have been divided without going through proper survey procedures and regulatory oversight are called "wildcat subdivisions."

But there have been issues and problems associated with the more or less successful ventures as well. Would-be future residents may have been fooled into purchasing a parcel with the expectation of more extensive provision of facilities and amenities beyond the sampling highlighted in the core showcase area or as depicted in the conceptual model: "Proposed lakes, eighteen-hole golf courses, swimming pools, and tennis courts may never materialize, and lot owners may be stuck with property they cannot give away, let alone sell for a profit" (Stroud 1995, 15). Whatever the level of truth in advertising or follow-up on promises made, these rural residential developments are a feature to be reckoned with across many areas of the West and indeed represent a problem that can only become compounded over time, as infill and attempts at build-out take place, perhaps straining the capacity of already deficient levels of infrastructure and provision of services.

Retirement migration will continue to shape the landscapes of the New West, at whatever fixed income level is involved. Indeed, the region as a whole is favorably portrayed by numerous retirement-oriented publications. Many of the rapidly growing locations that we describe in the next chapter are highly regarded for their retirement "ambiance" according to the latest edition of *Retirement Places Rated*, a measurement indicating "the presence of things that most persons agree enhance retirement living" (Savageau 2004, 6). This index of overall setting, reflecting a number of cultural and recreational amenities, perhaps more than other traditional factors such as climate or cost of living, has increased the amount of interest in putting out to pasture in some of the smaller towns of the western United States. Listed among the top 20 places in this roster of more than 200 locations are Bellingham, Medford-Ashland, Kalispell, Bozeman, Durango, Fort Collins, Santa Barbara, suburban San Diego, Santa Fe, Tucson, Flagstaff, and Cottonwood-Verde Valley (Savageau 2004, 7).

COMMERCIAL

Commercial land use in the New West ranges from the gentrified makeover of downtown storefronts to stand-alone super regional malls that may serve as destinations for a full day's shopping activity, much the same way that theme parks have become a self-enclosed entertainment node. Between those two ends of the spectrum may be found a wide assortment of commercial enterprises, each with varying degrees of neighborhood impact and potential land use planning concerns. Many of these types of commercial land use are not restricted to occurrences within the western states, of course, but in this region commercial development can arrive quite unexpectedly, especially for rural areas that have not previously encountered these kinds of land use patterns. Many small towns are struggling to retain the downtown businesses that give the place its liveliness and sense of well-being. Greater convenience and access by automobile are counteracting the traditional centripetal pull of these central business districts. The provision of everyday goods and services throughout much of the rural West as well as the edges of small towns is now sustained by retail establishments that tend to sprout like weeds along highways and roadsides. As with many places elsewhere across the country, the strip mall has replaced the downtown central business district. Often, in the case of rural housing subdivisions, there is no downtown close enough to these new residential developments that will serve as the requisite place to shop. Sometimes, larger developments that are primarily housing schemes will actually be mixed-use projects that also entail a more or less complete package of commercial retail space. This may result in decay or at least degeneration of the nearest downtown. Such was the case with the Rock Ridge development outside of Superior, Colorado, one of the numerous satellites surrounding the Denver galactic city. Residents of nearby Erie recently voiced opposition to a similar proposal entailing Vista Ridge subdivision with 2,500 homes and more than 100 acres of commercial land. These are just a few examples of the dynamic forces in commercial real estate development that are shaping the region.

In broad terms, the provision of retail space in the New West manifests several identifiable forms. First, there is an increasing recognition of the value of the central business district, the feeling that downtown matters. Conversely, as a community's population expands, and with it consumer demands that dictate wider variety and convenience, many downtowns are left behind as outlying commercial space is approved. Many smaller localities still cling to the outmoded notion that a new shopping center at the edge of town somehow confers modernity, sophistication, and respect. Even when downtowns manage to hang on to essential retail functions, too often the character of the central business district changes, as normal, everyday wares are now able to be purchased at "big box" discount stores and national chain stores located out along commercial strips. Eventually, those types of downtown establishments go out of business one by one. Rushing in (sometimes very slowly) to fill the vacuum of empty storefronts are other types of shops that may ultimately include specialty clothing stores, gift shops, antique shops, art galleries, and higher-end boutiques. Sometimes this is not an immediate transition, however, and filling in between times can be some less than desirable stopgap establishments that tend to give downtown a seedy, dilapidated appearance, such as discount "dollar store" outlets, tattoo and body piercing parlors, check-cashing franchises, and consignment shops.

Many places have attempted to encourage the continuation of central business district functions through a variety of techniques, ranging from local government enticements and intervention to participation in the patented-formula national Main Street program. Others have taken even more drastic measures to unify the design of their downtown, oftentimes leading to a "Disneyfication of Main Street" (Francaviglia 1996). Historic preservation measures may seek to freeze-frame a period of time in hopes of capitalizing on nostalgia. Whole towns may reinvent themselves as something else entirely in hopes of staying alive. Such was the story behind the transformation of Leavenworth, Washington, from obsolete logging town to a fabricated Bavarian village (Price 1997). Meanwhile, for those communities that have enabled unrestrained commercial development to occur on the outskirts of town, the identical retail landscape of strip malls, fast food outlets, automobile dealerships, and drive-through banks becomes all too familiar. Such is the dialectical dilemma facing small towns across the West: how to accommodate growth and the necessary commercial land use accompaniment without turning downtown into a theme park and the edge of town into a placeless assemblage of nationally ubiquitous franchises with their themed architecture and oversized signage (Gottdiener 1997).

As noted earlier, the pioneer settlement pattern for territories that eventually became the western United States was basically urban, with points of concentrated habitation starting out as either an oasis, perhaps a town emerging adjacent to some important resource such as an ore deposit, or else a stop or station along the rail line. Across the arid and semiarid expanses of the West, places with a reliable supply of water were few and far between, and thus became natural nodes of urbanization. Other towns served transportation or resource needs. What all of them had in common was a commercial core, those several blocks of retail establishments along a quintessential Main Street that formed the central business district. Geographer Richard Francaviglia (1996) has outlined a typology of commercial townscapes, which includes the three predominant forms found across the West. Towns oriented toward transport and marketing "are based on prototype designs that originated farther east, but are especially well-developed from Kansas and the Dakotas west to Montana" (Francaviglia 1996, 116). Here, Main Street is oriented either parallel or perpendicular to the railroad, and the train station then assumed a significant role in the economics and life of the population. Another map (1996, 120) correctly indicates the geographic extension for the occurrence of such a settlement type beyond the northern Great Plains, into those intermountain areas such as portions of the Great Basin and across the interior Northwest's so-called Inland Empire that were first settled in conjunction with railroad development. Southwestern townscapes, derived from Spanish traditions, typically were arranged around a central plaza with a church or cathedral, and the surrounding downtown civic and commercial buildings manifested unique architectural adaptations to the fierce desert sun, incorporating awnings and arcades in their design. The Mormon Culture Region, centered on Utah and the overlapping edges of adjacent states, evinces its own idiosyncratic style of Main Street, with unusually wide streets ordained by prophetic decree to be 2 chains, or 132 feet in width, and the church buildings to be prominently and centrally located. But whatever form it took, the essential function of downtown was always the same: to provide a highly accessible physical space where goods and services could be offered for sale to customers from the town and surrounding hinterland of settlement.

The challenge for many downtowns has been how to maintain their vitality in the face of increasing competition from outlying commercial districts. In all likelihood, downtowns will continue to function as providers of commercial space in varying degrees, although changes are everywhere apparent. One of the ways that towns have tried to encourage the retention of businesses is to change the layout of streets and parking places. Taken to extremes, this becomes a design alteration that Francaviglia (1996, 167) has termed "the malling of main Street":

> In the 1960s and 1970s, many Main Streets were closed to traffic in the hope that a pedestrian environment would improve retailing downtown (that is, increase the number of people), and Main Street would thus be able to directly compete with shopping centers that were drawing away its trade. Typically, the creation of a downtown mall involves closing the street and providing unlimited pedestrian access to shops. It reduces the noise, danger, and pollution of the automobile, and provides additional—often ample—space for street furniture, benches, sculptures, and lighting.

Some of these complete makeovers were not as beneficial as hoped, and a few places that tried this idea have returned to providing unrestrained access to the automobile. One of the more successful compromises has been to turn the downtown streets into one-way, single-lane conveyances for traffic, then taking the space of the removed lane and dedicating it to wider sidewalks. Grand Junction, Colorado, was among the first places to pioneer this method, and it has worked admirably for that community. Another variation involves bumping out the sidewalks at street intersections, to create a narrow one-lane ingress and egress to the block, and providing diagonal parking places rather than parallel slots along the street. This has worked well for downtowns such as Wenatchee, Washington. Other design amenities, including the replacement of concrete sidewalks with brick pavers, or the erection of stylized street lighting, may enhance the overall appearance of the central business district. As the typical New West townscape evolves, however, a more common metamorphosis is evident in the mixture of businesses that occupy the core retail space.

Specialized commercial land use is one of the hallmarks of the New West downtown business scene. The general merchandise stores of the past have given way to boutiques, gift shops, and single-genre mercantiles that now constitute a mosaic of different and distinct establishments. This can provide variety and interest for the retail customer, yet is also a discouraging trend in terms of keeping everyday needs in stock in downtown shops. Of course, in the more touristed locations, there will be a dozen different stores all offering the same kitschy souvenirs. But in those communities that have embraced New West sensibilities, and where substantial residential growth has taken place, consumer expectations have been raised regarding the opportunity to shop locally. Moreover, the mix of goods and services has dramatically shifted, and the kinds of articles and range of trade skills offered for sale now tend to skew toward the luxury or amenity end of the spectrum. It is not unusual, for example, to see holistic health services such as therapeutic massage or New Age counseling being advertised. These days, health food stores have evolved from their hippie co-op genesis to upscale yuppie markets, and may be found in many of the trendy New West downtowns. Generalized pet stores have now become specialized pet boutiques, such as the dog biscuit bakery that recently opened in Ellensburg, Washington. One of the more common enterprises to claim space and set up shop in a rejuvenated central business district is the art gallery.

Art is big business in the New West. Not only do new residents and tourists alike have more disposable income than in the past, but western art is nationally a hot genre these days. In terms of land use, this has several ramifications. In towns, artist supply stores and custom framing shops are part of the requisite commercial support system for the arts. Galleries and art studios are now common elements of downtowns or edge-of-town entranceways. But artists themselves may choose to market their own work rather than go through a broker or general gallery. Likewise, traditional Native American creations such as beadwork, jewelry, or woven textiles have become highly sought after commodities. In some areas, native vendors may set up stands alongside the road or at highway rest stops, a typical scene not only on the Navajo Reservation, but for many locations surrounding Indian country. In the same context, trading posts have expanded and have amplified their role of handling Native arts crafts and crafts for the tourist market. Generally, painting, pottery, basketry, textiles, jewelry, and sculpture may all be given individual outlets for display and sale by each artist who specializes in one of these media or techniques.

Larger galleries are also operated by brokers or dealers who handle the work of many artists and craftspersons. Moreover, the production of art sometimes requires much more elaborate facilities than a simple easel set up in adequate light. In the case of sculpture, for instance, studios may come to resemble small industrial plants, and these may have the potential for adverse impact on neighboring properties. Small towns and remote locations are no longer implausible settings for such activities, and planners across the New West need to be aware of their operational characteristics. For example, major bronze foundries may now be found in such tiny, out-of-the-way places as Choteau, Montana; Lander, Wyoming; and Joseph, Oregon. Indeed, diminutive and isolated Joseph has combined pride in its local foundry with other attractions by staging a music festival that also celebrates the village brew pub, an annual event known as "Blues, Brews, and Bronze." Welcome to the New West.

The surge in automobility across the country following World War II radically altered the geography of retail space. The importance of downtown urban centers as highly accessible marketplaces declined as outlying districts became targets for commercial developments that were capable of attracting just as many customers. In the western United States, as elsewhere, shopping centers sprang up at the edge of town where greater land availability and lower real estate prices combined to allow large stores or assemblages of stores to be constructed on short notice to meet the demands of increasingly mobile consumers. The term "shopping center" has been defined as "A group of architecturally unified commercial establishments built on a site that is planned, developed, owned and managed as an operating unit related in its location, size and type of shops to the trade area that it serves . . . [and] . . . provides on-site parking in definite relationship to the types and total size of the stores" (Casazza and Spink 1985, 1).

Developers soon began to elaborate upon this concept, from humble beginnings as a simple array of linear storefronts to the somewhat more sophisticated shopping plaza with open interior courtyard, on to today's regional malls, featuring a trademark fully enclosed climate-controlled shopping environment, complete with piped-in Muzak, food courts, and entertainment facilities such as video game arcades and multiplex cinemas. A patent formula of successful design ensures that nearly every mall will look the same: a pair or more of large department stores, ideally national chains, anchor either end of the project. Larger malls have additional anchor stores holding down the middle of the building, or at the terminus of any number of spokes. In between will be the usual franchise specialty shops that count on name familiarity, brand recognition, and symbolic status to stay in business. Variations in building size range upward from the basic regional mall to the so-called super regional mall, which must have "three or more department stores and at least 500,000 square feet of GLA [gross leasable area]" (Casazza and Spink 1985, 165). Surrounding the structure are the precise number of parking spaces, counted and arranged by code, with correct lighting and token landscaping meant to ameliorate the utter dreadfulness of so much asphalt. Regional malls and super regional malls may now be found on the outskirts of all of the larger towns and cities in the West. While it takes a car to get there, the duration of the shopping experience in a mall is primarily pedestrian, an irony that has not been lost on those trying to keep downtown businesses alive.

The strip mall, by contrast, is totally oriented to the automobile. Indeed, those sidewalks that local ordinances might require to be placed along the perimeter of these developments are conspicuous in their uselessness. Strip malls can assume several forms, according to the size and number of businesses that will fill the building's apportionments. Smaller facilities consist of a simple linear row of storefronts, almost as if a section of Main Street had been requested to vacate its downtown space and relocate out here along the highway. Strip malls have sprung up all over the country, of course, and are hardly limited to the western states as a signature commercial land use. But they have become all too common, and all too obvious, as symbolic manifestations of the spurt of new growth that has taken this region by storm.

Perhaps the most common new retail construction for rapidly expanding small towns across the West involves a large variety store, perhaps a local or regional chain, usually built in tandem with either a regional or national grocery outlet, along with a few smaller shops or lunch cafes nestled in between. Often they will show up seemingly all of a sudden on some neglected vacant parcel at the edge of town, much to the delight of some residents and to the utter dismay of others. Moreover, lately it seems that no new shopping center is deemed complete without either a genuine Starbucks or some other custom coffee vendor. Espresso stands that erupt out by the road depend on a drive-up window, which of course only adds to the overall automobile orientation of the site. In terms of the building's placement, the parking lot requirements, and other general site plan considerations, the design for such facilities has not changed much in fifty years. Which goes a long way toward explaining why rural western landscapes are rapidly coming to resemble every other place in the country, and suggests perhaps that the New West is not so "new" after all.

Although full-scale regional malls are still being constructed within the rapidly converted open space around the larger cities, the more typical commercial land use in smaller towns involves the recognizable discount retailing giants such as Wal-Mart, Kmart, and Target, among others. Nothing epitomizes large-scale New West commerce more than "the Big Box." It arrives on the scene sometimes after great anticipation, sometimes with dreaded fear, always stirring up mixed emotions. In some cases, comprehensive plans are revised and zoning is changed to accommodate the promised jobs and enhanced shopping opportunities desired by area citizenry. Take one recent example. During the summer of 2000, Wal-Mart proposed a 204,000-square-foot supercenter on 44 acres of land in a residential zone in Twin Falls, Idaho. It was slated to employ 500 people, obviously a huge boost to the local economy, but residents of surrounding residential areas naturally were concerned about impacts. No place is immune from the inroads made by these national chains. Another big Wal-Mart was recently built on the edge of Walla Walla, Washington, a town that has made great strides in protecting its compact, pedestrian-oriented urban core and enhancing livability.

By and large, outlying commercial development follows predictable patterns, and though speculation may sometimes overestimate demand, careful market area research by private development interests will usually dictate the scale and timing of any new proposals. Communities can therefore easily do their own research in order to anticipate what may be coming in the months or years ahead, and be better equipped to plan accordingly. Elected officials and concerned citizens would be well advised to become familiar with the standard categories and ranges of commercial developments that constitute likely scenarios for future projects. The Urban Land Institute has provided data on general characteristics of shopping centers, with information on classifications according to type of tenant, typical parameters for gross leasable area (GLA), usual minimum site area necessary, and the threshold, or minimum, population required to support each kind of facility.

Adequate parking allocations must also be maintained for any new shopping center, and these typically will range from 4 spaces per 1,000 square feet GLA for smaller centers, to 5 spaces per 1,000 square feet GLA for the larger malls (Casazza and Spink 1985, 65). And here in the New West, where SUVs and monster 4WD pickups reign supreme, you might as well forget about trying to squeeze any additional spaces into the lot by designating them "compact only." As one of the most visible elements of the built environment, and based on the amount of land area they take up, parking lots ought to be viewed as a form of land use in and of themselves (Jakle and Sculle 2004). In the growing small towns of the region, where it seems the majority of recently arrived residents prefer living in outlying areas in large houses on large properties and pedestrian life is not yet an option, parking lots are a necessary accompaniment to any new commercial development. Most of these communities have never needed sophisticated codes to address parking lot requirements, and this may result in little or no landscaping and a lack of other design considerations. Finally, for any new commercial land use, off-site impacts should be considered as well, and traffic counts must be predicted for peak hour trips undertaken by arriving and exiting customers.

Because of their increasing appearance in the rural and small town West, two additional types of outlying commercial developments should be mentioned here, namely the convenience store and the strip commercial zone. The 7-11 or Circle-K is likely to show up anywhere, and not only replicates and replaces the small grocery store of the past, but likewise combines that essential bread-and-milk function with today's version of the equally essential gasoline service station. Indeed, beginning in the late 1980s, many franchised petroleum companies started building full-fledged convenience stores rather than the traditional single-purpose gas station (Jakle and Sculle 1994, 80). These facilities are often the precursor to greater development pressures, so when such proposals arrive on a county planner's desk, ears might wish to perk up and pay attention.

The other type of commercial area that actually stems from misguided planning and zoning decisions is the strip commercial development, as explained, again, in the Urban Land Institute publication by Casazza and Spink (1985, 7):

> Strip commercial development, as distinguished from the "strip shopping center" (a frequently used physical description of a center with a linear configuration), is not a shopping center. Strip commercial can be a string of commercially zoned lots developed independently or a string of retail commercial stores on a single site where there is no anchor tenant and no central management, and where tenant mix results from leasing to available tenants with good credit, not from planning and executing a leasing program.

Way too often, local comprehensive plans will designate broad swaths of land areas adjacent to highways on the edge of town and, even worse, entrance roads *into* town, as commercial, under the impression that automobile accessibility is the single most important consideration for determining adequate provision of this land use category. What this *creates*, of course, is the commercial strip that nobody seems to approve of once it has been developed. Moreover, when a linear string of businesses emerges in the absence of a sign code or other effective guidelines that regulate advertising, the result is not only an unfortunate and preventable eyesore but a generic landscape that could be anywhere, one without any hint of regional identity or character. One interpretation of the significance of such a scene has been expressed in the widely cited exploration by Richard Horwitz (1985, 20):

> A cruise down the strip is far more than a visual experience. It is a kind of projective test for American culture. Like an ink blot, it may first engage the eyes but inevitably stirs the other senses. It is as ugly or beautiful, as inviting or horrifying, as our mem-

ories and dreams. A critique of the strip, pro or con, in terms of its formal, physical features is only a beginning. Its true meaning is to be found in the ways it is used, both pragmatically and symbolically.

And so the commercial strip becomes, in the words of geographer William Wyckoff (1992, 293), "a place exclusively claimed by no one, but used by everyone . . . a setting unabashedly evocative of American values, and one that prefigures, for better or worse, the future course of landscape evolution in countless American places."

But it need not be this way. The shopping experience does not have to be so inextricably oriented to the automobile (Beyard and Pawlukiewicz 2001). Several locations in California, including San Bernardino and Glendale, successfully experimented early on with major shopping centers in the heart of town, although this was perhaps not so difficult a transition for many areas of a region in which the established urban form had in fact been predetermined by the car: "In the western part of the United States, the first downtown centers were often merely suburban mall designs with some modifications—most notably, structured parking—inserted into the downtown of what was already an auto-oriented post World War II suburban community" (Casazza and Spink 1985, 14). One important thing to remember is that malls today do not have to look like the malls of yesterday. Under the direction of carefully drafted design review standards and with encouragement from local officials, commercial developers may find it to their advantage to build retail space that will blend into the existing urban mosaic of even the smallest town.

Mixed-use retail centers that combine commercial use with office space and other functions have more recently proven to be popular alternatives to the outlying shopping center. With the application of more intensive "new urbanist" designs, a blend of commercial, light industrial, office and warehouse facilities, along with residential space in a range of housing options, offers exciting new possibilities for combining work areas and places to live with shopping and entertainment opportunities (Bohl 2002). Even the "big box" no longer needs to be shunned and relegated to the highway. When Pacific Northwest regional grocery/variety chain Fred Meyer wanted to build in Ellensburg, Washington, the town welcomed the megastore to a neglected former industrial "brownfields" corner adjacent to the central business district that had once been the site of a lumber mill. The retail project development occurred in conjunction with tying the site to the downtown core by rejuvenating several blocks with period street lighting and attractive brick paver sidewalks.

Besides shopping centers and malls, strip zones and minimarts, and the isolated big box store, what else might show up on the commercial horizon of a rapidly growing community in the changing West? Our increasing cultural trend toward entertainment manifests itself in any number of imminent new land uses, some of them merely modified versions of their former selves. Few among us still remember the drive-in theater on the edge of town, but it has not gone away so much as moved indoors. While downtowns in most places are trying to retain the movie theaters and playhouses that were once a centerpiece of civic life, the multiscreen cinemax has conquered the hearts and minds of the populace, replacing the now defunct drive-in, sometimes literally in the same spot. It is perhaps ironic that this is one case where a decidedly automobile-oriented land use has actually declined in favor of an interior space that people negotiate on foot. Fast food restaurants, on the other hand, owe much of their appeal to the drive-through lane with its serving window and intercom-equipped menu board. Restaurants will, of course, continue to proliferate as Americans on the go eat more of their meals out of the home. Increases in the overall number of ubiquitous fast food franchises and the more formal sit-down establishments alike must be anticipated as a community grows and matures. Office buildings are another likely increaser, especially for an attractive and amenity-rich New West location. Curiously, even in the smallest of places, claims are often made that usable office space is at a premium in the central business district, while attempts at architectural trendiness and the expected highway exposure will require that an outlying virgin site be developed rather than the more sensible alternative of rehabilitating any vacant buildings downtown.

Although normally categorized in standard land use typologies as a public or semipublic use, churches are now being built on such a grand scale, and are targeting the same less expensive larger parcels beyond the edges of town, that we feel they ought to be included among commercial types of development. Traditionally, churches have been given free rein to locate where they wish. Even where land use planning and zoning are established functions of local government, an application for a new church building is often granted as an "outright use" in most zones. There is almost an unstated "hands off" policy when it comes to the locational decisions of churches or, for that matter, schools as well. But church officials and school districts alike are now seeking to expand while taking advantage of the best deal on land they can find. Typically the purchased parcel will be situated at a considerable distance beyond the currently built-up area. Furthermore, the latest trend in religious buildings is to go large, with structures that may hold a congregation numbering in the thousands. The physical building alone will likely be greatly out of scale with its surroundings, but then the impervious surface of its requisite parking lot must be considered as well. Consequently, the siting of one of these "megachurches" on its own can create conflicts with surrounding land uses that are decidedly more rural in character. But they can also act as a catalyst for further urbanization, stimulating nearby residential and commercial development. Likewise, when a new high school or middle school is allowed to be built out in the rural countryside, it will not take long for housing subdivisions and strip malls to welcome themselves to the neighborhood. Local communities need to keep these scenarios in mind when planning future land use beyond the built-up area.

Religious transformations of the landscape are not limited to urban and suburban zones, however, and here in the New West, large rural properties can sometimes be turned into retreat centers, utopian communes, or even attempts at full-scale "cities on a hill" (Fitzgerald 1986). Such was the case when a large ranch in central Oregon became the location for Rajneeshpuram, which stimulated one of the more colorful land use battles in that state's history. More recently, the Church Universal and Triumphant, or CUT, made neighboring Yellowstone National Park officials nervous with their plans to drill into geothermal resources beneath the ground of their upper Paradise Valley property in Montana.

Some commercial uses are perhaps better classified as recreational activities, albeit private enterprises that charge admission, because of the nature of the operation and, in some cases, the extensive use of land involved. Some of these activities are appearing in other parts of the country, to be sure, but they are often more visible out West where terrain and sparse vegetation allow for unobstructed views. For example, paintball "grounds" have become popular attractions for those who thrive on this particular adrenaline rush, and these facilities may now be found in even some of the more remote locations. Responding to the need to indulge in a similar, perhaps a more primal instinct, fee hunting has begun to supplement the marginal income of increasing numbers of farmers and ranchers. Upland game bird or waterfowl shooting opportunities are the more common operation, but these have been joined in some places by big game ranches, which can provide guides along with access. Fishing, which has become very big business in the New West, especially fly-fishing, is also intensifying rural land use in a commercial sense. Trout ponds, remembered by many as a kitschy roadside attraction in many parts of the West, have metamorphosed into exclusive and very lucrative fee fishing holes, in both stillwater settings and along private riverbanks and spring creeks. Several other commercial enterprises are outlined in the recreational land use section later. As these uses become more commonplace, we are witnessing the commodification of the rural West.

While some rural areas are liable to see an increase in commercial activity, the edges and entrance roads to most small towns across the region are almost certain to become developed along these lines. Several types of businesses are distinct land uses that ought to be mentioned here because they crop up time and again in the commercial landscapes of the New West. The drive-through coffee espresso stand, for example, once a signature of the Pacific Northwest scene, has diffused throughout the larger region. These can range from simple shacks erected by a local entrepreneur to standardized upscale national or regional franchises. As a town's population growth pushes its targeted market beyond established threshold levels, fast food chains will frantically fill in the spaces between farm implement dealers, feed stores, irrigation supply outlets, and what were once gas stations. As noted earlier, nationally franchised convenience stores with gasoline pumping islands have largely replaced the traditional automobile service station (Jakle and Sculle 1994). Other automobile-related businesses, such as tire shops and auto parts stores will also emerge here, again, more than likely accompanied by the themed signage of a national chain. Automobile dealerships are a commercial fixture of most towns with at least 10,000 population. Once strategically positioned in the heart of the commercial business district (CBD), especially in smaller towns, the latest trend has been for these dealerships to move out to the edges, either along one of the main arterials, or, if there is an interstate nearby, to a large, well-lit site at a highway exit.

One of the more emblematic land uses that proliferate in areas with New West tendencies are self-storage units. These will likely become a major element of the commercial landscape for places experiencing a housing boom and where migrants are arriving with moving vans while awaiting to take possession of a new home, or for recreation-oriented locations that have marked seasonal population shifts. Many people simply now use them to keep all the stuff that won't fit in the garage at home. Typically located in a highly accessible spot along one of the entrance roads into town, these businesses can differ greatly in terms of scale, both for individual unit size and in total number of units, and in overall design and complexity. There will usually be a small management office on-site and there may even be an all-hours attendant. The structures appear as a row of cheaply built, windowless barracks, internally divided into identical spaces fronted with a small roll-up garage door. Concrete or asphalt covers the driveways in between each block of units, at the ends of which the town or county zoning code may require token efforts at landscaping, what these days is straightforwardly referred to as "putting parsley around the pig" (Hayden 2004, 86). Security dictates that a high chain link fence surround the perimeter, perhaps topped with concertina wire. At this point the citizens who cherish living in a small town in the rural West need to ask: Is this what we wish to become?

Finally, we come to what might be viewed as a new hybridized setting for commerce and industry: the so-called Business Park. Certain more desirable suburban and even exurban areas can become so saturated with multiple replications of this form of land use they have assumed the shape of what Robert Lang (2003) has termed "*edgeless* cities . . . a form of sprawling office development that does not have the density or cohesiveness of edge cities." Whether coalesced across the landscape or when appearing more in isolated instance, most of these individual business "parks" are collections of low-profile buildings that squat along curvilinear tree-lined boulevards. Watch for them to pop up at interstate highway interchanges almost anywhere. They tend to emerge along the edges of rapidly growing small towns, and will harbor an assortment of offices and light manufacturing facilities or assembly plants, perhaps along with varying provisions of commercial retail space. When situated close enough to draw from an adequate consumer threshold, assorted shops might be sprinkled here and there among the office buildings, maybe a restaurant or even a hotel. Seen as a desirable and modern form of land use in most places, they are clean and ecofriendly green, and the statement they make is hard to misread: We have arrived. Here, amid the landscaped grounds of a campus-like setting we might well ask: What is commercial, what is industrial?

INDUSTRIAL

It is not merely the dramatic elaboration of residential and commercial landscapes that typify the changes taking hold across the West. The movement of industry to the western states during the last few decades of the twentieth century has coincided with the decline of manufacturing in the Northeast and upper Midwest, where enough layoffs, closures, and outright plant abandonments have occurred to warrant the label "Rust Belt." Within a continuous band of states, from Illinois through Massachusetts, each state lost manufacturing jobs for the three decades between 1960 and 1990. Conversely, for the eleven western states, every one gained manufacturing jobs during 1970–1980, and all of them but Oregon, Montana, and Wyoming gained for the decade from 1980 to 1990, with Nevada and Arizona showing the greatest percentage increases (Earle 2003, 96). Historically much of the West has been bound in a core-periphery relationship with owners and shareholders of large corporations with investment capital who lived elsewhere and who managed to glean the region of its abundant raw materials while providing only minimal local economic development options. Beef and leather, fish and furs, timber and paper, gold and silver, grains and forage, fruits and vegetables: These were the main components of the frenetic primary economic activity that initially shaped the western landscape and influenced its settlement pattern. It was not until the twentieth century that large-scale industrial operations materialized in the cities of the region. With World War II inducing production, a number of shipyards as well as aircraft manufacturing, together with the making of steel and aluminum, became important contributions to the military supply effort. Although some factories and assembly plants are still locating in the West as the migration from older manufacturing areas continues, the face of regional industry has undergone a makeover.

Clean, nonpolluting, often high-tech development is the hallmark of many newer industrial landscapes across the country, not just in the western states. Yet here in the New West, it is almost expected that innovative start-ups be heirs apparent to the legacies begun by the nascent computer industry—both hardware and software—in places such as California's Silicon Valley, Oregon's Silicon Forest, and the campuslike headquarters of Microsoft in Redmond, Washington. The next generation of manufacturing plants is now being sited, as western "technology parks" have expanded to produce silicon wafers, manufacture communications parts, or assemble precision instruments for biomedical and pharmaceutical applications. With a high-value and relatively lightweight product, transport costs are no longer an overwhelming factor in location to begin with, but one that has been further ameliorated by the territorial saturation of competing multimodal carriers like Federal Express and United Parcel Service. Being a classic example of a footloose industry—one not restricted by traditional locational constraints and transportation requirements—software companies, especially, are free to set up shop just about anywhere. Increasingly, anywhere translates to small towns out West perceived as having a high quality of life and abundant opportunities for outdoor recreational pursuits. Indeed, rather than being entirely footloose, locational choices for postmodern industrial enterprises are actually tied to amenity landscapes, either because the firm's owner wishes to reside there or as a means of recruiting quality employees. Even while operating in the age of instant and ubiquitous telecommunications coverage and just-in-time Internet commerce, the realization of these new locational factors is reshaping the region's geography (Kotkin 2000).

With little potential for conflict among either residential or commercial uses, the most recent trend is toward mixed-use developments, a sort of New Urbanism meets the corral. Where industrial development specialists once urged communities to develop self-contained industrial parks composed of wide streets, ample sewer and water connections, and provision of specialized utilities such as high-voltage electricity and natural gas lines, these days the impetus is on integration and the creation of safe and healthy communities where residents not only live but also both work and play. Such developments may include an established high-tech employer or an innovation incubator. Other industrial opportunities might focus on outdoor equipment manufacturing, with products ranging from backpacks to boats or recreational vehicles.

To be sure, the silicon and software crowd have commanded the spotlight and riveted the economies in many highly livable places. Micron in Boise and Hewlett-Packard in both Boise and Corvallis are just two examples. The retooling or refitting of old mills and the continuation of traditional commodity production should not be discounted, however. In some cases, a greater percentage of value-added comes about in the production of a specialty item or a more finished product. Such a strategy has the additional advantage of being able to utilize a skilled labor force already in place and eager to remain. For instance, the future of lumber manufacturing did not seem promising in Prineville, Oregon, a few years back, when the supply of marketable ponderosa pine from the nearby Ochoco National Forest was nearly depleted and all seven lumber mills shut down. But one plant has actively sought new sources of raw material and now imports lumber from South America for making higher value trimwork. Elsewhere, other lumber-oriented enterprises have begun to manufacture exotic species wood products. In Vancouver, Washington, for example, a former stud and planing operation has revamped its production equipment to make precision-milled flooring, a much sought after specialty item currently in great demand by builders of New West trophy homes.

AGRICULTURAL

Most people cannot think of the American West without thinking of cowboys and roundups, and indeed, beef cattle remain every bit as symbolic of western agriculture as when the unfenced open range was considered the primary resource. But many areas were developed as specialized intensive farming districts, especially where irrigation infrastructure delivered federally subsidized water throughout the growing season and enabled large-scale industrial cropping opportunities. In broad terms, when examining the generalized geography of the western states, particularly for the intermountain region, the predominant agricultural land use might be characterized as a mixture of very extensive grazing lands along with smaller areas of more intensive irrigated fields producing hay and other winter forage. This tried and true combination has worked to support cow and calf operations ever since the devastating blizzards of the 1880s made free-range cattle ranchers realize the need for growing winter feed as a required input to the open range system of raising livestock. Other than federal lands, where grazing permits are often an essential component of a ranch's resources, the open range has largely disappeared, fenced in by countless miles of barbed wire. Thus, many areas across the West still manifest the typical working landscape that fuses together private and public terrain. There is a primary ranch residence, often with a bunkhouse nearby for hired hands, some outbuildings, corrals, and a hay barn, surrounded by irrigated hayfields and perhaps some improved pasture or rangeland as the basic unit held in fee simple ownership. This privately owned parcel is accompanied in both actual practice and in terms of net worth by any number of grazing permits to utilize forage on larger holdings of public lands nearby, typically within multiple-use areas managed by state or federal agencies, primarily the Bureau of Land Management and the Forest Service.

But the standard beef cattle operation does not always ensure a means of livelihood anymore, given the volatility of market prices, the difficulty of keeping skilled labor employed in remote settings, and the increasing encroachment of land development opportunities that can raise property taxes beyond the means of ranching income levels. Running livestock on private lands alone is usually not enough to make ends meet in any case. Yet public lands have come under heightened scrutiny by increasingly urban-oriented user groups, who have in some cases issued calls to remove cattle and sheep from these areas. Ranchers have had to adapt to these changes in various ways. Specializing in distinct types of cattle beyond the common white-faced Hereford is one way to raise the profit margin, and beef products from specialty breeds such as Black Angus have become popular commodities. Fine-tuning this strategy further, another marketing advantage might be to capture a certain niche that will appeal to changing tastes and consumer demand: "Beef niches include certified organic, natural (no artificial ingredients with minimal processing), grass-fed (little or no grain finishing), locally raised (promotes local business) and conservation-based (animals raised on land protected according to certain stewardship practices)" (Sullins 2003, 8). Bison are another attempt to raise a specialty animal, in this case one that answers to the upswing in market demand for low-fat protein sources. But raising bison or other wildlife species such as elk and deer for the fresh meat market requires a huge initial cost outlay for breeding stock, along with expensive capital improvements in water supply, fencing, and security. There are product marketing agreements to negotiate, animal health risks that must be considered from a veterinary standpoint, special permits required, and resistance from both wildlife and cattle interests. Other varieties of exotic livestock, including llamas and alpacas, have also made an appearance, but this may represent more of a localized fad than a prevailing trend across the region.

For recent arrivals to the rural West, a herd of beef cattle grazing in the hills is part and parcel of the scenery that attracted them here in the first place. Potential conflicts between normal ranching operations and newly established residential land use notwithstanding, most people do not want cows removed from the landscape, and outsiders who relocate to ranching areas even seem interested in embracing token attempts at raising livestock themselves. Some ranchers, for their part, have begun to explore ways to supplement their traditional incomes through any number of forms of what might be termed New West agritourism. These can vary in the degree of visitor involvement in actual ranch operations, from daylong helping out with real chores to simply staying accommodated on-site in a guest cabin. This tradition extends back for nearly a century, of course, and the topic of dude ranches is covered in greater detail in the next section on recreation. One foreseeable result of these cultural changes transforming the region would be that grazing lands will remain part of the landscape across the West, even if the real money in agriculture becomes fixed somewhere else besides range livestock operations.

Agricultural land uses often have intensified in the New West, especially where irrigation water is available within arid regions. Other places have experienced a surge in part-time or hobby farms, with either a corresponding consolidation of commercial holdings into larger farms, or an abandonment of full-time operations altogether. There is a need for awareness and perhaps accommodation by many communities to the requirements of a radically restructured western agriculture. Global markets have engendered even greater specialization in crops, particularly those destined for export. Infrastructural support facilities such as large storage warehouses or transportation improvements such as loading platforms and intermodal transshipment staging areas often become part of a town's land use mosaic.

Viticulture has become almost a signature New West agrosystem. In areas where the larger commercial vineyards have become established, such as California's Napa Valley, Oregon's Willamette Valley, or Washington's Yakima Valley, small acreage owners may also engage in growing grapes on contract, or may even attempt to start up wineries of their own. One curious symptom of the agricultural transformation of the West may be seen in so many wineries starting up in more remote areas, often where vineyards have never been attempted before, by entrepreneurs hoping to cash in on wine's increasingly widespread appeal, or hoping to attract tourists as an income generator. Often they might combine their hobby farming/vintnering work with the all too ubiquitous bed-and-breakfast operation.

In some cases there is no distinct divide between large-lot residential development and part-time agricultural land use. Lot sizes can be deceiving, and often do not serve as useful parameters. Where commercial ranching has faltered because of diseconomies of scale or inflated land prices, part-time ranching may fill the vacuum, becoming a transparent justification for higher value land development: "In southwestern Montana, the spectacular scenery and the strong desire of out-of-staters to own hobby ranches lured affluent individuals into ranching. Typically they raised a few cows on a 200-acre spread" (Friedberger 1998, 205).

RECREATIONAL

We briefly take note of another category of land use that would seem to be an obvious increaser in our rapidly changing region. Recreational land use in the New West can take on a variety of forms and patterns, serving the needs of various recreational pursuits. These may vary from small, very site-specific activities to extensive facilities covering many square miles. With increased urbanization come increased expectations for the provision of urban recreational space. This would typically involve parks and greenways, ball fields, and playgrounds. These days, even in small towns, it seems that preference for soccer fields more commonly eclipses the traditional softball diamond. Across a region where state government budgets are often strained, state parks and camping areas typically cannot keep up with demand, and private campgrounds have been on the increase, particularly RV parks. Planners in counties experiencing higher population growth rates and many new migrants from urban areas may be seeing proposals for amusement and water parks, themed or otherwise. If it is deemed feasible by market research, chances are it will be built.

Among the more extensive recreational land uses, golf courses have become preeminent. Many new links are associated with residential subdivisions, and while stand-alone courses are still being constructed, few of those are public. Such a trend epitomizes the privatization of open space and commodification of scenery that manifests itself in any number of ways in the New West. Among other possible recreational pursuits requiring large areas of land are paintball battle-grounds and off-road vehicle tracks or rally courses. Finally, the infrastructure of spectator sports and musical entertainment would seem to best fit within the category of recreational land use. While professional sports stadiums might seem an unlikely candidate for New West locations, several small towns in Oregon and Washington have recently entered a fierce competition to lure a proposed NASCAR racetrack to the Northwest. One type of recreation facility that seems to be on the rise, sometimes in the most unexpected and remote sites, is the outdoor concert amphitheater. These venues often take advantage of an inspirational natural setting, such as Colorado's acoustically impeccable Red Rocks, which has hosted concerts for nearly a century, or the more recently established Oregon Garden. The most renowned outdoor venue in the New West, if not the whole country, is situated in remote semi-arid canyon country:

> Singular among all large concert venues in the Pacific Northwest is the natural out-door amphitheater overlooking the Columbia River in central Washington known simply as "The Gorge." In operation since 1986, it sits along an edge of one of the sculpted erosional scars created by the late Pleistocene flooding that scoured and carved much of eastern Washington into channeled scablands. The landscape is stark, with bare basalt escarpments rising in dark layers above the parched steppe. Although situated nearly adjacent to Interstate 90, there are no towns or cities within miles. The Gorge is indeed out in the middle of nowhere, at least by urban standards of what should seem an appropriate venue. (Kuhlken 2003, 294)

This place has won the national entertainment industry's Pollstar Award for "Best Large Outdoor Concert Venue" five years running since 1995. In terms of land use implications, the Gorge has had significant impact on the surrounding area. Gas stations, cafes, and motels along the highway routes leading to The Gorge have seen dramatic increase in business, and commercial land use has actually expanded in some areas because of concert traffic. While economic development boosters laud the place, there have been a number of negative consequences associated with the steady string of summer weekend concerts and the thousands of overnighting fans in the adjacent campground. These externalities range from traffic congestion and dangerous drug abuse to vandalism of private lands.

But what nature cannot provide, humans with an ear for profit will. Sometimes referred to as a "big shed," these open-air concert halls with their large stage and seating constructions are less dependent on environmental fortunes, and thus have the potential to be proposed almost anywhere. Of course a stunning view provides added incentive for site planning, and the open-sided Santa Fe Opera comes to mind as a paragon of this type. Most recently, the White River Amphitheater, built and managed by the Muckleshoot Tribe on rural reservation land south of Seattle, has also proven a very successful venture.

No discussion of recreation in the New West, however brief and summary, can fail to include the one recreational facility that provides a sense of continuity from former times. This is dude ranching, which might be considered the quintessential recreational land use of the American West. First organized as a commercial activity focused on the Yellowstone area more than a century ago, it has not lost its appeal:

> The dawn of the twentieth century saw the dude ranch movement expanding fast through Montana, Wyoming, and Colorado—and later into New Mexico—forming the bulwark of many local economies long after the financial glory days of ranching were but a distant memory. Like every other aspect of the Rocky Mountain tourist scene, it was fueled by a nation consumed by thoughts of nature. (Ferguson 2004, 195)

Indeed, as nostalgia over cow punching days on the open range blends with the current trend for catered adventure vacations, dude ranches have managed to fulfill both regional fantasy and the modern demand for a packaged travel destination. The Dude Ranchers Association, based in Cody, Wyoming, continues to set high standards and criteria for operators, and now has over a hundred members across thirteen states. Some might contend that the niche traditionally filled by dude ranches has been displaced, especially in the Southwest, by the higher end health spa. Examples of this particular recreational land use are on the increase, not only around larger urban areas like Tucson and Scottsdale, but likewise in the smaller towns that have become destinations for adherents to the New West lifestyle. Red Mountain Spa, outside of St. George, Utah, is one such place, where "the peace and solitude of the facility, daily fitness activities, hiking in Snow Canyon, healthy gourmet cuisine, and an array of wellness classes will set you on the path to lifelong fitness and health" (Red Mountain Spa 2005). In many ways, however, dude ranching may also be viewed as the precursor to the all-inclusive destination resort that has become so popular in our culture, and whose manifold forms are discussed in the next section.

DESTINATION RESORTS

We need to now consider the special circumstance of recreational resorts that have become so commonplace in many favored locations in the New West. There is a wide array of resort types that may be viewed as a land use hierarchy in terms of scale, function, level of luxury or amenity provision, and target clientele. While many smaller operations have been around for years, we have seen a dramatic increase in the large-scale destination resort that requires much more land area. It should prove useful to make ourselves familiar with the various possibilities and potential for resort development that might be encountered in the rural areas and small towns of the West.

At the top of the pyramid, in terms of both complexity and popularity, are the master-planned golf course resorts, which may encompass multiple eighteen-hole courses and, at a minimum, the obligatory pro shop selling clubs and lessons, a hotel, and generally several restaurants, gift shops, and boutiques. Further elaborations on the theme will typically include high-end residential properties lining the fairways along with the requisite clubhouse and swimming pool. Larger projects entail a full range of residential offerings, from massive single-family trophy homes to multiplex townhouses and time-share condominiums. Additional allocations of open space becomes part of the overall design, providing a scenic amenity away from the landscaped course itself. There may be an equestrian center, perhaps an ice rink. To capitalize on year-round recreational opportunities, many golf resorts in the mountains will seek to link up with nearby skiing locations by offering winter vacation packages. Indeed, many well-established golf course resorts will try to appeal to a wider clientele, to offer a wide range of activities that might entice a vacationing tourist or potential full-time permanent resident into purchasing time or property. But golfing still remains front and center at these places and drives the development potential for what might seem at first glance to be very remote, out-of-the-way locations that now lie in the rough. It is easy to underestimate the widespread appeal of this game across the country, and the resultant pressure on communities having enough available land where market analysis has determined the profitability of carving out a new course. Developers now vie for big name designers as a marketing ploy, and when a course is designated as having the likes of Arnold Palmer or Jack Nicklaus in its credit line, sales of country club memberships or residential properties will likely be enhanced. And it almost goes without saying that hardly any of these newer golf courses are being built as *public* facilities. One must buy into the entire package, or aspire to home ownership on the carefully manicured grounds, in order to play today's game.

Sometimes entire communities will become transformed by the establishment of a few key courses in the vicinity. Such has been the case with Bandon, formerly a sleepy little seaside town on the southern Oregon coast and now the latest darling among golfing resort destinations. Another area that is up and coming among golf enthusiasts is the Flathead Valley of northwestern Montana, where a number of championship courses have recently been built. More commonly, however, the destination golf resort will be a stand-alone venture, and while these become focal points, they may in fact be just one of the recreational draws that give certain places development advantages in the New West economy. Of course parts of the Southwest, particularly the deserts of California and southern Arizona, have long been known as golfing meccas, and resorts in the Palm Springs and Scottsdale areas continue to attract upper-end clientele.

But other regions have also taken a chance on staking a claim to the game, often insisting on high-quality and environmentally responsible development. One of the first of these "green" projects was Black Butte Ranch, in the ponderosa pine belt of central Oregon, in turn followed by Sunriver, just down the road south of Bend. This area, long considered an all-seasons outdoor playground, is now attempting to saturate the market by siting additional master-planned residential golf developments, including several in the Bend area, and to the north, around Redmond, Terrebonne, and Madras. Even blue-collar Prineville, an up-and-coming former lumber mill town, has become known for golf because of an award-winning ecofriendly design for its new course situated as an ideal land use in the floodplain of the Crooked River and that utilizes specially treated wastewater to irrigate its greens and fairways. Meanwhile Redmond, the fastest growing community in all of Oregon, has seen Eagle Crest grow into a major residential golf development that now dominates the landscape west of town.

Following that same pattern, one of the Northwest's newest destination golf resorts is located about sixty miles across the Cascade Mountains to the east of Seattle, along Interstate 90, again, similar to the preferred central Oregon setting noted earlier, in a native vegetation zone dominated by ponderosa pines. Originally known as Mountainstar, and started by the same folks who developed Redmond's Eagle Crest, the fledgling project is currently called Suncadia and has changed ownership and management a time or two before even getting off the ground. Plans are in the works for fifty-four holes of championship golf, along with a hotel and convention center and, of course, the ubiquitous time-share condominium complex. As is the case with development in most places in the New West, water resources have emerged as a significant issue. In an already overallocated Yakima River basin, the need to balance water needs becomes even more acute when it is realized that local Indian tribes are attempting to enhance salmon and steelhead fisheries on the river and its tributaries. The consideration of Native Americans as real players in the geography of resorts leads us to our final land use consideration, the development of casino gambling in the New West.

Finally, one recreational land use has dramatically increased across the region, and so we end our discussion in this section with a brief look at gambling. The gaming industry, as it prefers to be called, is no longer limited to the two largest urban areas of Nevada, long the protected bastions of this particular vice. In small towns and rural areas of that state, and wherever permitted in other states, there has been a trend toward developing large casino destination resorts (Schwartz 2003). Most significantly for the New West, Native American tribes have been given the legal leeway to build and operate casinos not only on their own reservations but in some cases on any other land owned by them (Lew and Van Otten 1998).

THE ROUTES OF CHANGE: GROWTH CORRIDORS

Transportation has emerged as a land use in its own right across the vast expanse of the rural West. Valleys, canyons, and coastal terraces serve as natural

FIGURE 2.6
Certain segments of the federal interstate highway system are here identified as growth corridors, where rapid development and future land use change can be expected. *Map by Ian Gray, CWU graduate program in resource management.*

transportation corridors along the shorelines and through the mountains. These landform-determined routes traditionally served to direct the emerging land use patterns of the region. Today, interstate highways generally follow these same traditional routes used for more than 150 years of American expansion. Railroads helped to shape the developed landscape of the late nineteenth century, while the

U.S. highway system of the 1930s to 1950s provided regional connections. But the interstates largely shaped the expansion of the developed Western landscape of the late twentieth century (Lewis 1997). In large part, former transcontinental highway routes such as U.S. 40 and U.S. 66 have been decommissioned where the interstates have been either built over them or beside them. The multilane, high-speed, limited-access thoroughfares connect all parts of the West to domestic and international markets. Land surrounding each highway interchange instantly becomes a potential commercial development site, and access routes to nearby towns and cities offer expanded development opportunities. Perhaps most importantly, the access afforded by the interstate transportation routes has effectively introduced millions of urban Americans to the West's natural landscape treasures, greatly encouraging an expanding tourism economy and land conversion and development for recreation and retirement housing. Broader regional access to adjacent towns and rural hinterlands is effectively enhanced by a distributive network of state and local highways, reducing travel time and expanding commuting opportunities for ranchers, farmers, tourists, and retirees alike. In this section we discuss a few selected New West growth corridors from the Pacific Coast to the Rocky Mountain Front Range as likely areas of future land use change.

The Rogue Valley Corridor

Interstate 5 is the most important north-south route in the far West, and has improved access to small communities and rural areas in northern California, Oregon, and Washington. Running from the Mexico border to Canada, I-5 follows the Central Valley of California, across the Siskiyou Range, into the Rogue and Willamette Valleys of Oregon and on to the Puget Lowland of Washington. Prior to 1968, U.S. Route 99, a two-lane highway, took a slow, tortuous path across the rugged terrain between northern California and Oregon, focusing traffic through each small town along its route. While the actual route did not go through the towns, Interstate 5 was built close enough to the southern Oregon municipalities of Ashland, Medford, and Grants Pass that the greater volume of travel-related consumers encouraged these communities to quickly extend commercial land uses to the highway interchanges. Southern Oregon's Rogue Valley was one of Oregon's fastest growing areas in the 1990s and continues to grow at an accelerated rate. The growth is due in large part to retired former California residents. The massive number of California travelers enroute to northern destinations such as Portland and Seattle or to other business or vacation destinations in the Pacific Northwest have found Southern Oregon's landscape, climate, and relatively low property prices quite appealing. At the state line a sign was once erected at the request of Governor Tom McCall in 1968, inviting Californians to "Enjoy your visit but please don't stay." The sign has since been changed to a more welcoming message. Visitors from the south *do* stay in Oregon. The forests, seashores, and rural landscapes are enchanting, there are no sales taxes, and residential parcels are quite reasonably priced by California standards.

Medford has developed into the regional commercial and medical center for Southwest Oregon. It is now the regional hub for air, truck, and rail transportation over an extensive region extending from California's northern border to the coastal and interior parts of southern Oregon. The physical limit of the growth corridor is quite narrow here, however. The Siskiyou Mountains rise immediately to the south and west, and the Cascade foothills are only a few miles to the east. U.S. Forest Service and BLM lands surround the Rogue Valley, a factor that largely constrains private land development to the lower foothills and valley floor. Growth management is one of land use planning's most important issues here, as prime orchard and vineyard land uses compete with the demand for residential properties and golf courses.

Rapid growth in the rural Rogue and Illinois River Valleys has increased local traffic congestion; caused air quality alerts, water quality problems, and the loss of prime farm and forest lands; increased the likelihood of slope failure on steep, erodible slopes; and greatly increased summer wildfire hazards in the desiccated chaparral and forest landscape.

A carved, overhead archway was erected many years ago leading to downtown Grants Pass. It proclaims: "It's the Climate," as the "livability" hallmark of the Rogue Valley. Winters are mild, summers warm, only a modest number of rainy days relative to northwestern Oregon. But with the growth of population, residential wood heating, industrial emissions, and increasing volumes of auto and truck traffic—air quality has become a significant episodic health problem in both summer and winter seasons. Due to descending, warming air from the Siskiyou and Cascade Mountains temperature inversions are common and the deep, narrow valley traps pollutants, causing frequent air quality alerts in both winter and summer seasons.

The Las Vegas—Cedar City Corridor

Interstate 15, another major north-south route, begins in San Diego, crosses the southern edge of the Sierras, and drops into the Nevada desert, effectively linking southern California with Las Vegas, then St. George, Cedar City, and ultimately Salt Lake City, Utah. I-15 then turns north into eastern Idaho and western Montana, and terminates at the Canadian border. The economic *boom* of Las Vegas and the accompanying residential *explosion* at nearby Henderson may be explained by many factors, including low cost land, water, and electric power; significant employment opportunities; personal and corporate tax benefits; resorts and casino recreation; and outdoor recreation opportunities on desert lands and at Lake Meade and the Colorado River—to name but a few. A high-speed interstate freeway connection to more than sixteen million people in southern California is certainly one of the factors that has influenced growth. As we discover in the next chapter, St. George and Cedar City are both experiencing phenomenal population increase and rapid conversion of rural lands to urban uses.

Although at a much smaller scale, a similar set of economic and residential growth incentives is found only an hours' travel east of Las Vegas on I-15 at Mesquite, Nevada. The recent development of large casino resorts and golf courses, and the construction of residential subdivisions at Mesquite, in the rural Virgin River Valley, is directly tied to the access offered by the interstate and its propitious location adjacent to the borders of the nongaming states of Utah and Arizona. Ample groundwater is presently available to meet immediate needs, and golf courses and residential tracts are quickly converting traditional ranch lands to high-density development.

The Front Range Corridor

Interstate 25 has benefited several emerging growth corridors, each offering dramatic views of rugged mountains, plateaus, and prairies. I-25 links with I-90 at Buffalo, Wyoming, connecting rural north central Wyoming with the regional service centers of Billings to the north and Cheyenne to the south. It is a high-volume north-south connector route that follows the Front Ranges of the Rockies from Buffalo, Wyoming, near the Montana border, south to Denver, on to Albuquerque, and finally terminating at El Paso, Texas. Regional specialized medical, transportation, financial, and government services are available to residents along the corridor via short air commutes, but the interstate brings these services within reasonable travel time to rural residents and small but fast-growing communities in the northern corridor, such as Sheridan, Storey, Big Horn, Buffalo, and Casper.

Known as the Queen City of the Plains, Denver is the gateway hub of services to the Intermountain West. It is the focus of travel routes along the Front Range and to the interior West from the Great Plains. Interstates 80, 70, and 25 merge at Denver, following the historic routes across the Plains. Denver's continued growth is metro-complex as the preeminent regional center for government, business and commerce, industry, and transportation services. However, much of the New West–type growth is occurring in surrounding communities and rural counties along the Front Range of the Rocky Mountains. Boulder, a largely residential community, has attracted growth based on educational services, quality of life, and carefully cultivated small town charm. Boulder's extreme attractiveness resulted in the rapid conversion of surrounding ranch lands to high-value home sites. To manage growth, the city and county of Boulder began an open space land purchase program to maintain viewscapes and to preclude excessive development on ranchlands. Presently, the city and county governments hold title to the largest tract of real estate in the county.

Greeley, Loveland, Colorado Springs, and Pueblo, all traditional towns and cities of the plains, have greatly expanded their rural residential patterns with improved transportation connections along the Front Range. The key to continued development of this High Plains growth corridor is the availability of water. Presently, agricultural tracts are being purchased by developers who are most interested in securing water rights, a resource more valuable than the land itself.

The Rio Grande Corridor

To many visitors from the eastern United States, Santa Fe epitomizes the essential southwest. The rapid economic and residential growth of Santa Fe in the upper Rio Grande Valley has been enhanced by distinctive Southwest architecture; American Indian and Hispanic cultures; and the natural landscape with its rounded hills dotted with piñon pine, deep blue skies, and the distant snow-capped peaks of the Sangre de Cristo Mountains. Interstate 25 has contributed greatly to the development of both Santa Fe and the entire Albuquerque metropolitan area, a fast-growth center for residential, industry, and commercial expansion. Presently, land use transformations are taking place south of the Albuquerque area toward Socorro.

The Inland Empire Corridor

In the Pacific Northwest, Interstate 90 connects Seattle and the greater Puget Lowland with central Washington, crossing the Cascades at Snoqualmie Pass to the north of Mt. Rainier. The I-90 route traces through the northern Columbia Basin with its industrial-scale agriculture and into the Spokane-Coeur d'Alene Valley, where it becomes an agent for land use change once again. Meanwhile, another interstate highway, I-82, takes off from I-90 and heads south out of Ellensburg to the Tri-Cities, providing access to the string of agricultural service centers of the lower Yakima River Valley. Many of these towns, especially Yakima itself, are seeing increased retirement activity.

The traditional heart of the so-called Inland Empire, Spokane offers regional services and an attractive setting with rolling forested hills, lakes, and streams. With a population nearing 400,000 and a built-up area growing rapidly toward the east, Spokane has nearly merged with urban developments across the state line around Coeur d'Alene. Once hailed as the next big urban-industrial heartland by past boosters, the manufactured label "Inland Empire" never did reach its expected potential (Morrissey 1997). The area has nevertheless benefited greatly from its geographic position along the primary route connecting the northern plains with Seattle and the Pacific Rim. Interstate 90 has enhanced residential expansion with easy access to Sandpoint and Lake Pend Oreille and small communities across the Idaho Panhandle and into Missoula and the Clark Fork, Blackfoot, and Bitterroot Valleys of western Montana. Further east, some of the most observable growth in Montana is adjacent to the interstate highway between Butte and Billings. In central Montana, the route forks into I-94 to North Dakota, and south to eastern Wyoming and Rapid City, South Dakota.

The Columbia Gorge Corridor

At Portland, Oregon, Interstate 5 connects with the east-west I-84, a historic route that utilizes a unique water level passage through the central Cascade Range, connecting the Pacific Rim with the Rocky Mountain Region and the Great Plains. The Columbia River route serves rail, highway, and barge traffic alike. Portland and neighboring Vancouver, Washington, are the chief beneficiaries of the commerce generated by combined port, rail, and highway connections. I-84 serves several Oregon and Washington towns, the latter by bridge connections, within the Columbia Gorge. The exceptional scenic beauty of the Gorge features deep, blue waters, precipitous forested cliffs, and numerous waterfalls. In a forty-mile west-to-east traverse, one encounters a series of natural ecotones that transition from a west coast marine forest climate to a semidesert steppe.

Originally known for high-quality apple, pear, and cherry orchard crops and forest products, Columbia Gorge communities now also serve as recreation destinations for those seeking the thrill of high-energy water sports such as wind surfing and parasailing. I-84 provides direct access from Portland and serves as a natural growth corridor to the east. Demand for residential and commercial parcels is exceptional. The communities of Cascade Locks, Hood River, and The Dalles, Oregon, and Stevenson and White Salmon, Washington, however, are each limited in growth potential not only by physical landscape constraints imposed by the precipitous walls of the Columbia Gorge, but also by a set of rigorous growth management regulations enacted to protect natural scenic qualities within the Columbia River Gorge National Scenic Area.

Anticipating eastward residential and commercial expansion from Portland along the I-84 corridor, the Columbia River Gorge Bi-State Commission was formed by an act of Congress in 1986 to administer land use in the unique natural scenic area that covers more than forty miles of the Cascade Corridor demarcated by the Sandy River on the west and the Deschutes River on the east. The area includes two states, six counties, thirteen urban areas, two national forests, and significant tracts of Bureau of Land Management (BLM) land. The objectives of the planning effort are clearly aimed at growth management, but include both conservation and economic development policies. Priority issues include preservation of unique scenic amenities, enhancing information on historical and cultural heritage, promoting outdoor recreation, and conserving existing agricultural and timber lands. The objectives and policies are set forth in the Columbia River Gorge Management Plan, and the land use regulations are enforced by local governments (Abbott, Adler, and Abbott 1997).

The Oregon Trail Corridor

Pendleton, Oregon, and the surrounding communities of Hermiston, Irrigon, and Milton-Freewater are located on the eastern edge of the Columbia Plateau, at the base of the Blue Mountains. Pendleton is a small but rapidly growing town on I-84, and it serves as a regional transportation, medical, and commercial center for northeastern Oregon and the southeastern Columbia Basin. Pendleton's cowboy image and New West charm derives in large measure from the Pendleton Roundup, a week-long series of rodeo events similar in style to Cheyenne Frontier Days or the Calgary Stampede. Crossing the Blue Mountains via Mecham Summit, a historic but steep and winding pass, I-84 enters the Grande Ronde Valley, where the highway follows the historic route of the Old Oregon Trail south to the Idaho Border. The towns of La Grande and Baker City not only share the economic benefits as inland port authorities astride the major transportation route, but also provide recreation access to the Snake River Canyon and spectacular views of the Wallowa and Elk Horn Mountains. East of Boise, the interstate serves the rich agricultural heartland and major population centers of southern Idaho, curving south and east across the Snake River Plain, connecting that city with Twin Falls, Pocatello, and Idaho Falls. Some of the fastest growth in the Pacific Northwest, associated with the expansion of technological enterprises and the food processing industries, has occurred in the Boise Valley and the nearby Snake River Plain.

The Carson Valley–Reno Corridor

Emerging on the east from the Wendover Range, Interstate 80 follows the Humboldt River drainage west across the Great Basin to Reno. From Reno, the interstate turns south, joining U.S. Route 395 through the Carson Valley and finally crossing the Sierra Nevada Mountains south of Lake Tahoe en route to Sacramento. The Carson Valley–Reno growth corridor is a rapidly developing residential and commercial area benefiting from its location relative to Reno, Sparks, and Carson City, Nevada's state capital. As a retirement relocation, Nevada is most attractive to Californians, who seek tax advantages and lower real estate prices. Regional commercial, medical, education, and government services are offered within reasonable travel distances. Alluring scenic and recreational amenities are offered by Mt. Rose, Heavenly Valley, and other major ski destinations. Lake Tahoe, the Truckee River, and Pyramid Lake offer world-class fishing and water recreation advantages.

CONCLUSION

In this chapter we have sampled the different types of development patterns and noted some of the more typical land uses that might be expected to occur in the New West. These landscape alterations are already taking place at various scales and at different locations throughout this rapidly changing region. In the next chapter we embark on a tour across the eleven western states, and take note of where the current hot spots are in terms of rapid population growth and increased urbanization. Throughout our exploration of the region, we will encounter actual examples of some of the patterns and prototypes described in this chapter, and we will be able to typify the kinds of places that are experiencing the more substantial transformations in land use and local character. Based on this firsthand knowledge of current trends and the geographic areas within each state that have already attracted substantial in-migration, we are able to predict just where these types of land uses and development patterns may turn up next.

REFERENCES

Abbott, Carl, Sy Adler, and Margery Post Abbott. *Planning a New West: The Columbia River Gorge National Scenic Area.* Corvallis: Oregon State University Press, 1997.

Beyard, Michael D. *Business and Industrial Park Development Handbook.* Washington, D.C.: Urban Land Institute, 1988.

Beyard, Michael D., and Michael Pawlukiewicz. *Ten Principles for Reinventing America's Suburban Strips.* Washington, D.C.: Urban Land Institute, 2001.

Blakely, Edward, and Mary Snyder. *Fortress America: Gated Communities in the United States.* Washington, D.C.: Brookings Institution Press, 1997.

Bohl, Charles C. *Place Making: Developing Town Centers, Main Streets, and Urban Villages.* Washington, D.C.: Urban Land Institute, 2002.

Bookout, Lloyd W. Jr., *Residential Development Handbook.* Washington, D.C.: Urban Land Institute, 1990.

Booth, Douglas E. *Searching for Paradise: Economic Development and Environmental Change in the Mountain West.* Lanham, Md.: Rowman & Littlefield, 2002.

Borne, Lawrence. *Dude Ranching: A Complete History.* Albuquerque: University of New Mexico Press, 1983.

Carpenter, Susan, and Martha Willman. Living at Runway's Edge. *Los Angeles Times,* July 3, 2001.

Casazza, John A., and Frank H. Spink Jr. *Shopping Center Development Handbook,* 2nd ed. Washington, D.C.: Urban Land Institute, 1985.

Clifford, Hal. *Downhill Slide: Why the Corporate Ski Industry is Bad for Skiing, Ski Towns, and the Environment.* San Francisco: Sierra Club Books, 2002.

Dickinson, Peter A. *Sunbelt Retirement: The Complete State-by-State Guide to Retiring in the South and West of the United States.* Washington, D.C.: American Association of Retired Persons, 1986.

Earle, Carville. *The American Way: A Geographical History of Crisis and Recovery.* Lanham, Md.: Rowman & Littlefield, 2003.

Ferguson, Gary. *The Great Divide: The Rocky Mountains in the American Mind.* New York: W. W. Norton & Company, 2004.

Fishman, Robert. *Bourgeois Utopias: The Rise and Fall of Suburbia.* New York: Basic Books, 1987.

Fitzgerald, Frances. *Cities On a Hill: A Journey Through Contemporary American Cultures.* New York: Simon & Schuster, 1986.

Francaviglia, Richard V. *Main Street Revisited: Time, Space, and Image Building in Small-Town America.* Iowa City: University of Iowa Press, 1996.

Friedberger, Mark. Cattle Raising and Dairying in the Western States. In *The Rural West Since World War II,* edited by R. Hurt, pp. 190–212. Lawrence: University Press of Kansas, 1998.

Fulton, William. *Guide to California Planning.* Point Arena, Calif.: Solano Press, 1991.

———. *The New Urbanism: Hope or Hype for American Communities?* Cambridge: Lincoln Institute of Land Policy, 1996.

———. *The Reluctant Metropolis: The Politics of Urban Growth in Los Angeles.* Baltimore: Johns Hopkins University Press, 2001.

Gottdiener, Mark. *The Theming of America: Dreams, Visions, and Commercial Spaces.* Boulder, Colo.: Westview Press, 1997.

Hall, Kenneth B., Jr., and Gerald A. Porterfield. *Community by Design: New Urbanism for Suburbs and Small Communities.* New York: McGraw-Hill, 2001.

Hart, John Fraser. *The Rural Landscape.* Baltimore: Johns Hopkins University Press, 1998.

Hart, John Fraser, Michelle J. Rhodes, and John T. Morgan. *The Unknown World of the Mobile Home.* Baltimore: Johns Hopkins University Press, 2002.

Hayden, Dolores. *Redesigning the American Dream: Gender, Housing, and Family Life.* New York: W. W. Norton & Company, 2002.

———. *Building Suburbia: Green Fields and Urban Growth, 1820–2000.* New York: Pantheon, 2003.

———. *A Field Guide to Sprawl.* New York: W.W. Norton & Company, 2004.

Horwitz, Richard P. *The Strip: An American Place.* Lincoln: University of Nebraska Press, 1985.

Jackson, Kenneth. *Crabgrass Frontier: The Suburbanization of the United States.* New York: Oxford University Press, 1985.

Jakle, John A. Landscapes Redesigned by the Automobile. In *Making of the American Landscape,* edited by Michael Conzen, pp. 293–310. Boston: Unwin Hyman, 1990.

Jakle, John A., and Keith A. Sculle. *The Gas Station in America*. Baltimore: Johns Hopkins University Press, 1994.

———. *Fast Food: Roadside Restaurants in the Automobile Age*. Baltimore: Johns Hopkins University Press, 1999.

———. *Lots of Parking: Land Use in a Car Culture*. Charlottesville: University of Virginia Press, 2004.

Knight, Richard L. What Happens When Ranches Die? *Colorado Rancher and Farmer,* October 1994, pp. 8–9, 18.

Knight, Richard L., George N. Wallace, and William E. Riebsame. Ranching the View: Subdivisions Versus Agriculture. *Conservation Biology* 9 (1995):459–461.

Kotkin, Joel. *The New Geography: How the Digital Revolution Is Reshaping the American Landscape*. New York: Random House, 2000.

Kuhlken, Robert. Manufactured Homes. In *St. James Encyclopedia of Popular Culture,* edited by Tom Pendergast and Sara Pendergast, vol. 3, pp. 263–265. Detroit: Gale, 2000.

———. Louie Louie Land: Music Geography of the Pacific Northwest. In *The Sounds of People and Places: The Geography of American Music from Country to Classic and Blues to Bop*, edited by George Carney, pp. 277–312. Lanham, Md.: Roman and Littlefield, 2003.

Lang, Robert. *Edgeless Cities: Exploring the Elusive Metropolis*. Washington, D.C.: Brookings Institution, 2003.

Lew, Alan A., and George A. Van Otten. *Tourism and Gaming on American Indian Lands*. New York: Cognizant Communication Corporation, 1998.

Lewis, Tom. *Divided Highways: Building the Interstate Highways, Transforming American Life*. New York: Viking Press, 1997.

Low, Setha. *Behind the Gates. Life, Security and the Pursuit of Happiness in Fortress America*. New York: Routledge, 2003.

McKenzie, Evan. *Privatopia: Homeowner Associations and the Rise of Residential Private Government*. New Haven: Yale University Press, 1994.

Morrissey, Katherine G. *Mental Territories: Mapping the Inland Empire*. Ithaca: Cornell University Press, 1997.

Olson Richard K., and Thomas A. Lyson, eds. *Under the Blade: The Conversion of Agricultural Landscapes*. Boulder, Colo.: Westview Press, 1999.

Ozawa, Connie P., ed. *The Portland Edge: Challenges and Successes in Growing Communities*. Washington, D.C.: Island Press, 2004.

Popcorn, Faith. *The Popcorn Report: On the Future of Your Company, Your World, Your Life*. New York: Doubleday, 1991.

Price, Ted. *Miracle Town: Creating America's Bavarian Village in Leavenworth, Washington.* Vancouver, Wash.: Price & Rodgers, 1997.

Putnam, Robert D. *Bowling Alone: The Collapse and Revival of American Community.* New York: Simon & Schuster, 2000.

Rasker, Ray. *A New Home on the Range: Economic Realities in the Columbia River Basin.* Washington, D.C.: The Wilderness Society, 1995.

Red Mountain Spa. 2005. <www.redmountainspa.com/about/index.html>. [accessed 19 August 2005]

Robbins, William G. Landscape and Environment: Ecological Change in the Intermontane Northwest. In *Indians, Fire, and the Land in the Pacific Northwest,* edited by Robert Boyd, pp. 219–237. Corvallis: Oregon State University Press, 1999.

Salamon, Sonya. Cultural Dimensions of Land Tenure in the United States. In *Who Owns America?: Social Conflict Over Property Rights,* edited by Harvey Jacobs, pp. 159–181. Madison: University of Wisconsin Press, 1998.

Savageau, David. *Retirement Places Rated,* 6th ed. New York: John Wiley & Sons, 2004.

Schwartz, David. *Suburban Xanadu: The Casino Resort on the Las Vegas Strip and Beyond.* New York: Routledge, 2003.

Starrs, Paul F. *Let the Cowboy Ride: Cattle Ranching in the American West.* Baltimore: Johns Hopkins University Press, 1998.

———. An Inescapable Range, or the Ranch as Everywhere. In *Western Places, American Myths: How We Think About the West,* edited by Gary J. Hausladen, pp. 57–84. Reno: University of Nevada Press, 2003.

Stroud, Hubert B. *The Promise of Paradise: Recreational and Retirement Communities in the United States Since 1950.* Baltimore: Johns Hopkins University Press, 1995.

Sullins, Martha. AFT Helps Ranchers Add Value to Product. *American Farmland* 24, no. 1 (2003):7–8.

Travis, William R., David M. Theobald, and Daniel B. Fagre. Transforming the Rockies: Human Forces, Settlement Patterns, and Ecosystem Effects. In *Rocky Mountain Futures: An Ecological Perspective,* edited by Jill S. Baron, pp. 1–24. Washington, D.C.: Island Press, 2002.

Wyckoff, William. Denver's Aging Commercial Strip. *Geographical Review* 82 (1992):282–294.

A Geographic
Land Use Digest

This chapter provides a broad perspective into the kinds of land use change and development patterns taking place across the eleven western states. We initially delineate the established outlines of urban and suburban geography for each state, and then proceed to examine primarily the spatial circumstances of rural and small-town growth trends and potentials. These specific examples should prove instructive for those wishing to anticipate the kinds of development that may occur in any given area having an equivalent setting or similar geographic conditions. The next chapter looks at the current status of land use planning within each state and features some of the more innovative ways that planners have handled the need to accommodate these new growth patterns and development pressures.

Now let us take a look at what has been happening in each of the western states, beginning with the Idaho panhandle pointing to high noon, then rotating clockwise through the remainder of the West. One note on the accompanying state maps: several counties are highlighted within each state, indicating the fastest growing counties by percentage growth rate for the decade 1990–2000, as tabulated by the U.S. Census Bureau. The maps do not show the same number of counties for each state since the same numerical parameters are not used for every state because of inconsistent ranges in these data. For example, Wyoming only has two counties highlighted, Jackson and Sublette, and the ten-year population growth rate for those counties was 63% and 22%, respectively; Colorado, on the other hand, had more than a dozen counties that experienced an annual growth rate of well over 5%, including Douglas County, the fastest growing county in the nation, which increased its population over that decade at a whopping rate of 191%! In the interests of cartographic clarity, these percentage numbers are not given, although on every map, the darker shading indicates the fastest growing county in that state, while the next lighter shading indicates the next several fastest growing counties. For every state, a selection of towns and cities is also depicted to locate places discussed in the text and to show that the fastest growing counties of the New West are nearly always rural.

IDAHO

Idaho, with a total land area of 83,574 square miles, ranks second smallest of the eleven western states. Private land holdings are limited as a result of large areas of public land predominantly managed by the two main federal resource agencies, the Bureau of Land Management (BLM), watching over the relatively uninhabited deserts of the far south, and the Forest Service, with huge holdings throughout the center of the state and extending northward to the Canadian border. Indeed, the central portion of the state contains some of the largest intact, officially desig-nated wilderness in the lower forty-eight, including the Selway-Bitterroot and the River of No Return Wilderness Areas. Such a vast extent of public land has con-strained Idaho's settlement geography, but has also acted to stimulate pockets of potential development where easy access to recreational pursuits is available. Con-centrations of urban areas in the state thus exhibit a bimodal spatial distribution, and are mainly situated along the two major east-west transportation corridors comprising railroad routes and, more importantly for settlement patterns, inter-state highways: I-90 across the former mining district of the panhandle, and I-84 following the wide arc of the Snake River in the south.

The Idaho Panhandle

The northern panhandle area includes the growing recreational community of Coeur d'Alene, along with the neglected mining towns of Kellogg and Wallace; while to the north, amid a slightly more remote landscape of lakes and forests, are the small settlements of Hayden Lake, Sandpoint, and Bonners Ferry. Recreational use dominates this landscape: golf courses are plentiful; Silverwood Theme Park appeals to those seeking thrill rides and water slides; and a popular state park with camping facilities now occupies the site of a former World War II military train-ing center. Many of the in-between private lands are in the process of being de-veloped as low-density recreational or vacation homesites, while a few favored locations, such as Sandpoint, are feeling the pressures of unrestrained growth. There, traffic congestion has been an increasing problem for residents, and in 2004 the controversial solution to alleviate downtown snarl was the construction of a highway bypass. Sandpoint is auspiciously situated along the northern shores of Lake Pend Oreille, at the base of Schweitzer ski area. Although not strictly a ski town, the local economy is still dependent on tourism. This has acted to limit work options to the relatively small number of service jobs that are available, and few opportunities exist for skilled employment. Coeur d'Alene, in another lakeside setting to the south, finds itself somewhat more fortuitously within the economic sphere of Spokane, Washington, just across the state line to the west. As a result, much of the sprawling large-lot residential development north of Coeur d'Alene can be attributed to jobs and other connections with Spokane. One particular area, the Rathdrum Prairie, is of particular concern for several reasons: An increase in residential land use has provoked conflict with the normal field-burning practices of bluegrass farmers, and greater withdrawals from the underlying Spokane Valley aquifer, the only source of drinking water for the nearly half a million people who depend on it, has caused problems with water quality and quantity. As an example of the kinds of residential properties increasingly for sale throughout the West, here is a description for a typical three-bedroom house in Rathdrum: About 15 miles outside of Coeur d'Alene, this wooded five-acre property is entirely fenced and has a three-stall horse barn and an outdoor riding arena. Three man-made ponds, connected by a brook and stocked with koi, are in front of the house, which is 3,800 square feet. It has three full and two half bathrooms, granite counters and a great room with a 22-foot vaulted ceiling. A two-bedroom, one-bathroom apartment is above the horse barn.

Open space in this area has been a topic of even more fervent debate, and recent inventories suggest that nearly 85% of the prairie already has been developed. Meanwhile, Kootenai County has embarked on a team effort termed the Open Space Project, which will consider the purchase of conservation easements (Taylor 2004). The county also hired an Albuquerque consulting firm, Consensus Planning, Inc., to come up with a "regional planning strategy" that will analyze existing codes and regulations within an area that is "facing numerous challenges regarding extension of urban services; conflicting land use goals and policies causing planning gridlock; protection of a sole source aquifer; preservation of rural character, and open space" (Consensus Planning 2004).

For a number of years this part of the country has carried the unfortunate stigma of being the home of white supremacists and other neo-Nazi hate groups, dangerous fanatics who do not exactly make for good neighbors in the New West. Such a dysfunctional social landscape, coupled with numerous pollution problems resulting from decades of hard-rock mining and smelting of lead, zinc, and silver ores, has acted to retard the residential and recreational development of the area. Much of this organized hatred was centered around the Aryan Nations compound at Hayden Lake, which was dismantled after a successful lawsuit forced the group into bankruptcy. With the death of Aryan Nations founder Richard Butler in September 2004, northern Idaho residents must have breathed a sigh of relief and can now look forward to the day when the scourge of racism is no longer associated with the region.

Not nearly as ephemeral, the impacts of mining, both environmental and social, have indeed been severe. More than fifty years ago, Joseph Kinsey Howard (1949, 55) once described the bleak geography: "Here, in the northern half of

Shoshone County, half a dozen towns with a brief history of human and elemental violence, of fantastic fortune and corrosive poverty, cling to scarred and slipping hillsides or sprawl across barren clearings which once were green parks in America's noblest white pine forest." Although large-scale operations have all but ceased, the local effects of past activity linger. Poisoned streams, tracts of contaminated soils now identified as EPA Superfund sites, and still barren hillsides mark the legacy of mining and smelting in this area. Clearly, the future of the Coeur d'Alene mining district is not promising, for it lacks the overall charm and associated amenities of neighboring Kootenai County to the west, which was one of the three fastest growing counties in Idaho for the decade 1990–2000, with a 55% rate of population increase. As illustrated in figure 3.1, the other two fastest growing counties are Boise County, just northeast of that city, and Teton County, along the Wyoming border.

At the southern base of the panhandle may be found the anomalous inland port city of Lewiston along with the nearby university town of Moscow, which benefits from its close association and linkages with Pullman, Washington, just eight miles away, where Washington State University is located. Moscow seems minuscule for being the home of the University of Idaho, but it is still one of western Idaho's main culture centers. Yet despite its codependent interaction with Pullman, this town is perceived as being too isolated and has only witnessed modest residential and commercial growth. Nevertheless, the university manages to sponsor nationally renowned artistic events such as the annual Lionel Hampton Jazz Festival. To the south, Lewiston maintains the capacity to negotiate freshwater barge traffic on the Columbia-Snake system and thus functions as a shipping port for commodities such as wheat grown in the nearby Palouse and wood chips and lumber products from the surrounding forest lands. One of the more salient natural resource controversies in the New West concerns the four dams along the Snake River upstream from its confluence with the Columbia, and the navigational locks that facilitate commercial water transport this far inland. Proponents of salmon recovery programs have initiated efforts to have these dams removed, and should that come to pass, then Lewiston's fate may well be sealed into being merely another backwater former mill town.

Snake River Plain

Upstream from Hell's Canyon, the wide Snake River plain provided a natural arena for pioneer settlement, which in turn was followed by cooperative irrigated agricultural pursuits and attendant town building over the past century. Much of that parallel process has been fashioned and ordained by the socioreligious energies inherent in this northern extension of the Mormon culture region (for geographic elucidation of the region in its entirety, see Meinig 1965; Francaviglia 1978; and R. Jackson 2003). In his excellent environmental history of this basin,

FIGURE 3.1
Idaho, showing the fastest growing county for the decade 1990–2000 in darkest shading, the next fastest growing counties in lighter shading, and selected towns and cities discussed in text. Data source: U.S. Census Bureau. *Map by Ian Gray, CWU graduate program in resource management.*

Mark Fiege (1999) relates how early pioneers first settled along several tributaries of the Snake, exotic streams such as the Bruneau, the Boise, the Payette, and the Weiser, which derived their flow from the better watered terrain of higher elevations. In the low-lying desert country, irrigation became an absolute necessity in order to grow grains and other produce, which at first were sold to nearby mining camps. Railroad development further prompted both urbanization and homesteading, and a string of agricultural market and service towns sprang up along the broad arc of the Snake River. Despite a noteworthy attempt by historian Peter Boag (1997) to evoke a more refined sense of place and regional identity for the area, the pall of industrial agriculture now lays claim to most of these lands, primarily yielding enormous quantities of potatoes for the mass market. Additional exports include alfalfa and other hay crops. This is a landscape of large-scale corporate farming. There is nothing New West about this place, and rapid population growth has only really occurred, and can only be anticipated, at the base and at the point of the river course's long scimitar blade, in the Boise-Caldwell area on the west, and at Idaho Falls to the east.

Boise has been earmarked as one of the chosen few, a rapidly growing medium-sized city within an attractive setting fostering a high quality of life, frequently named in the top ten lists of best places to live in the nation. For some, such a designation elevating the place to celebrity status is a curse, and for others, a blessing. The effects of in-migration are especially pronounced in the Boise area, where "there seems to be the belief that equity-rich Californians, moving to Idaho to escape a spoiled quality of life, are creating many of the state's growth-related woes" (Smutny 1998, 315). Long-time residents who liked things the way they were are now faced with the negative consequences of inevitable growth, while new arrivals bask in the pleasantly moderate climate dominated by bright sunshine in a cloudless sky and enthusiastically proceed to set down roots in this refreshing capital city that not only has been able to attract clean, high-tech industries, but also maintains a tradition of supporting the arts, education, and civic events (MacGregor 2003). During the decade between 1990 and 2000, Boise's growth rate of 37% eclipsed even the dynamic figure of 28% tallied for the state as a whole. Culturally, the town has made it a point to leave behind its pioneer past and has rushed to embrace what is cosmopolitan or fashionably chic, and so sushi has replaced rocky mountain oysters. There are abundant recreational opportunities offered by city and regional parks, bike paths, and a stunning public riverfront, all surrounded by the famed Idaho wildlands in the back of beyond. It is an explicit recipe for continued growth, and one that calls for ever greater sophistication on the part of local officials in attempting to accommodate population increase while preserving the celebrated quality of life. In a speech before the Idaho legislature, the newly elected mayor of Boise, David Bieter, recently expressed the desire to safeguard his city's renowned livability by reminding the lawmakers that their state is in the midst of a profound transition from historically rural to predominantly urban, and that "Boise must have clean air . . . mass transit, mixed-use development" (Kemmis 2004, 9).

Exceptional among locations in the Intermountain West, Boise carries on an established tradition of being attentive to growth management needs and developing a sound planning process. Mileposts in the modern era of planning were reviewed by historian Merle Wells (1982, 124):

> Local government assumed planning functions for their areas when Boise's expansion raised issues of growth management that required community attention. Boise obtained a California professional consultant's report, which was used as a basis for adopting a comprehensive management plan, on April 27, 1964. Ada County also accepted a comprehensive plan in 1964. Planners had to consider regulation of commercial and residential expansion that would prevent the replacing of farm land, irrigated at great cost, with development that could not use existing water rights and storage . . . planning was necessary to avoid excessive service costs for scattered commercial and residential development, as well as to guard against the ruin of valuable irrigated tracts for agricultural purposes.

Boise is also one of the fortunate few western cities that have managed to attract substantial high-tech investment and employment opportunities. Beginning in 1973, when the Hewlett-Packard electronics plant first opened, the city has successfully followed a recipe that enhances its natural scenic resources and makes use of an abundant supply of developable land: "Campus-style commercial and industrial parks, with large office and production facilities, placed in an attractive open setting of broad lawns and trees, offered Boise firms a superior environment by 1976" (Wells 1982, 127). By the beginning of the 1980s, Hewlett-Packard alone had a labor force of 4,000 employees working in a million square feet of office and production space. Other high-tech firms that have found Boise to be a favorable location include Micron and Preco Electronics. According to data compiled by the American Electronics Association, the Boise metropolitan area experienced a 52% growth rate in high-tech employment during the 1990s, and the city is now ranked second among smaller "cybercities" in the country, those places having between 15,000 and 25,000 technology workers. Boise's former mayor Brent Coles is quoted as saying, "We offer a way of life that many larger cities don't have with our affordable housing, the great outdoors, and negligible commute time" (American Electronics Association [AEA] 2000).

Entrepreneurial activity is not limited to high technology, of course, and this corner of Idaho is able to lay claim to other commercial and industrial accolades. While the city has come to be viewed as part of the "new corporate frontier," many locally established firms have made good, setting up the foundation for future success stories, as David Heenan (1991, 77) pointed out: "Boise has earned its reputation as a serious business center over many years." Food and drug megavendor

Albertson's, along with timber conglomerate Boise Cascade, agribusiness giant Simplot, and the large engineering and construction firm Morrison-Knudsen are all hometown firms, and all require substantial office space as well as research and development facilities. But being bigger does not always account for everything. Acclaimed men's fashion designer Robert Comstock, for example, a fifth-generation Idahoan, maintains three homes in different parts of the state, but keeps his company's headquarters anchored in Boise. Indeed, local economic activity is so vibrant and varied that newspaper reporter Mark Trahant once suggested that "Idaho's capital could be a prototype for the New West economy" (Trahant 2000).

Development patterns around Boise manifest a wide range of styles, densities, and genres, from the all-too-common homogeneous tract homes on curvilinear streets with numerous cul-de-sacs to more forward-thinking "new urbanist" designs for mixed use: master-planned communities featuring internal commercial districts, industrial areas, and even schools, along with parks, playgrounds, greenways, and other recreational amenities. Varied examples of this so-called neotraditional approach may be seen in both the Harris Ranch and the Hidden Springs developments. The promotional advertisement for Harris Ranch emphasizes its geographic and environmental setting: "nestled between the foothills and the Boise River, just upstream from downtown, where the air is cleaner and colors brighter . . . natural surroundings on the network of trails and open spaces that abound." There are several different housing schemes within the project, with various lot sizes and corresponding densities. By contrast, Hidden Springs is an outlying bedroom community attempting to become its own identifiably discrete village. Its houses are perfectly executed replicas of 70- to 100-year-old designs, with front porches and white picket fences each enclosing a petite front yard. There are no driveways, for garages do not face the street but are behind the house, accessible by alleyway. There are street trees and sidewalks, and old-fashioned lamp posts.

Such details are part of the prescription called for by a remarkable group of designers and architects, who have found that by modeling the classic American small town, the resultant place functions coherently, the feel of the space is correct in the context of proportional scale and pedestrian orientation, and in terms of design and appearance it looks the way customers want it to look. Tried and found to be truly effective elsewhere, this new urbanist template fostered by Andres Duany, Elizabeth Plater-Zyberk, and Peter Calthorpe, among others, has yet to be successfully amalgamated to the avowed need for privacy, elbow room, and long vistas sought after in the wide open spaces of the New West. Here on the outskirts of Boise, and in other western locations such as Bozeman, Montana, and Prescott Valley, Arizona, a grand experiment in merging the two paradigms is currently underway.

At the other end of the Snake River arc, a major north-south arterial, Interstate 15, connects Pocatello with rapidly growing Idaho Falls. While the largest city at the nucleus of this region has made some effort to address growth issues, the smaller satellite jurisdictions surrounding Idaho Falls have not. As a result, development is running rampant in places like Ammon, where both residential and commercial land use has been driven by the demands of the automobile. An irony that should not be lost on local elected officials are the repercussions of such sprawl, which has had a direct influence on the continued decay of the central business district of Idaho Falls. Meanwhile, Pocatello residents have embarked on an ambitious planning effort geared toward articulating a vision for their area that encourages contiguous urban expansion catering to the needs of pedestrians, while revitalizing downtown. Plans are also under way for implementing the Portneuf Valley Land Trust, an effort aimed at conservation of outlying open space and resource lands.

To the east of Idaho Falls lies Teton County, which recently has experienced one of the highest percentage population growth rates in the state. This area, celebrated far and wide during fur-trapping rendezvous days as Pierre's Hole, remains very picturesque in terms of natural scenic resources, being situated in a transition zone between forested highlands and arid plains, and is in close proximity to the Teton Range and other popular public lands playgrounds. Increasingly, as the housing crisis in Jackson, Wyoming, becomes ever more acute, service workers and others who cannot afford to live in that town are now making the commute from domiciles in Driggs and surrounding residential areas within Idaho. Massive new tract housing developments have been built in Teton County to house these workers. Moreover, an Idaho land use watchdog group reports that in this county, "Large golf course resort developments are a major trend. . . . Teton Springs will more than double the population of Victor when complete" (Idaho Smart Growth 2003). Thus, spillover effects from ultradevelopment in high-amenity locales will continue to combine with the undeniable charms of the local landscape to induce frighteningly rapid growth for this region, and local officials had best prepare for it.

Isolated Interior Settlements

Other towns in the interior of the state are few and far between, and include Challis, Salmon, and Stanley, all of which are located in scenic mountainous terrain and thus have the potential for new growth and development. Stanley, especially, is well situated to take advantage of the recreational opportunities provided by the rugged Sawtooth Range, whereas both Challis and Salmon are somewhat more arid, and the mountains there are not as forested. Challis is a small community supporting the mining and ranching needs of the surrounding area, and its remote location prevents any significant economic transition from taking place. Farther north, the larger community of Salmon likewise maintains its extractive resource orientation to ranching and logging traditions for the time being, but is also witnessing increasing visitation associated with nearby wilderness use and river rafting trips. Salmon is also in close proximity to Montana's Bitterroot Valley just across the mountains to the north. Thus, it is somewhat better positioned to become part of the New West, perhaps whenever the cost of living in already discovered locales increases beyond reach.

Among the scattering of communities across central Idaho, McCall is suitably primed to incur the spillover growth from the Boise area. Taking advantage of a pleasant waterfront setting along scenic Payette Lake, the town holds several civic and social events, including a music festival and a winter carnival. Numerous ski resorts nearby ensure year-round recreational opportunities. Guidebook author Bill Loftus (1994, 151) wrote that McCall "embodies the best of Idaho: friendliness, beauty, and plenty of room to play." There is also an airport, which is home to one of the West's crackerjack smokejumper units, and there are other offices for land and resource management agencies. While becoming increasingly cautious of the potential surge of new inhabitants, town officials still follow standard economic development planning, and small industry would find a welcome mat waiting for them here. In addition to McCall, there are several other communities in the surrounding area, including Lakefork, Donnelly, and Cascade. All in all, this region imparts magnetic potential for rapid growth and prototypical New West development patterns. Whether McCall and its surrounding area can absorb the coming wave of new arrivals without being overwhelmed by sprawl and congestion, or experiencing stress and strain to existing infrastructure, remains to be seen. The decision to plan for and anticipate such growth needs to be made now, before the demand for housing and support services reaches an unmanageable level.

Ketchum–Sun Valley

Among the invigorated growth poles of Idaho, New West sensibilities are most prominently displayed in the Ketchum–Sun Valley area. These two communities in the Wood River Valley represent a tangled tale of one old town (Ketchum) being eclipsed by old money deliberately fabricating a resort complex (Sun Valley) that has gone through several incarnations, and that, in turn, is largely being supplanted by even more recent infusions of capital and development initiatives (Ketchum again). Complicating matters, a third additional focal point of growth in this area is the master-planned community of Elkhorn. But it all began with skiing, for Sun Valley may be said to have started the ski industry in the West. The establishment and management of tourism and winter recreation in this isolated spot, at first during the 1930s under the direction of the Union Pacific Railroad and subsequently by other corporate interests, is elucidated most elegantly by environmental historian Hal Rothman (1999, 178), who describes the economic transitions and social displacements that are often irrevocable terms for communities participating in "a devil's bargain":

> Tourism in the American West is at its core colonial, grafting new sources of power and financing atop existing social structures, bringing idealistic and romantic value systems supported by outside capital to places where the majority of residents have yet to experience material prosperity, and promising an economic panacea but delivering it only to privileged segments of the public. When it succeeds, tourism changes the economic structure of communities and surrounding regions, redistributes power from local people to outsiders with capital, and packages and transforms the meaning of place to successive waves of people, from "old-timers" to the newest "neo-native" arrivals, who seek to pull the figurative door shut behind them.

Hollywood types have been attracted to Sun Valley from its earliest operation, and the resort still clings to its exclusive airs. Much of the surrounding newer residential development has been stimulated by the deliberate attempt at concentrating wealth in the past, perhaps seeking to further the historical circumstance of setting out to make a playground for the rich and famous. Although skiing and other snow sports remain the principal draw, this area is now regarded as a major summer recreation destination as well, and serves as the south gateway community to the Sawtooth Recreation Area.

The town of Ketchum has risen dramatically from its modest blue-collar beginnings as a railroad town to a place where only the wealthy can afford to live. Motion picture celebrities along with prominent political figures like Teresa Heinz Kerry now call the town home, at least for a portion of the year. Housing prices have jumped outrageously, and one real estate agent reports that even upscale properties that used to fetch a million dollars now command ten or fifteen million dollars (Boone 2002). These new seasonal homeowners are less likely to become involved in local issues, and the resultant culture and community ambiance have changed drastically. Property taxes have gone way up, forcing a number of homeowners to sell out and leave. Many local residents blame this infusion of new wealth for destroying the fabric of community: "The small-town atmosphere— what the dwindling number of natives believe attracted the rich and famous—is in danger of disappearing as lower-, middle-, and now upper-middle-income families are forced out" (Boone 2002, B4). Service workers now commute from more affordable addresses located as far away as Twin Falls, and nearby small towns such as Hailey and Shoshone are beginning to feel spin-off effects of migration out of the higher priced domains. But because the Wood River Valley has been a high-amenity landscape for many years, new development proposals are subject to intense scrutiny. Several recent projects have failed to pass muster, and at least some residents of Blaine County remain ever vigilant in their opposition to any semblance of runaway growth that would negatively impact their perceived quality of life.

MONTANA

Widely regarded in the popular imagination as "the last best place," Montana has witnessed perhaps some of the more blatant landscape transformations in the American West. Once heavily reliant on mining and grazing and to a lesser extent, logging, the natural resource–based economy of the state has taken a dramatic turn. Rather than such directly extractive activities, natural resource use these days encompasses an appreciation and consumption of scenery and recreation. Moreover, people are not satisfied with just visiting, but increasingly wish to set down roots by establishing either a primary or secondary residence. No longer a mere vacation destination or target for ephemeral summer tourists, Montana is now experiencing unprecedented in-migration, and rural real estate in the more favored locales is aggressively being marketed to the new clientele. Ranches are no longer being sold for raising cattle, but rather as equestrian homesites or fly-fishing retreats. In many ways it is the externally projected, idealized image of Montana that people have in mind when they decide to move there. That overarching big sky, those high, rugged mountain ranges and broad verdant valleys, the abundant wilderness full of wildlife and recreational opportunities, and the state's indubitable stature as a fly-fishing mecca have all combined to provide an enormous pull-factor for in-migration.

Literary endeavors likewise have helped to shape Montana's reputation for rugged livability, from the historical novels of A. B. Guthrie to the stark realism and landscape portrayals within the poetry of Richard Hugo and the short stories of William Kittredge, both of whom nurtured legions of students at the University of Montana's influential creative writing program. Award-winning writer Richard Ford also once lived here while his wife Kristina held the position of Missoula city planner, and he has placed several of his settings within the state. One of the finest novelists in the country, Thomas McGuane, has long called Montana home, and the characters of his more recent books caricature the newly arrived clueless. McGuane has embraced the western ethos in other activities besides writing, and was once honored as state cutting horse champion. The views from his ranch in the Paradise Valley south of Livingston became too closed in with new dwellings a few years back, and he has since relocated, at first further east to the Big Timber area, and more recently to a ranch near Boulder, south of Helena. Several other prominent authors have opted for small-town life, establishing residency long before it became fashionable to move to Montana: science essayist and natural historian David Quammen, who lives on a quiet tree-lined street in Bozeman; and the indefatigable travel and adventure writer Tim Cahill, inhabiting a similar setting in smaller and more laid-back Livingston. Both of these writers have at times taken on local themes in their nonfiction offerings, and both knowledge and mythos of the place have been enhanced as a result.

Besides attracting luminaries of literature, Montana enjoys the additional cachet of a burgeoning arts scene. Notable painters (with their studio locations indicated in parentheses) include Russell Chatham (Livingston), Marshall Noice (Kalispell), Ted Waddell (Manhattan), and Clyde Aspevig (Livingston). Sculptors and artists working with other media have found a home here as well. Land use implications of this creative activity include the commercial space required for displaying and selling pieces of art, which may be a remodeled downtown storefront or a stand-alone structure along a highway or road outside of town, each requiring considerations for parking. Then there are the working studios, which, in the case of glass or metal sculpture, can resemble industrial operations that involve potential nuisances such as excessive noise, or environmental health and safety issues such as fumes or the hazards of welding processes, glass-blowing furnaces, or smelters and foundries. While the arts certainly contribute to the overall health and vibrancy of a community, care must be taken to accommodate the processes of their creation in a way that does not negatively impact adjacent properties and the surrounding area.

Celluloid reality created by Hollywood has contributed to Montana's mystique as well, and movies such as the wildly popular *A River Runs Through It* have helped to stimulate additional migration of outsiders to what has come to be perceived as a backcountry haven. Other films that have used locational settings within the state include *Missouri Breaks* and *Rancho Deluxe*, both of which adapted screenplays written by McGuane. Another aspect of Hollywood's influence on the growth potential of rural Montana may be seen from the increasing number of actors who have purchased land and built homes there, including Jane Fonda, who once occupied a spacious ranch with former husband Ted Turner southwest of Bozeman; long-term Paradise Valley denizen Jeff Bridges; and Andie McDowell, who lives part of the year on a property near Missoula. For whatever reason, having celebrities as neighbors is an attractive prospect for some people, and this has further stimulated new development.

But these scenes and the supportive mythology mostly refer to the western portion of the state, which is posting the effects of population increase, while the eastern plains ponder an exodus and an ongoing process of marked depopulation. Ten Montana counties east of the Great Divide lost population during the 1990–2000 decade. These northern plains are geographically part of what some have come to term "the big open" or "the buffalo commons," conceptual areas that have been the focus of certain intentional (and inherently controversial) proposals to dislocate the human population (Popper and Popper 1994; Matthews 2002). Across the northern-tier states of the West, an idealized scenery composed of mountains and rivers and forests has come to represent what people most want and what they want to live near to. Thus, among the more favored locations are three areas of concentrated growth illustrated in figure 3.2: (1) the northwest part of the state around Whitefish and Kalispell, with both Flathead County and Lake County showing substantial percentage population increase; (2) the area around Missoula, especially south of town in the Bitterroot Valley in Ravalli County; and (3) from the Bozeman vicinity to the northwest, involving the three counties of Gallatin, Jefferson, and Broadwater.

Other specific places, such as the previously mentioned and once aptly named Paradise Valley, now likewise manifest symptomatic New West malaise.

Gateways to Glacier

Several towns in northwest Montana owe much of their appeal to being gateway communities for Glacier National Park and various other public recreation lands. Nearby is Flathead Lake, the largest natural body of fresh water in the West. The most populous community in this area is Kalispell, whose county courthouse commands a small space that the business route of U.S. Highway 93 is forced to go around, faintly resembling but failing to emulate a Southern courthouse square. Outlying byways have been completely overcome by strip malls and the loose assemblages of similar commercial land use. Rapid growth around Kalispell

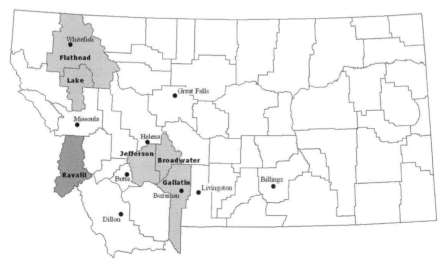

FIGURE 3.2
Montana, showing the fastest growing county for the decade 1990–2000 in darkest shading, the next fastest growing counties in lighter shading, and selected towns and cities discussed in text. Data source: U.S. Census Bureau. *Map by Ian Gray, CWU graduate program in resource management.*

has created not only traffic congestion but a palpable deterioration in sense of place. Other towns are located at either end of the north-south–trending lake, and have likewise done little to contain sprawl. The population of the Flathead Valley now exceeds 70,000. By far the most desirable place from a New West perspective is Whitefish, hailed by one tourist promotional brochure as "the closest thing to a tony resort community west of Bozeman." Similar in setting to Sandpoint, Idaho, it is a small lakeside community at the foot of a low-key skiing facility known as Big Mountain.

Whitefish is a former logging town turned recreation headquarters, with Glacier National Park being a major tourist draw. Ecotourism has taken hold here, and one of the newest commercial attractions is an above-the-trees canopy walkway stretching 750 feet between a pair of observation platforms where visitors might learn about the ecological workings of coniferous forests. But the town has also thrown its hat into the ring of competing for most-favored golf destination in the Northwest. This singular game with its large-scale terrain appropriations and other support accoutrements has become an increasingly essential element of a New West lifestyle. Another surprisingly common recreational facility across the West is represented east of town by the Big Sky Waterpark, while winter sports enthusiasts take advantage of nearby Big Mountain Resort. These recreational amenities found throughout the surrounding area have made Whitefish a desirable address, either for a seasonally occupied home or a more permanent, year-round habitation. Real estate sales have responded accordingly, and land values have soared. Consequently, growth management issues are on the local political agenda, and many residents have come to recognize the need for regional planning.

Kalispell itself only holds about 15,000 people but has become something of a celebrity destination, with several movie stars and popular music icons maintaining vacation properties nearby. It has a lively and impeccably clean downtown graced with turn-of-the-century architecture. Along Main Street, renowned painter Marshall Noice's studio and art gallery occupies what was once the Silver Dollar saloon, which typifies the kind of commercial land use now found in the growth centers of the New West. Although his paintings hang in galleries in places like Telluride, Park City, and Santa Fe, Noice considers Montana to be more inspirational than other parts of the West partly because "it's bigger and better" (Schneider 2004, 120). What positions Kalispell firmly in the New West are not just the hordes of retirees and second-home owners, but the type of employment opportunities that are being developed by local expertise and talent. North of Kalispell, for example, Sonju Industrial maintains a 15,000-square-foot factory with a workforce of 40 people. Owner and company president Dick Sonju began with an automotive painting and body shop and expanded into a small anodizing operation in 1999. Recently, Sonju landed several contracts to supply aerospace giant Boeing with aircraft parts, and the firm is planning on constructing a new facility and hiring additional workers (Choate 2004).

Missoula and the Bitterroot Valley

Missoula, home to the University of Montana, sits nestled in the snug canyon of the piscatorially endowed Clark Fork River. The town's compact central business district contrasts sharply with the suburban-style strip commerce of its southern flanks, one of the few openings in the terrain where growth might proceed unchecked by topographic constraints. The terrain has a direct effect on the city's seasonal air-quality problems. During winter the atmosphere above the city frequently becomes stagnant from a cold air inversion layer, which traps particulates spewed from countless wood stoves used for home heating. Yet there have been few attempts at managing the growth of new residential and commercial development. Kristina Ford, currently city planner for New Orleans, once served as planning director for the city of Missoula. She later wrote an excellent book describing some of her experiences in attempting to shape the patterns of growth in this small western town that was only then starting to come out of its shell. Ford attributes the failure of planning in Missoula to a combination of vague zoning regulations, weak state subdivision laws, and a reluctance on the part of local citizens to become involved, to the point where public participation in planning was often limited to sporadic input regarding specific projects rather than long-term engagement in the whole process (Ford 1990).

Houses cover the short-grass hills south of town, and new developments are now merging with the already established subdivision patterns of the lower Bitterroot Valley. Many of the new residents, in what must seem for them an effort to fit in, aspire to own a log home, or at least one of those manufactured cedar prow houses that seem like glorified A-frames. But a local company has a different idea: concrete structures that are designed to look like log homes. Entrepreneur Dick Morgenstern knows the concrete construction business firsthand, having run one for twenty-five years. Not one to rest after retirement, he has since established Concrete Log Systems, which now markets simulated logs cast from concrete, poured into molds that have been fashioned from actual logs. As reported recently in the Missoula newspaper, "The company has developed patented technology to build a home from concrete logs," and its attention to simulating minute structural details has yielded favorable results:

> You have to really get up close to the logs, or even touch them, to see that they are not made of wood. The logs have a rich texture and depth to them. Even the log's end rings are visible. Each has been stained by a local faux painter to add to that real-wood appearance. (Fitzsimmons 2004)

The concept has struck a chord with property owners who desire to build dwellings in forest lands prone to wildfire hazard. Morgenstern explains: "Insurance companies don't want combustible homes built in wooded areas, but people still want the rustic look of log homes" (Fitzsimmons 2004). The company's web site also reports the recent completion of their own 2,400-square-foot faux log office building in Missoula (Concrete Log Systems 2004). For those people wishing to have a real wood log home without the hassle of building it from scratch, these are available as fabricated kits designed and put together by several firms located in Stevenson and Hamilton.

The lovely Bitterroot River Valley extends in a nearly straight line upstream south from Missoula and affords spectacular views of the Sapphire Mountains to the east, and the even loftier and more rugged Bitterroot Range to the west, which forms a topographic wilderness boundary with Idaho. Homesteaded during the period 1860–1890, the rich bottomlands were claimed throughout the entire valley, and now a closely connected string of communities extends from Lolo south to Sula, with Stevensville, Hamilton, and Darby being the largest towns. But it is the land outside of municipal boundaries that is exhibiting the most noticeable effects of New West urbanization. This area manifests one of the densest local road networks in rural Montana, providing easy access to private lands on either side of U.S. Highway 93, which parallels the river. Thanks to Ravalli County's hands-off policy regarding land use and subdivision, the creation of numerous small parcels proceeds unabated, and population continues to soar. The county experienced an astounding 44% growth rate during the decade 1990–2000 and now contains an estimated population of nearly 40,000. Planning guidelines allow for the implementation of neighborhood plans and "voluntary zoning districts" to be drawn up by petition of local residents within specific areas. But from the looks of things, it seems that property rights have taken precedence over government regulation, and many people who work in Missoula tend to look here first in their search for a country lifestyle. As one indicator of the commuter landscape created in the Bitterroot Valley, it has been reported that the mean travel time to work for Ravalli County residents is twenty-three minutes, which is somewhat longer than the state average of eighteen minutes.

The Bozeman Area

In many respects, Gallatin County has been adopted as the recalcitrant poster child of Montana's New West. A population growth rate of nearly 35% for the decade 1990–2000 has stimulated land use transformations across the rural countryside, swallowing open space and the rustic views that originally drew people here in the first place. Sprawling exurban subdivisions of large-lot ranchettes now carpet the slopes of most of the upland terrain surrounding Bozeman, the county seat that is both a quintessentially western and perfectly winsome college town, and that should be viewed as a major catalyst for all this growth. This highly desirable area has become a key target for in-migration, and recently made the list of "preferred places" in *Forbes* magazine:

> The Gallatin Valley in southwestern Montana has proven especially popular with
> telecommuters because it offers woodland scenery yet is still close to Bozeman's

amenities. Buyers in search of recreational or working ranches have also gravitated to the Madison Valley, just west of the Gallatin, for its natural beauty. (Rohleder 2000)

Of course, with several nearby ski areas (Bridger Bowl, Big Sky, Moonlight Basin), along with prime blue-ribbon trout streams galore in the immediate vicinity, the town has for a number of years been known as a base of operations for outdoor tourism and recreational forays, including serving as the larger first-tier gateway to Yellowstone National Park. Following its "discovery" as a potential domicile by outsiders, however, Bozeman has blossomed into something else entirely, and has since become a magnet for savvy entrepreneurs, equity refugees from higher priced California, and the trendy equestrian set alike. Those radiant scenic hillsides and lush creek bottoms all around Bozeman that once comprised larger ranch holdings have metamorphosed nearly overnight into smaller parcels that have somehow slipped through the loopholes or allowances of the minimal zoning guidelines of Gallatin County. Realtors and developers have carved up most of the larger holdings into more marketable offerings of twenty to forty acres. Counterintuitively, rather than limiting sprawl, these larger lot sizes have paradoxically encouraged the conversion of natural resource lands to super-sized residential tracts. Along with such extensive development naturally comes the demise of the open space and scenery that people who are building or buying houses there initially craved. Because of the propensity to accommodate the demands for larger lots, more and more land is needed for fewer new homes. Although the tentacles of this exurban octopus must now reach farther out from city limits, this voracious gobbling up of rural land would not have been nearly as rapid nor as complete without the requisite amenities, the cultural attractions, and the marketplace functions of Bozeman.

The city itself has exhibited somewhat more sophistication in accommodating and welcoming new growth, and there are numerous amenities that would be the envy of any town. Home of Montana State University, Bozeman's municipal landscape is also graced by the presence of the Museum of the Rockies, both of which are situated a few blocks south of the central business district. Commercial land use patterns have proceeded through a sequence of changes that typify what is happening elsewhere in the West. Not so long ago, Main Street was a drab assemblage of sad-looking storefronts, some of which were vacant, while others might as well have been. Businesses that anchor normal retail activity in a healthy town were barely hanging on, such as hardware and sporting goods stores, or the movie theaters. As is the case with small towns everywhere, not just in the West, the commercial land use of Bozeman was shifting out toward the edge, along the main highways leading into town, in this case to the north, along Seventh Avenue in the direction of Interstate 90, and more emphatically to the west, along Highway 191.

At first, one strip mall after another, each with its own capacious parking lot, leapfrogged their way sequentially outward from the central business district.

Banks, restaurants, gas stations, and specialty stores filled in the gaps, making the strip continuous. Then in 1981, an interior-spaced mall opened at the far western edge of the strip, and downtown merchants wondered how much longer the core area could hold on. But as residential development began to revolutionize land use patterns in the Bozeman vicinity, so too did the downtown begin a renewal period that continues to this day. In many cases, the types of shops have changed to ones that cater to a more upscale clientele. The five and dime is gone of course. Gift stores are more expensive than before, espresso coffee shops have replaced the old cafes, and art galleries seem to be elbow to elbow vying for attention.

Bozeman appears to be striving toward the Santa Fe, or Jackson, model of a New West downtown, and this is one that is likely to be mimicked in other similar locations, wherever amenity-driven landscape change has taken place. And it is one that, if followed devoutly to its endgame, will terminate the normal marketplace functions of a downtown for all but the well-heeled new arrivals or those visitors seeking to relocate. But under careful guidance, and with public-private cooperation, there are also redeeming components to this kind of central business district renaissance, elements that are more egalitarian and can be enjoyed by long-term residents and newcomers alike. Along Bozeman's Main Street, for example, the movie theaters have been saved from demolition, and several bookstores are able to operate successfully. There are close to half a dozen bicycle shops, and several outdoor suppliers. A brewpub has opened at the east end of town, and at least one of the older hotels has been refurbished and its restaurant rejuvenated. There are banks and professional offices. The library and various government facilities are situated within the city's hub as well. Last we checked, the post office was likewise still downtown, on the ground floor of the federal building, or at least a small remnant of the post office, for the main postal facility has indeed wandered off to a northern entrance road, following the national trend of relocating to an outer arterial site. Yet for the most part, Bozeman has what should be encouraged to prevail in any rapidly growing western town: exactly this kind of medley of offices, public buildings, and upper end shops mixed in with the more down-home, everyday businesses. When thrift stores and secondhand sporting goods outlets are able to share the streets with art galleries and expensive boutiques, then all is not lost in the central business district. The final ingredient for successfully maintaining a healthy downtown is affordable residential units, whether those are owner-occupied townhouses or second- and third-floor apartments over the business blocks. Fortunately, Bozeman historically has been well appointed with these kinds of diverse living arrangements, and this situation needs to be maintained into the future.

Industrial development has taken off as well, providing an enviable and relatively stable employment base beyond what is offered by Montana State University, local civil servants, or the retail sales and service economy. Much of this new development has occurred along the western outskirts of town and beyond.

Belgrade, a small community west of town, has managed to groom some of its land deemed useful for industrial purposes, cashing in on its proximity to the municipal airport and abundance of large tracts of level ground accessible by rail or interstate highway. But closer-in smaller industrial developments have served the growing community's needs perhaps just as well. One example is the office and warehouse complex along Simmental Way, on the northern edge of town near Exit 305 off Interstate 90. One of the first tenants within this tidy cluster of office buildings and small assembly plants should serve as an instructive example of the kinds of industrial activity that are so characteristic of the New West.

Starting with little more than some revolutionary ideas sketched in a notebook, maverick backpack designer Dana Gleason and business partner Renée Sippel-Baker created what would become the premier brand name of pack for serious hikers and anyone else looking for comfort, functionality, and quality. Gleason collected a core cadre of intensely loyal employees plucked from local sporting goods stores, and the hometown manufacturing firm grew steadily. The company was so successful that it eventually became the target of takeover by a larger corporation, and this has resulted in subsequent outsourcing of production overseas. Thus, Dana Design packs are no longer made in Bozeman, and, some would say, are likewise no longer anything close to what they once were. But other firms have established plants here, much to the delight of local economic development officials pursuing the gospel strategy of diversification.

In the same small industrial park where Dana Design operated their enterprise, nationally renowned instrument maker Gibson established a guitar manufacturing center in 1990. There is a photograph of the facility's exterior with an understated matter-of-fact caption on their web site: "In this unobtrusive building in the heart of Big Sky Country, the artisans at Gibson Montana build the finest acoustic guitars in the world" (Gibson Montana 2004). After praising the virtues of Gibson's handmade process, online vendor Folk of the Wood (2004) goes even further in framing the location of the Gibson plant in terms of geographic conditions:

> Even though they might get a little more snow up there, the environs of Bozeman, Montana are a guitar builder's dream come true. Extreme heat and high humidity are natural enemies of wood. Bozeman has neither. There are other advantages to Montana in addition to ideal climate. Gibson's acoustic guitars rely heavily on its builder's sense of creativity and concentration. Living in "Big Sky Country" appears to nurture both of these needs. It seems that looking out over a range of snow covered mountains every morning makes for inspired guitar building—which, in turn, makes for inspired guitars.

Another local company builds the kind of fiberglass drift boats that are viewed as being indispensable for floating and fly-fishing Montana's rivers. The Yellowstone Drifter Boat Company actually started back in the 1970s in nearby Livingston and subsequently relocated to Jackson, in the Big Hole Valley. During the 1990s, the company moved to Bozeman, and was eventually sold to the firm's current owners, who have since expanded the line with new designs (Hostetler 2004). This is one good example of local craftsmanship targeting a product that stays in high local demand. An alternative business strategy would be to conduct more widespread marketing of local products, or at least ones that can be identified with the region. To the west of Bozeman, a little beyond Belgrade, is the community of Manhattan, close by the Gallatin River. From there, a company advertises its wares on the Internet and claims to offer the "largest online selection of western furnishings and western decor," specializing in log furniture such as beds and sofas, or willow chairs (Timberline Furniture 2004).

Such grassroots manufacturing endeavors help keep the local economy alive and serve as examples of relatively benign land use change. But it is the once rustic countryside of the Gallatin Valley that has been utterly transformed by New West development. Here, large-lot subdivision of land, often resulting in parcels ranging between twenty and forty acres, has carpeted former open grasslands and foothills of the mountains in most directions, but primarily to the north and to the southwest of town. The sprawling end result of so many incremental decisions to allow building permits for all these exurban ranchettes has raised an alarm among many, who point to the ineffectiveness of county zoning regulations and the frailties of code enforcement. Part of the problem has been that most of the development has been according to code, wherein large minimum lot sizes were considered a preventive measure and a restrictive palliative to edge-of-town tendencies toward sprawl, and would thereby serve as a restraint on rural development. No one ever figured on *that* many people wanting to spend *that* much money on a bare, treeless lot *that* far from the edge of town.

All is not sprawl, however, and some of the newer compact developments are offering an alternative that seems to be capitalizing on public outcry over lost open space, while simultaneously commodifying the sense of community so noticeably absent in more conventional subdivision designs. Baxter Meadows, emerging from a former working ranch north of town, is the name of one such project that has recently been formulated somewhat along these more intensive New Urbanist principles. The master plan for this 440-acre development calls for "a mixed-use traditional town" encompassing residential neighborhoods, 130 acres of commercial zoning, and 150 acres of open space. More than one-third of the project displays the tight rectilinear grid of streets that have become requisite in neotraditional town planning, although the intersections with surrounding rights-of-way appear offset and skewed, causing undesirable insularity. In one residential area, bungalows and other front porch–dominated vernacular designs line the sidewalks along Gallatin Green Boulevard, a wide lane with planted street trees, a perfectly delightful addition to any urban mosaic. But seemingly all alone standing out here on the plains, it makes for a somewhat disconcerting scene. Cattail

Drive, one wag claims, is named appropriately enough for the wetlands that were filled in to enable paving the road and platting the zero-lot-line parcels.

To its credit, Baxter Meadows will offer a wide range of housing options in a variety of densities, including a number of innovative "live-work units," which feature multistory condominium units situated above a street-level shop or office space. Yet the majority of residential properties are geared toward individual single-family dwellings, and nearly a third of the entire development is devoted to higher priced "estate lots." Attention to recreation has been given full rein, however, with a planned equestrian center and a dedicated regional park situated in the middle of the development, with interconnected pathways leading to ball fields, ponds, natural areas, and an amphitheater, along with a site set aside for a future YMCA facility (Baxter Meadows 2004). Historic preservation efforts have focused on turning an existing barn into the community center. Commercial space is slated for retail establishments, restaurants, and offices, all within walking distance, while the provision of communications infrastructure emphasizes state-of-the-art fiber optics. Despite its design flaws and compromises, Baxter Meadows is a commendable step in the right direction toward constraining the centrifugal forces of land use conversion that are overpowering many smaller cities and towns across the West. In Bozeman, developers have begun to recognize the profound changes that are currently underway, and have sought to accommodate the demands of rapid population growth bringing a new culture to the area.

Gateways to Yellowstone

Although the national park itself is primarily situated in Wyoming, special mention must be made of Yellowstone's three major gateway communities that are located in the state of Montana: West Yellowstone, Gardiner, and Red Lodge. As is the case with a number of other communities sprinkled throughout the West, fortune has granted these places a special dispensation from the laws of decline, simply by virtue of their geographic proximity to a national park and other public recreation lands. As such, they have been labeled "gateway communities" (Howe, McMahon, and Propst 1997). While several have long served as logistical supply points for tourists, others have only lately assumed that role following the demise of other reasons for being. The one true town in its own right, Red Lodge has become a gateway community by spatial default, drawing on its location along the park's northeast entrance road. It was originally established as one of any number of "central places" that primarily functioned as social and economic nodes within the northern Rockies ranching and farming settlement system. Perhaps because of its genesis, Red Lodge exudes a charming authenticity that easily lends itself to New West transformation. Downtown shops that had once seen better days have been rejuvenated, and several blocks of the central business district have come alive with cafes, bookstores, and other establishments associated with the tourist trade. New migrants have begun to refurbish vernacular dwellings in the core area, resuscitating what was once a comatose residential setting (Wiltsie and Wyckoff 2003).

Unlike Red Lodge, which is situated at some distance from Yellowstone's northeast entrance, the more unabashedly tourist-oriented service centers of West Yellowstone and Gardiner both sit directly against the boundary line of the national park. Each of these towns has long served the need to provide a place for gas stations and automobile service facilities, overnight accommodations, and cafes and restaurants for visitors to the park. But there are striking differences that are readily apparent when comparing these places that have such a similar function. The physical geography of the two sites could not be any more of a contrast: Gardiner is set in a dramatic perch amid tall peaks and straddling the channel between two entrenched canyon segments of the great river that churns off the forested plateau to the south and emerges downstream some distance from town into its broad valley. West Yellowstone is splayed out as a lackluster grid of streets, many of them unpaved, surveyed across the featureless flat expanse of a lodgepole pine thicket. Gardiner, with its older, established half a Main Street facade facing the park and its highly symbolic stone Entrance Arch, has retained a certain genuine historic character that is utterly lacking in West Yellowstone. At one time the terminus for the rail spur that connected to the Northern Pacific mainline at Livingston, Gardiner has also served as headquarters for the main concession company, in its manifold iterations over the years, that operates and manages the hotels and restaurants at numerous nodal locations within Yellowstone under licensing agreement with the National Park Service. Situated at the lowest elevation entrance to the park, this area is usually open and accessible year-round. West Yellowstone, at a higher elevation, has become the snowmobiling capital for winter visitors who wish to witness steam clouds over the geyser basins and wintering herds of elk and bison along the Firehole. The endless controversy over snowmobile visitation to the park is centered on this town, where many local merchants see their fortunes tied to deregulation. The iconic portrait of the ranger at the West Yellowstone entrance booth wearing a gas mask to avoid breathing the fumes from a line of snowmobiles waiting to enter the park provides summary argument against allowing unrestricted access for this seasonal mode of touring.

One of the most beautiful landscapes in the entire United States is formed by that segment of the Yellowstone River flowing between Gardiner and Livingston. Aptly named Paradise Valley, this place captures the imagination of many a visitor to Yellowstone Park who is fortunate enough to travel this route. At river's edge along the riparian bottomlands may still be found majestic galleries of cottonwoods, while the settlement landscape on the floor of the valley has until recently comprised a functional mosaic of pastures, irrigated hayfields, and the farmsteads, barns, and corrals of working ranches. Towering over all are the majestic peaks of the Absarokas to the east and the Gallatin Range on the west. In a revealing case study undertaken as a master's thesis by geographer Eric Compas (2001), it was shown that this valley has attracted increasing numbers of new residents moving here from out of state. Once devoted almost entirely to cattle ranching, current purchases of land for different purposes have dramatically increased its cost: "Aesthetic and recreation values have been at the heart of this new ownership pattern, rather than the extractive economics that drove the previous wave of settlement" (Compas 2001, 12). As might be expected, parcelization of larger holdings has occurred, but this has taken place primarily along the existing network of roads that provide transportation access along with proximity to utility infrastructure such as electric power. Additional concentrations of subdivision activity, particularly for smaller sized parcels, has become most evident along the river, which "shows the importance of the river for recreation and aesthetic value" (Compas 2001, 19).

Development Potential

Among the larger urban areas of the state, Billings, inexplicably, will continue to grow, as will, to a lesser extent, Great Falls. Helena is perhaps the best prospect for undergoing rapid future development at an urban level, building upon its function as the small to mid-sized seat of state government, and further capitalizing on the scenic and recreational amenities of the surrounding countryside. Elsewhere, some of the most unlikely locales now are poised for new development, including the old mining landscapes around Butte and Anaconda. Butte, once so thoroughly dependent on copper mining, and consequently tainted with a town vista still dominated by its monstrous abandoned open pit that is now a toxic pond, would hardly seem a candidate for admission to the New West. But recent population surge and a host of new homes in the hillsides around town tell a remarkable story of changed perception and renewal. Commercial development has begun to reshape the place as well, and Butte is currently attempting to reconcile its ambivalent respect for a "bittersweet legacy of mining," which originally built the town, with its aspirations to embrace a new "landscape of consumption," which will "create a growth machine that spurs economic expansion" (Wyckoff 1995).

Further west, the former company town of Anaconda during the mid-1990s installed an innovative new golf course by refashioning the old tailings that had come to dominate a counterfeit terrain contaminated by mining: "Jack Nicklaus designed this golf course by transforming abandoned slag piles into tee areas and 'black' sand traps" (Berger 2002, 66). Measuring a lengthy 7,700 yards, Old Works Golf Course has now become one of Montana's top-rated links, partly as a result of the skillful use of local conditions and culture: "Incorporating numerous mining relics throughout, sculpting broad, gracefully flowing fairways, and peppering the sides of his massive greens with the beautiful ebony sand traps, Nicklaus managed to reclaim an enormous amount of integrity on a site that was scarcely a good enough environment for a rodent" (Penner 2004, 2). As it flows across the course, Warm Springs Creek, once a dead zone, now has trout again and serves as a focal point for the renewed landscape. Reclamation efforts normally do not have such dramatic results, and this has utterly changed the perception of this place that once tied its livelihood to the ecologically disastrous processes of copper mining and smelting. Nevertheless, it has not yet yuppified the area: "Not your typical golfing Mecca dotted with gated communities, white sand beaches, and three figure green fees, the town of Anaconda is like a breath of fresh air for the purists of the game" (Penner 2004, 3).

As the legendary open spaces of Montana's more favored locations become wiped out by the homes and lifestyles of all the new arrivals, and the sought-after rustic authenticity of the mythic western landscape becomes tarnished by the reality of suburban-style development, where else within this state might fall victim to such a transformation? The scenic mountain and foothill areas to the east of the great Continental Divide seem likely enough possibilities, including the currently sparsely settled vicinities of Big Timber, Columbus, White Sulphur Springs, and Choteau. Mere wide spots in the road, if the road happens to parallel great trout fishing, also need to be prepared for change: places such as Ennis, Twin Bridges, and Wisdom have already begun to experience parcelization of former ranch properties into homesites. To the west, several as yet relatively "undiscovered" valleys between the Rockies and the Bitterroots likewise seem ripe for New West transformation. There are exceptionally large holdings of private lands situated amidst national forests between Missoula and Helena, primarily in Powell County but also within Granite County, much of it quickly accessible by the interstate highway. South of there, finely situated Philipsburg, with its mining heritage, abundant recreation options nearby, and a downtown designated a national historic district, has all the markings of a New West outpost. As unlikely as it may seem right now, places that don't feel they would ever need regulations like zoning are too often the ones caught by surprise.

One real sleeper would seem to be the tiny town of Dillon, county seat of expansive Beaverhead County and home to an institution of higher education formerly named Western Montana College, now labeled, somewhat awkwardly, University of Montana Western. This community seems to be hiding behind its supposed remote location in the far southwest corner of the state. But the intersection of several main roads and highways with Interstate 15 enables easy access to the scenic riches of southwest Montana, and this area could become the next locale to claim the title "last best place." In town, the newly restored Union Pacific depot, the local attention to art and architecture, and the upgraded status of the university all point to civic pride and great potential. The surrounding area is replete with historic and cultural resources, such as significant Native American and early pioneer sites, ghost towns and old mining camps, and the first territorial capital at Bannack. There is the nearby 80,000-acre LaCense ranch, a working quarter horse and black angus cattle operation known for its horse-whisperer style educational programs and "the only ranch in the United States certified to sell recreational quarter horses trained in Parelli natural horsemanship methods, providing you with a safe, sound, highly educated equestrian partner that you will enjoy for years" (LaCense Montana 2004). Numerous public lands recreational attractions, especially wildlife refuges, likewise bring in visitors who engage in hunting, fishing, and, increasingly, nonconsumptive appreciative viewing of various species such as swans and other waterfowl. There are hot springs and ski slopes, and plenty of backpacking and mountain climbing options in the vicinity. Moreover, Beaverhead County continues to be an important agricultural player, ranking number one in the state for both beef cattle and hay production. By corollary, private land is in abundant supply, should rural residential development loom on the horizon. Now is probably the time for city and county government to learn how they might best shape and guide future growth in this region.

WYOMING

Aside from Jackson, long considered a western lifestyle capital and tony trendsetter, this least populous state is one of the more recent targets of New West development. With its larger towns situated on the edge of the Great Plains, Wyoming has long been ruled by cattle and oil interests. The extractive industries that once dominated the state politically and economically have hardly advocated an appreciation of scenery and environmental values by local residents. Moreover, places like Rock Springs are notorious examples of the boom and bust cycle of equally rapid growth and decline and evince little in the way of attractions, amenities, or civic pride. Other less destitute locations, though still closely aligned with energy resource exploitation and development, have shown modest growth, including the small cities of Casper, Gillette, and Sheridan. State capital Cheyenne and cowboy-and-college town Laramie, situated in the far southeast corner of the state, have shown less inclination to take off in terms of population expansion. It has been the smaller towns, those remote, out-of-the-way outposts of tourist catering and outfitting, that are now bursting at the seams, manifesting spillover residential and commercial development into formerly rustic countryside. These diminutive towns are for the most part classic "gateway communities," serving as entrepots not only to the national parks but also to national forests and other recreation areas.

Wyoming's Gateway Communities

Faced with so many public land recreation options in the northwestern and northcentral part of the state, a tidy collection of communities has developed over the years to take care of visitor needs. They are still doing so today, but there's a new twist: many of the visitors are deciding to become residents, either seasonal or permanent. Lander and Pinedale, small villages straddling the sublimely beautiful Wind River Range, are prime examples of the type. These mountains, once mistakenly believed by Frémont to contain the West's loftiest summit, nevertheless hold some of the finest alpine environments in the country and are a vast public wilderness playground for the more primitive recreational pursuits. In the sprinkling of small settlements at the base of the mountains, dozens of outfitter and guide services are listed in the local business directories. But backpacking and hunting suppliers and snowmobile repairmen have been joined by New West entrepreneurs vending llama rentals or scenic helicopter flights, while former cattle ranches have traded in the lariat for the floating fly line.

At Pinedale, nearly a dozen motels and lodges offer accommodations either in town or around the several glacially carved lakes on the way to the mountains. Yet these days, people are not just visiting but are staying, and Sublette County, as illustrated in figure 3.3, has become the second-fastest-growing county in the state.

FIGURE 3.3
Wyoming, showing the fastest growing county for the decade 1990–2000 in darkest shading, the next fastest growing counties in lighter shading, and selected towns and cities discussed in text. Data source: U.S. Census Bureau. *Map by Ian Gray, CWU graduate program in resource management.*

Coming into Pinedale from the west, it is hard to remain focused on the scenic mountain backdrop with all the new houses going up on the flats, but then your gaze takes in the large ridge to the north of town, a glacial moraine, and it quickly becomes evident that the New West has invaded here. For what conceivably might have been conserved as one of the area's key identifiable topographic landmarks has now become the setting for view lots and whatever passes for trophy homes in these parts.

Besides scenic resources, there are increasing residential conflicts with wildlife habitat, specifically with seasonal corridors used by pronghorn. On a hill just west of Pinedale known as Trappers Point, a new subdivision has further constrained a migration bottleneck for these herds that travel south from the Tetons to their Upper Green River Valley wintering grounds. Complicating this particular conflict is a renewed rush to issue exemptions for natural gas exploration, and local BLM projections foresee something on the order of 10,000 new wells, a tripling of the number currently active in this area, over the next decade (Gordon 2004). Yet residential development shows no sign of slowing down, either, and local builders with an eye to the future are starting to take note. There is now a firm in Pinedale that constructs custom-designed houses, advertising "unique hand-crafted log homes" built primarily of lodgepole pine and Engelmann spruce, but with an ecofriendly slant, as the firm's web site explains: "standing dead trees are harvested using environmentally responsible methods" (Logcrafters 2004). Even while questioning the ecological validity of removing potential wildlife snags from the forest, we can only hope that the process leading to the actual placement of these new homes gives more thought to environmental values than in the past.

Like Pinedale on the west side, the community of Lander is in a similar situation on the east side of the Winds, a tidy, compact village that boasts several bookstores along with a number of specialty coffee houses such as the Magpie, the Global Cafe, and the Wildflour Bakery. Of course there are the ubiquitous wilderness outfitters, but there is also the Lander Golf and Country Club, with its eighteen-hole course available for public play. There is a paved pathway along the Popo Agie River as it flows through town. The recently remodeled Grand Theater keeps alive the tradition of main street cinema and showcases an alternative film series on weekends. For fine art enthusiasts, there are public tours of the Eagle Bronze Foundry, which casts some of the largest bronze sculptures in the country. And there are arranged walking excursions through historic downtown, which is also billed as the future home of the Museum of the American West, although that name (and web domain) has already been commandeered as a new title for the former Autry Museum of Western Heritage in Los Angeles. But Lander is not the only small town in Wyoming that has placed its bets on the potential draw of a museum.

Further to the north, Cody has long enjoyed its status as funnel for the east entrance to Yellowstone National Park, and the equally compelling recreational riches of adjacent Shoshone National Forest. It retains a vibrant downtown, with many shops, restaurants, and overnight accommodations, including the celebrated Irma Hotel, established by Buffalo Bill Cody and named after his loving wife. Town officials have kept traditions such as the rodeo and parade alive, and have welcomed and nourished as a civic centerpiece the Buffalo Bill Historical Center, which has since expanded to include four collateral facilities: the Plains Indian Museum; the Draper Museum of Natural History; the Cody Firearms Museum; and the Whitney Gallery of Western Art, featuring what has become a hot genre nationally these days. In addition, the center sponsors a summer institute that brings in notable scholars to offer courses and deliver presentations on various aspects of the changing West. During 2004, lectures were presented by Colorado State University professor Richard Knight on "Speaking Western: Honest Conversations in the New West" and University of Texas-Arlington geographer Richard Francaviglia on "Believing in Place: A Spiritual Geography of the Intermountain West." In conjunction with cultural resource specialists from the National Park Service, the Buffalo Bill Historical Center also offers day-long tours of a number of historically significant ranch properties in the Big Horn basin. All told, visitors to Cody have been charmed, and more and more of them have decided to relocate or retire here. The outskirts of town, with an abundance of open space, has naturally been deemed most desirable, and as a result nearly the entire North Fork Shoshone Valley has now been parceled out and is up for sale. Figure 3.4 illustrates the conversion of cattle ranches to large-parcel recreational homesites.

FIGURE 3.4
Former cattle ranches with their irrigated hayfields are being divided and sold as large parcel recreational homesites in the North Fork Shoshone River Valley, west of Cody, Wyoming. *Photograph by Robert Kuhlken.*

Jackson Hole

Jackson, along with Santa Fe, may be viewed as a capital city of the New West. The dramatic structural downwarp at the foot of the spectacular Teton Range is known as Jackson Hole, while the town that has grown up at the southern edge of this ecologically rich marshy plain is named Jackson—although these two to-ponyms are sometimes used interchangeably. Jackson Hole contains the headwaters of the Snake River, and much of the land is in public ownership, primarily as Grand Teton National Park. Although the entire park encompasses a rich diversity of environments, it is this lower elevation area that provides very important wildlife habitat, most notably for a resident elk herd that depends on it for critical winter range. There exist some small pockets of private property intermixed with the public domain north of town, and numerous houses have been built on these exclusionary large lots, but so far it appears it has been mainly landowners much appreciative of the scenery and who seem willing to design homes that make an attempt to blend in.

Lands surrounding Jackson Hole are under Forest Service management, thus contributing to the circumstance that nearly all of Teton County, an astounding 97%, is in public ownership. Faced with limited land availability, the town's growth spurt has been constrained on the north by the national elk refuge, and in most other directions by national forest ownership. Consequently, the expansion of urban development has been squeezed along two transportation corridors: U.S. Highway 191 heading south, and State Route 22 to the west. Nevertheless, the area's supreme scenic beauty and public recreation bounty continue to lure wealthy outdoorspeople bent on owning a piece of the action, as travel writer Kimberly Seely (2004, 59) noted recently: "With ranches in the shadows of the Teton mountains and houses only a few feet from the Snake River, the valley of Jackson Hole has always offered a unique Western experience. But recently it has drawn scores of second-home buyers, and real estate prices in some areas have increased by 80 percent over the past five years."

Affordable housing is one of the main casualties of increased capitalization of properties in the Jackson area. Much of this simply stems from the law of supply and demand: "With only 3 percent of the county in private hands, property around Jackson Hole doesn't come cheap; few houses cost less than half a million dollars" (Seely 2004, 59). Although a range of housing types are on the market, they are priced well above what might be considered an affordable range for real estate. Houses in excess of 5,000 square feet of living space adorn the small residential parcels scattered here and there along the river, or perched on hillsides of glacial till. Asking prices for these properties typically can range from a mere million dollars to a staggering fifteen million dollars. Time-share condominiums, such as those offered by the Four Seasons Residence Club, offer one alternative to outlandish fee simple ownership in Jackson, but this option does nothing for the service employees and other permanent residents who simply cannot make the kind of mortgage payments required to own a year-round home, and more than likely do not have the wherewithal to even rent the all-too-rare apartment units in town. For those who can afford it, however, there are still large ranches for sale, along with those very expensive custom-designed homes in lovely settings. But larger parcels are more often voraciously eaten up by grandiose development corporations that are keen to accentuate the natural amenities of the area with lifestyle add-ons such as common open space, swimming pools, spas, and security patrols for the many exclusive lots that are usually less than an acre each.

Jackson is considered to be one of the more favored locations in the New West largely because it is surrounded by stunning scenic amenities, abundant public lands, and well-developed recreation facilities, but also because it is easily accessible by air. It has professional-level ski runs, a riveting backdrop of mountains, and an airport that handles commercial jet aircraft. Paradoxically, the town itself has been reworked into a represented image of the small western frontier outpost people want to believe still exists, even while the types of businesses are decidedly high market. Fancy shops catering to an upper-class clientele, and those who want to consider themselves as such, emanate outward for several blocks from the public town square, with its famous corner entrance arbors fashioned from elk antlers. There are art galleries and pine log furniture studios, jewelry stores full of turquoise and silver, sweet-smelling shops hawking authentic Indian blankets or baskets or pottery beneath the piped-in soundtrack of Native American flute Muzak, and an untold multitude of western clothing vendors. Exclusive designer fashion outlets sit side-by-side with kitschy souvenir joints, as tourists scramble around recording each other on videocams, while nouveau-western outfits scream cowboy chic as their well-to-do wearers stroll down the wooden boardwalks to window shop. In the winter months, simply make the seasonal switch to the latest in active ski-wear woven from space-age textiles, and the scene remains the same.

Local responses to managing this kind of appeal and consequent growth have been mixed. Ad valorem taxes are anathema in Wyoming, which has some of the lowest rates in the nation, and private property rights still reign supreme. There are, however, enough people who care about conservation of natural resources to make a difference. Moreover, there are many private property owners who wish to preserve the beauty and integrity of their parcels, and prevent further development. Toward that end, the Jackson Hole Land Trust has been instrumental in orchestrating conservation easements, whereby development rights are donated in perpetuity in return for an even lower tax burden. Visitors along with long-term and seasonal residents alike have joined forces in promoting greater attention to regional planning: "In all seasons, the area draws a conservation-minded, egalitarian crowd passionate about outdoor pursuits and united in their desire to preserve the unparalleled landscape" (Seely 2004, 59). The expression of that aesthetic has found functional outlet in an organization known as the Upper

Snake River Conservancy, which espouses a regional planning effort that takes into account scenic and environmental values.

Growth Potentials

Elsewhere in Wyoming there are hints of things to come along the upper reaches of the North Platte River, where that stream drains the western slopes of the Medicine Bow Range. Parcelization of larger holdings has great potential to modify the landscape around the small communities of Saratoga and Encampment. In the context of tourism and sport, this valley actually functions as a northern extension of the Colorado mountain parks, which are described in more detail later in the chapter. Already the scene of increased recreational pursuits, this area is known for its horseback riding and snowmobiling opportunities, and there are a number of bed-and-breakfast facilities as well as more elaborate guest ranches nearby. The place seems ripe for much more intensive amenity-driven development, perhaps including a golf course resort or two. How successfully such projects might be integrated into the local economy and environment without becoming intrusive nuisances will be up to county officials and concerned citizenry.

Nestled up against the eastern flanks of the Bighorn Mountains is the vibrant community of Buffalo, which is attempting to enter the New West by pledging its allegiance to the Old West. This is, after all, in the words of the Chamber of Commerce web site, "a place of sheep herders and cattle barons, renegades and rustlers," which also cites Butch Cassidy's local exploits along with the Johnson County Cattle War as major historical attractions. Downtown, in addition to the obligatory museum, there are antique shops and art galleries, a quaint old-fashioned soda fountain, and the restored Occidental Hotel, which figured prominently in Owen Wister's novel *The Virginian*. As might be expected, a rodeo is an annual spectator event, but everyday participant recreation is likewise given full sway, with what is claimed to be the largest outdoor swimming pool in the state, and (what else?) a highly rated championship golf course. For good measure, a hiking trail now extends ten miles along Clear Creek, from the town west to the mountains (Buffalo Chamber of Commerce 2004). Outside of town, the historic TA Ranch takes dude-ranching a step further, with its remarkable historic preservation efforts. Guests may opt for the traditional guest ranch experience or indulge in a fly-fishing vacation; but in the true New West spirit of multitasking, there is also a business conference center. Storey and Big Horn, hardly places at all, are emerging as potential trophy home settings, and former ranchlands, with a view in close proximity to the Powderhorn PGA golf course, are being parceled off at a swift pace. Figure 3.5 provides a panoramic view of the setting near Big Horn.

Finally, one place located in the northern interior of the state offering plausible retirement amenities is the presently very small town of Thermopolis. With but a single stop light directing vehicular traffic for a population of merely 3,500,

FIGURE 3.5
Residential development is converting these ranchlands with a view overlooking the
Powderhorn golf course at Big Horn, Wyoming. *Photograph by Philip Jackson.*

it is the county seat of Hot Springs County, which itself only counts a total of
5,000 souls. Civic pride centers around one of the world's largest hot springs, developed as a state park that offers free admission to the soaking pools; nearby pastures within the park hold a resident herd of bison. As the local economic
development council boasts on their web site, the town "enjoys a quality of life
most places only dream of . . . the area remains unspoiled and relatively undiscovered, beckoning the visitor, the new resident, or the new business." In that regard, local land use regulations are intentionally lax, and this is set forth as one of
the "further essentials" for an estimable quality of life: "*Reasonable* county and
town planning and zoning regulations *keep property protected but official intrusion
limited*" (italics added). A notable business success story is highlighted by the
council, which relates how one sheet metal fabricating firm relocated to Thermopolis from Denver and has enjoyed expanded opportunities for marketing its
products, including landing a contract to supply Yellowstone National Park with
bear-proof garbage dumpsters. The town's economic development director, Curt
Pendergraft, points out that remote location and meager population are no longer
obstacles to business success and that there are certain advantages that can only be
offered by a small town such as Thermopolis situated in an attractive rural setting.

UTAH
Beginning with the 1847 establishment of Salt Lake City, sacred nucleus of the
Mormon faith at the western base of the Wasatch Range, the entire state of Utah
was more or less colonized intentionally and systematically. A pattern of cooperative irrigation enterprises and the platting of self-sufficient, compact agricultural

communities soon gave rise to industrial production and full-scale urban and commercial expansion along the Wasatch Front, where sprawl has become a signature element of the landscape throughout the 100-mile stretch between Brigham City and Provo. It was not hard to see this coming: More than fifty years ago Dale Morgan (1949, 181) noted that Salt Lake City "has grown vigorously through a century by reason of the economic energy of the Wasatch Oasis." Population growth is expected to continue for this entire conurbation, and how well such development is managed depends on the level of interest and willingness to engage in land use planning within each of the individual municipalities, as well as the five different counties for unincorporated lands. Without coordination among these multiple jurisdictions, there can never be a coherent, consolidated approach to accommodating new growth and integrating it into existing development patterns and infrastructural capabilities. It may well be that a united, multilateral stance taken by a consolidated government agency such as that presented by the Wasatch Front Regional Council is best suited for such a task. Among their manifold programs are those addressing air quality, congestion management, corridor preservation, natural hazard mitigation, transportation systems, and open space planning (Wasatch Front Regional Council 2004).

Rapid urban growth of this type is neither a hallmark of the New West nor unexpected and is, of course, occurring in many regions of the country. Within Utah, however, there are several locations that manifest remarkably changed cultural geographies over a short time span, and these places are worth examining in greater detail. For example, a case study of one particular community near the Wasatch Front would reveal some of the dramatic changes that can occur when scenery and recreation are close at hand to population centers. Among a handful of hardrock mining communities that once peppered these mountains, resuscitated Park City has emerged as Utah's premier resort town. Here, both visitors and residents alike are able to enjoy recreational pursuits through the four seasons, and affluent migrants have been buying up houses as second homes or vacation getaways (Ringholz 1996). But New West growth has also taken hold in the state's smaller communities well to the south of this decidedly more urbanized area, primarily in the gateway towns near national parks and other public land recreational facilities, and in the southwest corner of the state, in the area known as Dixie. County growth trends for Utah are illustrated in figure 3.6.

Redrock Gateway Communities

Southern Utah is considered by many to be unusually blessed with scenic attractions, largely derived from the geological predominance of the Colorado Plateau and the many canyons carved across it by tiny streamlets and mighty rivers alike. Canyon walls and cliffs formed by exposed layers of sandstone in many different shades, sometimes brilliant white but most often red or orange,

FIGURE 3.6

Utah, showing the fastest growing county for the decade 1990–2000 in darkest shading, the next fastest growing counties in lighter shading, and selected towns and cities discussed in text. Data source: U.S. Census Bureau. *Map by Ian Gray, CWU graduate program in resource management.*

have lent color and character to this arid region. Mesas and buttes are interspersed with other erosional remnants of a vast sedimentary plateau, including distinctive topographic features such as hoodoos and badlands. Plateau surfaces—sparsely vegetated tablelands locally known as slickrock—have their own visual appeal as the stark rolling surface of the sandstone shelters a picturesque ecological community of piñon-juniper. Relief is quite varied, however, and large areas of mountainous terrain comprise forested "islands in the desert." Past economies were based upon consumptive resource use, including logging and uranium mining, or were agriculturally based, with small irrigated fields along watercourses, dryland farming wherever possible, and grazing. The communities that supported these lifeways are still there, but are rapidly undergoing change and are having to accommodate new residents with different values and ideas about the natural environment.

The recognition of scenic resources and recreation has been operative here for some time, of course, but tourism as an economic enterprise was fairly limited by isolation, bad roads, and a less than welcoming attitude by long-time locals. All of that has changed along with public perception and attitude, reflected in much more substantial investments by resource management agencies in visitor facilities and infrastructure. The larger national parks of southern Utah evolved for the most part from earlier, less intensive designations as national monuments, and these include Arches, Canyonlands, Capitol Reef, Bryce Canyon, and Zion. Smaller units of the Park Service still include Natural Bridges and Cedar Breaks National Monuments. Visitation figures for all of these places have increased steadily over the past several decades. Zion's traffic has reached the point where congestion on its main canyon-bottom dead end road precipitated a decision to restrict automobile access during the summer, and now all visitors are required to use the shuttle bus service. Located in between these parks are the national forests of the higher elevations, along with extensive public lands under the aegis of the Bureau of Land Management, providing a more primitive recreational experience unsupported by the usual tourist-related conveniences. So-called national recreation areas round out the picture, many of them associated with canyon tributaries of the Lake Powell impoundment, itself a major attraction. During his final days in office, President Clinton elevated the status of a huge chunk of these lands by creating the Grand Staircase-Escalante National Monument (GSENM). The small towns of southern Utah that serve as immediately adjacent gateways to all this wondrous country include Moab, Monticello, Torrey, and Escalante.

Moab was once a dusty uranium-mining town laid out along a comparatively quiet reach of the Colorado River, far enough away from anywhere else to have the freedom both to be itself and to be left alone. With the demise of atomic energy and the relative unlikelihood of nuclear warfare, the town's vitality deteriorated into a slow and seemingly inexorable decline, as measured by the half-life of whatever managed to hang on. Its gradual renewal first began when Arches National

Monument was upgraded to a national park, and visitation to Arches and to nearly adjacent Canyonlands National Park increased dramatically. One of the more idiosyncratic attributes of Arches is the notable imprint of the late writer Edward Abbey, who worked there several seasons as a ranger and whose excellent book *Desert Solitaire*, which was based on that experience, has earned legions of enthusiastic readers along with continual accolades from conservationists. It is largely through Abbey's writings that the canyon country of Utah has been changed forever in the popular mind from a desolate wasteland to a place of beauty and reverence. And no location has felt the effect of this transformation in perception more than once sleepy Moab.

Even as mining and the processing of uranium ore began to decline, tourism had started to take up the slack in the local economy: "With its mild climate and low rents, Moab attracted a growing number of retirees and a small arts community" (Amundson 2004, 153). When visitation to Arches National Park began to rise, this town underwent a metamorphosis of sorts. Motels and tourist lodges moved from ramshackle to upscale, while other types of businesses became established that would have been foreign to the former mining supply center. There are now camping and backpacking outfitters, several bookstores, gourmet coffee shops, tourist gift boutiques, numerous clothing outlets, and a couple of laid back nightspots, including a brew pub at the south end of town. Storefront windows are saturated with iconic images of Kokopelli, the legendary Native American hump-backed flute player, who is said to have wandered the canyon country seducing young maidens. This shadowy figure could well be considered the mascot for the current generation of wanderers in this part of the New West, where leisure activities and appreciation of scenery have replaced natural resource extraction efforts. The town's makeover might all have occurred anyway given this change in popular perception and use of the surrounding public recreation lands. But what has most put Moab on the map is a phenomenon that continues to fuel the supercharged local economy: mountain biking. Moab is now a mecca for the fat tire crowd. There are several bike shops offering repairs and rentals. Maps and guidebooks point the way to nearby places to ride. Fleets of shuttle vans with rooftop bike racks scurry about, as illustrated in figure 3.7, ferrying riders to and from the many designated single tracks in the vicinity, including the famed Slickrock Trail, which traverses the sandstone plateau overlooking the town.

Along with the increased intensity in commercial use, Moab's residential landscape is in the midst of pronounced upheaval. Infill of vacant lots in town with newly constructed houses is one rather desirable result, but it doesn't end there. The hillsides that line the edge of town were platted into lots some time ago, and have seen a diverse scattering of dwellings placed there over the years, comprising a wide variety in style, quality, and workmanship. A few of these developments are filling in sporadically, while the rest are being avoided as new money seeks its own virgin ground. At a slightly higher elevation, on Johnson's Up-On-Top Mesa, a

FIGURE 3.7
Downtown Moab, Utah. Many businesses now cater to the mountain bike crowd.
Photograph by Robert Kuhlken.

proposed luxury resort recently caused a good bit of controversy. As approved by
the Grand County Planning and Zoning Commission, "Cloudrock" was slated to
comprise a 200-room hotel, 150 condominium units, and more than 100 single-
family houses on two-acre lots, while further plans for developments at the site include an outdoor amphitheater (Church 2001). The most recent actions by
county officials called for a scaled-down version of the approved project, but then
any subsequent decision was tabled, effectively stalling the process for the foreseeable future.

South of town, irrigated bottomlands of the Spanish Valley are now being
carved up for residential subdivisions of many shapes and varieties. A townhouse
complex known as Rim Village has recently taken up a large area of land on the
valley floor, despite the relatively high density resulting from the attached units.
Over by the golf course, a new perpendicular cul-de-sac of near-zero-lot-line
"ranch homes" arrayed in staggered pattern was being constructed during the
spring of 2003. As explained on the sales brochure:

> Coyote Run is an exclusive Ranch Home planned development. Inspired by the
> Ralph Lauren Western look , it is "Old West" authentic. We've combined the privacy
> of individual homes with the carefree maintenance of a planned community. Coy-
> ote Run is carefully sited between the Moab golf course, redrock canyon walls, and
> the green ranchlands of Spanish Valley.

It's not all that bad, really, for density is within tolerable parameters, and the structures do look nice. The design for each dwelling unit includes exterior pathways and porches, for that "new urbanist" dash of pedestrianism, yet with a two-car garage as a reality check. But in a photo we took of a pair of real estate for-sale signs along a fence out on the road, we were most struck by the irony inherent in the juxtaposition of the two illustrations (figure 3.8). Perhaps when we once again start to build passive solar-powered multifamily units constructed from earth materials and situated well away from floodplains and off of rich agricultural soils, we may then begin to remember the lessons lost now for nearly a millennium.

For thirty miles or so upstream from Moab, the Colorado River winds through remote and gorgeous slickrock country. State Highway 128 parallels the twists and turns of the river's course along the left (south) bank all the way to a place called Dewey Bridge, where the road crosses over to the other side and continues north to the community of Cisco and a connection with Interstate 70. On this reach of the Colorado there are no serious rapids, and flatwater recreational rafting is a popular pastime, while several basic public camping areas (no electricity, no water) have been set up in the tamarisk groves. From Dewey Bridge downstream, the riparian terrain alternates between close-in canyon walls and more open, parklike amphitheaters where the river manages to maintain a sizeable floodplain. Several of these flats are the setting for former working cattle ranches that have been

FIGURE 3.8
Real estate signage south of Moab, Utah, displays unintended ironies. *Photograph by Robert Kuhlken.*

transformed into tourist facilities. These enterprises include Red Cliffs Lodge and Sorrel River Ranch, with its exclusive restaurant where reservations are required.

North of the river is the backcountry of Arches National Park, while south of the river encompasses a series of tributary canyons under BLM stewardship, including several with designated hiking trails as well as a technical rock-climbing site at Fisher Towers. These BLM lands merge into Forest Service holdings higher up, culminating in the volcanic La Sal Mountains. Thus, private lands are limited to properties along the river, and except for a few small housing subdivisions on hillsides across the road from the guest ranches, developers have not managed to carve up the area or eradicate its outstanding scenic resources. There have been a few close calls, however, including a recent dramatic incident that ended when a brand new adobe house was purposefully demolished by the latest landowner.

It was at Dewey Bridge, on lands lining both sides of the river, that Moab businessman John Ogden planned to build a residential and commercial development with ostentatious trappings, to be called "Rio Colorado at Dewey." Streets were laid out, paved, and curbed, accompanied by underground utilities and fire hydrants, while exotic tree plantings attempted a boulevard look. It all seemed so incongruous and out of place. At least that's what Jennifer Speers thought when she purchased the entire fledgling development. Figure 3.9 is a photo of the single house nearly 4,000 square feet in size and valued at $600,000 that had already been constructed in the residential tracts.

FIGURE 3.9
This new adobe structure was the only dwelling in the incipient development once known as Rio Colorado at Dewey, some fifteen miles upriver from Moab, Utah, before conservationist Jennifer Speers bought the entire subdivision and razed the house. *Photograph by Robert Kuhlken.*

Speers purchased the property with the full intent of putting a stop to the development, both actual and potential. She proceeded to salvage from the house anything of value and then pulled the gutted adobe dwelling to the ground. An avowed conservationist with the advantage of a family inheritance at her disposal, Speers simply did not think it was right that urban development should encroach upon a place so remote and serene. She has since applied for and received a zoning change from the Grand County Council that will limit any future development on the property, and was seeking a way to more permanently prevent such action by attaching a conservation easement (Church 2004).

Well to the south of Moab, former agricultural service centers Monticello and Blanding were once best known for the dryland peas grown on the surrounding plateau. Increased tourism to the lesser visited parks and monuments nearby has helped to push these two towns toward their new role as purveyor of travel amenities and recreational pursuits. Bed-and-breakfast facilities have sprouted in the fields where previously crops were harvested, while horseback riding rentals have replaced intransigent range riders doggedly herding cow and calf operations toward financial ruin. These days, everyone can play at being a cowboy in a heavily romanticized New West. Moreover, with their low cost of living, both Monticello and Blanding have the potential to attract residents looking to build retirement or vacation homes. Further south, in the San Juan River country, the tiny communities of Bluff and Mexican Hat are profiting from the popularity of rafting the river, along with the newer craze of cruising desolate slickrock country with off-road vehicles. With far fewer urban amenities, a dearth of water resources, and little suitable land to build upon, it is unlikely these communities will change all that much. That suited the late environmental writer Ellen Meloy just fine, who until her untimely death in 2004, lived in tranquil anonymity near Bluff. Her several books, which are a lasting testament to the carefully examined life among landscapes of a changing region, include *The Last Cheater's Waltz: Beauty and Violence in the Desert Southwest* (1999) and *The Anthropology of Turquoise: Meditations on Landscape, Art, and Spirit* (2002).

Toward the center of the state are several small villages that have recently been roused to the possibilities of New West economic undertakings. As Highway 24 slices across Wayne County, it links together a series of communities to the west of Capitol Reef National Park, from Loa to Grover, where irrigated hayfields and pastures tell of a settled agrarian landscape. Although Capitol Reef has been an established national park for some time, it has only recently achieved a level of popularity that would necessitate the construction of additional support infrastructure in adjacent towns. Thus, at the western gateway to the park lies Torrey, which has witnessed a wave of new commercial and residential development just over the past few years. Motels and tourist cabins have been built, along with combination gas station–convenience stores, gift shops, and surprisingly upscale restaurants and cafes, such as the Capitol Reef Inn and Cafe and the Cafe Diablo. Art galleries feature local weavers and painters along with more widely recognized work. A number of older houses along the highway continue to be remodeled and turned to commercial use, and there are still some shining examples of local vernacular architecture intact.

Beneath a grove of towering cottonwoods providing luxuriant shade, a visitor wishing to purchase a cappuccino or latte can cross the little wooden footbridge spanning the irrigation ditch and enter Robber's Roost Bookstore, where proprietress Michelle maintains an eclectic and astutely stocked reading larder along with well-oiled espresso machinery. Having moved here several years ago from the congested world of southern California, she gave up her job as a seasonal ranger in the nearby national parks to pursue this pioneering occupation of bookseller-barrista, so representative of life here on the rediscovered frontier of the New West. It is a noble endeavor, and we wish her well. This particular bookstore also serves as a cultural-ecological focal point, for it occupies the former residence of local writer and conservationist Ward Roylance, who passed away in 1993, the same year that he acted as cofounder of the Entrada Institute, which continues to function out of the building. This nonprofit organization, "dedicated to preserving the red rock country and its heritage through arts and education," sponsors programs throughout the year, and the institute remains "a gathering place for the local art community" (Leach 2000, 40). Beyond the boundaries of what might be construed as the linear central business district of Torrey, real estate signs advertise the offering of smaller and smaller parcels for sale. While the place in no sense faces the kinds of land use transformations that have overtaken Park City to the north, or Moab to the east, in terms of relative deviation from the traditional norm, Torrey's metamorphosis is still a big deal. In this tiny corner of Utah, where until just recently a magpie's call might have been the loudest intrusion on the overarching quiet, the welcome mat is out, and momentous changes are on the way.

Running south from Torrey, Highway 12 traverses the formidable heights of Dixie National Forest and descends to the colorful plateau tablelands at Boulder, where a new bed and breakfast with a tavern plays host to visitors who may take some time to tour the Anasazi State Park. Continuing south, the road skirts past the BLM recreation and picnic area at Calf Creek Falls, which has been prominently featured so many times in national magazines that the would-be visitor often requires placement on a ranger's waiting list to snare a coveted parking spot. From there the route veers west and into Escalante, once a somnolent Mormon farm and ranch community, now turned lively gateway town for the newly minted GSENM. These public recreation lands, encompassing most of the intricate canyon system of the Escalante River and its side tributaries extending north from the impounded Colorado River at Lake Powell, have always been here for the curious to seek out and ponder their mysteries. Indeed, when one of us (RK) was a graduate student taking geography courses from the other one (PLJ) at Oregon State University during the late 1970s, it was common for several of us who preferred the field over the classroom to take a quick road trip down this way for spring break. We would disappear down Harris Wash, or Scorpion Gulch, and reemerge days later from some different side canyon, having discovered for ourselves the intoxicating combination of outdoor adventure and wild seclusion. Back then, you had to already know how to get to these places, because big brown recreation roadsigns were nowhere to be seen, and printed guidebooks were unavailable, and we learned to stock up on last-minute necessities in northern Utah, for there were no supply depots hereabouts.

Well, that has surely changed, brought on by the new official designation for these lands, and Escalante now boasts several camping supply shops, along with cafes and restaurants complete with deck seating. At the lower end of town more changes are anticipated, for the village has just installed sidewalks and designer lamp posts, along a street edged with a series of newly planted shade trees on a drip irrigation system. This is certainly nothing to write home about elsewhere, but it is revolutionary here in Escalante, and some locals are not so sure they see the sense of it. One young person we spoke with recounted how her father, a long-time rancher, was dead set against the street trees in particular, because they wasted good irrigation water. But these are the changes that typify New West development even in the smallest of locales. At the edge of town are several art galleries, which were never here before, while the nearby desert hills provide a setting for Turn-About Ranch, advertised as a "proven, unique program for troubled, defiant teenagers on a self-destructive path." These adolescent dude ranches featuring tough love are more common than one might imagine, and it seems the more remote the location, the better. Finally, the shift in perception and appreciation of surrounding public lands, primarily used for grazing in the past, is reflected in the newly constructed Escalante Interagency Office Visitor & Recreation Information Center. The facility is open year-round and efficiently combines outreach efforts directed by officials of the Forest Service, the Park Service, and the Bureau of Land Management.

In a very interesting and most pertinent case study of change in the New West, a recent master's thesis by another Oregon State University graduate student examines the effect that creation of GSENM has had on local economy and culture and delves into the complex feelings of anger and frustration that have been aroused in residents of both Boulder and Escalante, who "felt purposefully left out of the democratic process that usually precedes national monument designation" (Leaver 2001, 4). After conducting ethnographic fieldwork in the two communities, Jennifer Leaver found that such anger may be recognized as "a reaction to the threat GSENM poses to local cultures by limiting (and, in some cases, prohibiting) traditional practices, increasing environmental regulations, and attracting outsiders, such as tourists and newcomers" (Leaver 2001, 7). Moreover, as one economy stands to be replaced by another, area residents are not so keen to participate in the transition:

> Similar to environmentalism, tourism is also viewed by many longtime Boulder and Escalante locals as a threat to their local culture. Tourism infringes on local territoriality, encourages the infiltration of outside ideas (via urban tourists and newcomers) and stimulates awareness of the area which can lead to increased in-migration (population growth) and local displacement. (Leaver 2001, 14)

Leaver (2001, 16) concludes her study by offering a number of recommendations for "ways in which residents can seek interactive and innovative community solutions as the Old West and the New West collide."

Utah's Dixie

St. George is the county seat of Washington County and de facto capital of the southwestern Utah district colloquially known as Dixie. Geographer Richard Jackson (1978, 334) related how early leaders of the Mormon Church "constantly encouraged the settlement of the regions south of the Wasatch Oasis" because they perceived these areas to have better agricultural potential due to warmer temperatures and a longer growing season. This region has also been thought of as a desirable place of final retirement or seasonal escape ever since Brigham Young himself established a winter residence there. But now they are coming in droves, and "few communities in the West are feeling the strain of accommodating new arrivals as profoundly as is St. George" (Starrs and Wright 1995, 431).

Surrounded by a palette of colorful mesa tops to the west and south, and adjacent to what has been until very recently the irrigated farmlands of the Virgin River Valley, the town itself is well-endowed with both scenic vistas and country charm, but it has been utterly unprepared for the development frenzy that has taken place over the past few years. Not that they can claim they didn't see it coming. What had been a sluggish agricultural service center of 4,000 souls began to feel sharp growth pangs after an upscale golf course was constructed during the 1960s, followed thereafter by a series of master planned communities that quickly extended the outer limits of the once compact urbanized area like the pulsating lobes of a voracious amoeba that suddenly feels the need to feed. As Raye Ringholz (1996, 25) relates:

> It wasn't long before Bloomington, a planned community catering to golfers and equestrians, greened the sandy wasteland with a private country club and complex of condominiums and homes. The population of St. George soared to about 7,000, with nearly 14,000 in all of Washington County. Once the attractions of the region became recognized, transformation into a resort environment came fast.

Growth since that initial spurt has only accelerated, with St. George expected to have 85,000 people by 2020, while Washington County's population is on track to double during the first two decades of the twenty-first century and should total more than 150,000 by then (Ringholz 1996, 28).

Much of the surge in Dixie's urbanization has derived from retirement, or even second home construction, but a good percentage also comes from younger migrants seeking employment opportunities in what is perceived as a healthier place to raise a family. Unfortunately, the physical parameters of the town could not contain the growth, and as a result landscapes have been rapidly modified on a large scale. The mesa slopes enveloping town have been carved up for residential subdivision, and the formerly productive valley agricultural lands are also being converted to residential use, with lot sizes ranging between one-quarter acres to five and ten acres. This will undoubtedly cause problems in irrigation water allocation and delivery, despite promises in the real estate advertising that water rights will be assigned to each lot. One cannot fail to notice the irony inherent in this kind of land conversion from large fields of fertile farmland to small individual fee simple properties, each holding an individual water right, occurring in an arid region where cooperative irrigation schemes initially enabled successful settlement.

Many of the newer subdivisions include large houses, some containing four or five thousand square feet, with corresponding four- or five-bay garages. Swimming pools and motorized toys are prevalent. Several developments are obviously equestrian oriented, with fenced pastures in addition to the non-xeriscaped lawns. Names for these subdivisions might reflect the physical terrain ("Crimson Cliffs Estates"), vanished societies ("Indian Knolls"), displaced wildlife, albeit exotic introductions ("Pheasant Meadows"), or, in a new twist, former land use ("The Fields"), this one advertising "agricultural serenity . . . landscape required . . . protective covenants . . . majestic views." Some of the old farms have adapted to the new reality, and offer horse boarding facilities. Yet agriculture has all but vanished, and wheeled sprinkler lines are probably seeing their final year of watering what will be a final crop of alfalfa in this valley. Beyond the immediate vicinity of town and the adjacent Virgin River Valley, numerous large new developments are taking place, in all directions, northeast toward Hurricane and Zion National Park, northwest toward Snow Canyon, and southwest toward Mesquite and Las Vegas.

But it is not only new residential subdivisions that are making their mark along the edges of St. George. When we visited in 2003, large industrial parks were being constructed in the valley bottom just southeast of town, and these are filling up with tenants as fast as the utilities and infrastructure can be installed. Geographers Paul Starrs and John Wright (1995, 432) noted nearly a decade ago that Washington County had experienced "a 180 percent increase in new employment between 1989 and 1994 . . . leading employers are the Wal-Mart regional distribution center, E.S.A.M. Electronics, Quality Park Products, and Pace America Motor Homes." Newer industrial enterprises taking advantage of the dedicated industrial park setting include Anderson Components, Deseret Laboratories, and a huge Blue Bunny ice cream plant.

Well beyond this residential and industrial mosaic, several development patterns and trends are transforming the outer peripheries of the St. George area. Southwest of town, in the flats just upstream from where the Virgin cuts its dramatic canyon into uplifted sediments, and even more so to the northwest, in the desirable Snow Canyon area, large-scale golf course subdivisions hold sway. Let us examine one of these master-planned projects in greater detail.

North of town, along Route 18, one of the most conspicuous displays of wealth occurs in the form of the master-planned golf community known as Entrada at Snow Canyon, shown here on the map in figure 3.12. This development contains a dozen or more separate pods, one of which, Kachina Springs, features artificially constructed stream channels as part of a pumped water system that also provides each backyard with its own private waterfall descending over a carved ledge of red-tinted concrete, illustrated in figure 3.11.

As it raced toward build-out, prices for bare lots in Kachina Springs ranged from $150,000 for a quarter-acre parcel, to $280,000 for a homesite just three-quarters of an acre in size. Typical dwellings being constructed reflect the popular trend of blending faux-adobe walls with stacked sandstone columns, set in a manicured landscape of half-grass, half-dryland garden.

The growth machine of greater St. George has deliberately targeted Californians seeking more affordable retirement options. Although normally assuming a more or less passive stance, the frantic pace of new construction has alarmed even local jurisdictions, and they are beginning to address the environmental effects of the ongoing urbanization. The dry canyons and rimlands surrounding St. George, for example, comprise crucial habitat not only for the threatened desert tortoise, but also for the Gila Monster, and in fact may represent the northernmost extent of that rare lizard's natural range. Research conducted by Central Washington University biology professor Daniel Beck indicates a critical loss of habitat that can be attributed to road pavement and exotic landscaping of residential parcels in the canyons north of St. George. Local officials have initiated measures at conserving the wildlife habitat that remains by setting aside scenic natural areas, such as Red Cliffs Desert Reserve, that will remain as undeveloped open space.

COLORADO

This beautiful state, situated astride the heart of the Rocky Mountains, perhaps best symbolizes the landscape changes taking place within the New West. In many ways, Colorado has always manifested the kind of growth patterns we are attempting to elucidate across the entire region. In that regard, this state might be

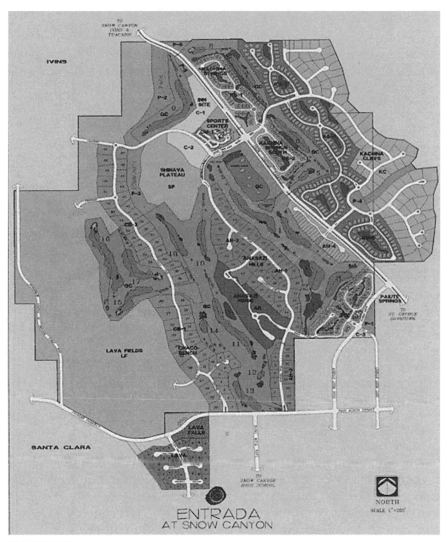

FIGURE 3.10
Master plan for Entrada at Snow Canyon, a massive phased development northwest of St. George, Utah. *Source: <www.entradarealty.com>.*

seen as both exemplar and harbinger of the trends and development pressures that much of the rest of the West is also beginning to experience. From the gold rush fever that seemingly overnight created sprawling urban scenes deep in the rugged interior, to the "instant city" of Denver that in similar fashion emerged as an important entrepot where the plains meet the mountains, population growth

FIGURE 3.11
Artificially constructed waterfalls and stream course in the back yards of residential
lots for sale at Kachina Springs, one phase of a massive development called Entrada
at Snow Canyon, northwest of St. George, Utah. *Photograph by Robert Kuhlken.*

and urban development in Colorado has been on a fast track from the very beginning (Barth 1988; Wyckoff 1999).

The interior of the state manifests complex and irregular geography. This part
of the Southern Rockies stretches across a fairly wide east-west extent, and there
are numerous named mountain ranges, isolated valleys, and broad high-elevation
intermontane basins known locally as "parks." Here are the celebrated mountain
peaks, the alpine lakes, the flower-filled high meadows that combine to create
some of the most desirable scenery in the West. Here too are the once dilapidated
mining towns that have gyrated into a more lucrative future as hip ski towns and
the ranching service centers suddenly turned upside down by new arrivals with
expensive new tastes. In examining the ever-increasing pace of land use conversion from agriculture or forestry to residential development in the Colorado
mountains, Theobald (2000) charted data across a spectrum of housing densities
and discovered that the exurban-scale category, defined as containing between six
and twenty-five dwelling units per square kilometer, was actually growing the
fastest. Outskirts of small communities that never needed zoning or any other
land use regulations have become overwhelmed almost overnight by massive new
developments of low-density starter castles. The place has likewise become an all-
seasons recreational mecca, and vacation homes are being constructed just as fast

as people can get a building permit. Consequently, as illustrated in figure 3.12, central Colorado contains several of the state's fastest growing counties.

We focus our attention, however, on those places to the east and to the west where urbanization and growth management has commandeered the agenda of many local governments: the Front Range on the east and several distinct regions in the western portions of the state.

The Front Range

The largest cities in Colorado are all located along the so-called Front Range, the eastern face of the Rocky Mountain escarpment. From the southern outskirts of industrial Pueblo to the northern edges of Fort Collins, home of Colorado State University, rapid urbanization continues apace. Denver has grown well beyond its earlier ring of suburbs, a situation epitomized by the site of the new regional airport out on the eastern plains far from the urban center. Outlying satellites and former stand-alone towns alike now find themselves within the orbit of one of the largest conurbations in the interior West. Many of these communities are faced

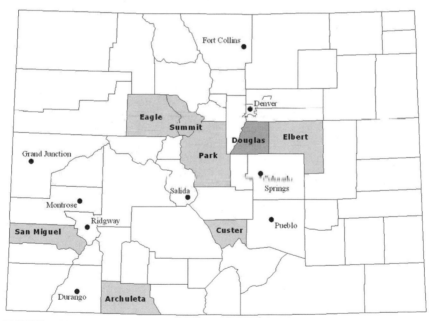

FIGURE 3.12
Colorado, showing the fastest growing county for the decade 1990–2000 in darkest shading, the next fastest growing counties in lighter shading, and selected towns and cities discussed in text. Data source: U.S. Census Bureau. *Map by Ian Gray, CWU graduate program in resource management.*

with the problem of trying to accommodate new growth while maintaining the quality of life that continues to attract new residents. A number of innovative projects have emerged from that attempt, many of them following the "new urbanist" prescription. At one town north of Denver, for example, a fairly high-density residential plan is richly endowed with open space: "In Prospect New Town, an 80-acre development located on the former site of a tree farm in Longmont, Colorado, nine pocket parks are all located within a two-minute walk of the neighborhood's 338 housing units" (Schmitz 2003, 59). A number of other projects within the metropolitan area have followed suit and understand the logic of high-density, mixed-use, transit-oriented development, especially in the context of urban infill situations. This includes the proposed reshaping of the Stapleton Airport site, which lends itself to the urban village concept because of its size (nearly 5,000 acres) and accessibility within the urban matrix; over the next fifteen years the project is slated to house 30,000 new residents in 12,000 dwelling units (Weber 2003). Urban redevelopment is one thing, yet the real challenge, as everywhere in the New West, will be how best to shape the settlement frontier, that elusive, ever-expanding edge of the built environment.

Situated between Denver and Colorado Springs, Douglas County has the dubious distinction of being the fastest growing county in the entire country. Massive new developments such as Highlands Ranch now sprawl across the rolling countryside at the foot of the mountains. Scharff (2003, 6) has depicted activity space here as emblematic of women's roles in a new social ecology that both emanates from and creates its own rapidly replicative setting:

At the end of the twentieth century and the beginning of the twenty-first, the hourly, daily, and weekly journeys of women, as much as anything else, delineate the postwestern landscapes of places like Highlands Ranch, Colorado, a burgeoning suburb in the fastest growing county in the United States. What had once been rolling prairie has become not simply a land of cul-de-sacs and For Sale signs but more, a metastasizing landscape of single-family dwellings, strip streetscapes, massive malls, and families inventing new forms of fissure and connection, stretched across the bounds of geography and genealogy.

South of here, just beyond the utterly suburbanized divide of Castle Rock and Black Forest, the city of Colorado Springs has grown dramatically from its earlier more tranquil existence, first as a health resort, then as a military-industrial outpost of the Cold War. This particular urban ink blot has now coated the landscape with California-style development in all directions. Further south still, steel mill town Pueblo hardly shares in the pace and scale of what is happening throughout the rest of the Front Range; its predominantly blue-collar and Hispanic minority population help compose a different scene altogether.

Southwest Colorado

This corner of the state contains some of the most rugged terrain in the lower forty-eight. Even John C. Frémont, popularly known as "The Pathfinder," lost his way here. A legion of miners pursuing silver and gold rapidly pushed the Utes out of the way and eventually started settlements, some of which linger to this day while others have deteriorated into dust. Former mining communities like Ouray are experiencing a new influx of people chasing dreams of living the small-town life deep in the mountains. These migrants are fixing up dilapidated Victorian-era housing stock on back streets and sometimes opening businesses on Main Street that cater to increasing numbers of tourists. Other towns, having sprouted from ranching and agricultural roots, are likewise seeing a boom in population, as more new arrivals view them as viable alternatives to the urban-suburban morass of the Front Range.

Durango, in the far southwest corner, is a delightful little village. At an elevation of 6,500 feet above sea level, its lively downtown sits at the bottom of a draw hemmed in on all sides by mountains. The settlement was founded in 1879 by the Rio Grande Railroad, which was able to extend its tracks here in 1881 for the purpose of extracting gold and silver ore from the mountains. The minerals have largely played out, and what the region now mines is spectacular scenery. This has resulted in several successful ventures for Durango. Fort Lewis College, billed as "Colorado's Campus in the Sky," occupies an elevated plateau directly above the central business district. One of the state's smaller four-year institutions of higher learning, Fort Lewis has the unfortunate reputation as a party school among the many out-of-state students who come here primarily seeking the pursuit of recreation rather than knowledge. But the school is also, remarkably, a place where Native American students are able to pursue a degree in a carefully cultivated atmosphere of tolerance and encouragement, with complete financial assistance, and as a result, Indians form fully one-fifth of the student body population.

In addition to the college, Durango has another rather unique asset, one that brings in tourists by the multiple carload: the Durango and Silverton Narrow Gauge Railroad, which uses authentic steam-powered locomotives to haul sightseers back and forth across the mountains to the little mining town of Silverton, forty-five miles away. In land use terms, this represents a significant permutation, and an alchemy that is being emulated elsewhere. This historic and ever so scenic railroad line that once hauled metallic ore has been resuscitated as a nationally known leisure escapade and now serves as a model for similar ventures across the West, including rail excursions and dinner trains in other remote places like Verde Canyon, Arizona; Lewistown, Montana; and Prineville, Oregon. The mountains of southwest Colorado, once so formidable and feared, now hold the capacity to delight and satisfy the romantic recreationist. With challenging ski slopes in the vicinity, more wilderness than a person can explore in a lifetime, and Mesa Verde

National Park just down the road, it is little surprise that sleepy Durango has become one of the New West's growth poles.

To the north of Silverton and Ouray, beyond the rugged mountainous terrain, tiny Ridgway has grown by leaps and bounds over the past decade or so. Adjacent to the older village grid, newly paved streets harbor an assortment of dwellings that manifest a startling variety in size and style. Population growth brings physical changes to former ranching service centers such as Ridgway, which are seeing for the first time unfamiliar infrastructural components like underground utilities, street lamps, sidewalks, and gang mailboxes. Some residences have put the shingle out to become bed-and-breakfast establishments, while several abandoned storefronts have been refurbished and are again open for business. On the outskirts of town, along the highway, commercial land use has taken some strange alternative paths, emerging in one case as a low-budget cowboy-kitsch tourist trap called Frontier Town. Of course the more standardized convenience store–gas stations continue to reproduce themselves here as well.

In the surrounding countryside there have been changes too, and this story has been told most eloquently by Peter Decker (1998) in his book *Old Fences, New Neighbors.* Decker, a one-time state bureaucrat and former university educator, was drawn to the area for its open space and ranching traditions. In 1974 he purchased a working cattle ranch just west of town and attempted to fit in with the locals. Of course, other newcomers seemed to be pursuing the same thing, with varying degrees of success. As a result, the local environment, culture, and political ecology began to shift dramatically. Decker has documented these transformations along with his own participation in the geographic drama of trying to set a course for a place in the midst of profound change. He concludes that the injection of outside capital into the region and the purchase of ranch properties by people who don't need to raise cattle for a living are actually what has saved the wide open spaces of Ouray County. Decker figures that having rich neighbors like Ralph Lauren just might be the only thing that prevents parcelization and subdivision of large holdings when long-time ranchers are ready to retire and get out of the business.

West Central Colorado

The west central part of the state, while never very far from mountainous terrain, offers something that is getting hard to find in Colorado: affordable residential lots, and plenty of level ground to site them on. One town, Gunnison, was an early entrepot for the entire western mining district. The other urban places in this region—Grand Junction, Montrose, and Delta—have their origins as market and service centers for large-scale irrigated agricultural district. As a consequence of that legacy, these days rural residential parcels, typically between five and twenty acres in size, come with the probability of a watered pasture for horses, which is a configuration in high demand in today's western housing market. Flying across the country on a clear day, looking down over the south-facing slopes of the Grand Mesa in the vicinity of Delta, one easily notices the large areas of land already subdivided and gridded with access roads. It will be up to local officials, and the constituency they represent, to decide if the process has gone on long enough or whether to keep the floodgates flung open for more of the same. Isolation and Native American resistance to settlement had retarded pioneer incursions into this area. These days, however, the so-called western slope basks in the benign glow of its mild winters that once stimulated a rapidly growing agricultural economy but has now engendered a new settlement frontier based on its recreation-oriented communities and lowland terrain.

Because of the difficulties in displacing the many bands of Ute Indians who continued to utilize their extensive territory, this region underwent pioneer Euro-American settlement comparatively late in the game. Following the 1880 Cession, what had been perceived as desolate and nearly worthless land became available for homesteading and potential agricultural transformation. This necessitated cooperative irrigation projects, large-scale transportation improvements, and an emerging urban support network, as explained by geographer William Wyckoff (1999, 226):

> The removal of the Utes allowed for legal settlement across western Colorado, and the building of railroad lines offered a spatial infrastructure to facilitate development. Yet it would remain the job of the farmer and the canal-builder to reshape lowland landscapes of the western slope in ways that endure to the present.

Indeed, the several towns that developed early on in this region are key centers of New West development today, and none represents more of a fulcrum for twenty-first-century landscape change than the oasis community of Grand Junction.

Grand Junction sits on the floor of the Colorado River Valley and enjoys the notable scenic and recreational amenity of Colorado National Monument on its doorstep. This is redrock cliff country, the first such geography encountered for people arriving from the east, which makes it that much more dramatic. High above the town to the east is the elevated forested plateau known as Grand Mesa, a vast public playground administered by the Forest Service. And for all practical purposes, Grand Junction can also be thought of as the eastern gateway community for the Utah national parks, with Arches, Canyonlands, and Capitol Reef each within easy reach of less than a day's drive. Add to that locational situation a relatively mild climate, fresh produce from the farms, and fruit from the numerous commercial orchards, and it is little wonder that Grand Junction has blossomed over the past few decades. The municipality has always been rather forward thinking and was one of the first communities in the country to widen downtown sidewalks and rearrange parking to create a pleasant pedestrian mall. As the county seat of Mesa County, the town serves as administrative and jurisdictional focal point for one of the largest counties in western Colorado. It also is pleased to play host to the campus of Mesa State College, a mainly four-year baccalaureate institution with increasing graduate degree offerings, which immediately places Grand Junction among the select few small towns in the West that can make such a claim.

The incomparable scenery of the surrounding cliffs and the high forested mesas to the east have caught the eye of those who continue to change these kinds of landscapes with typical New West development patterns. The promotional web site for a residential golf course subdivision on the outskirts of town proclaims a "dramatic blend of golf and nature" while highlighting some key points of what has become the obvious draw for new residents: "While dramatic scenery is a commodity in western Colorado, rarely will you find the sweeping 360-degree panoramic views that dominate the landscape at Redlands Mesa." Developers proudly refer to the 2001 rating of the Redlands Mesa links by *Golf Digest* as "the #1 best new affordable golf course in the nation." Affordability, of course, is only relative, and in this case might be more accurately gauged by the developer's offering of 6,000-square-foot luxury homes. Further reading reveals a refreshing albeit unintended honesty regarding their endeavor, for the website claims that when developers "initially stepped foot on this remarkable land they sensed their mission would be driven by the preservation of the high desert environment, while capitalizing on the beauty and mystery of the setting" (Redlands Mesa 2005). Here we witness the underlying leitmotif of much New West development: the paradox that scenery and spectacular views will be *capitalized upon,* all the while simultaneously *preserving the environment.* This happens to be a transparent and somewhat clumsily crafted mythology aimed at guilt-free consumerism. But it must work, after all, for the market is saturated with similar sentiment, and many a sales pitch now includes the emphatically asserted ideas of environmental preservation and a new kind of development proposal that not only blends in but actually harmonizes with the physical setting. The truth of the matter is a different story. Dramatic scenery *has* become a commodity, but once sold, thereafter becomes used, and somewhat tarnished in the process. Development radically alters the environment, not just in terms of lost vistas, but ecologically as well. You cannot inject irrigated fairways consisting of carefully groomed exotic grasses into a shrub-steppe ecosystem and say that you have blended golf with nature. Despite this all-too-typical rush to the frontier amid the environs of Grand Junction, it is a credit to local planning efforts that the town itself continues to be a delightful and charming community.

As historian Kathleen Underwood (1987, 23) has written, "Grand Junction would become the dominant town in an economic and political hierarchy on the western slope that emerged within a decade after its founding and which remains relatively intact to the present day." Although it was never a preordained "instant city" like Denver or San Francisco (Barth 1988), there was never any doubt that the chosen site, deemed so favorable for settlement by its founders, would develop into an urban center: "Between 1881, when Grand Junction was nothing but sagebrush and tumbleweeds, and 1900, when the town had elm-shaded streets, these settlers struggled to shape their community" (Underwood 1987, 7). Early pioneers were engaged in a deliberate effort to establish an important central place. In 1882, a year after deciding upon the town's location, they systematically laid out a hierarchy of streets and proceeded to "set aside a full block for city and county buildings—a bit premature as Grand Junction would not be named county seat for another year" (Underwood 1987, 12). But that same year, the Denver and Rio Grande Railway arrived, allowing shipment of agricultural products and facilitating import of needed supplies such as building materials. The railroad's decision to install maintenance shops and a locomotive roundhouse further boosted the town's importance, and "Grand Junction became the principal rail center between Pueblo, Colorado, and Salt Lake City, Utah" (Underwood 1987, 27). What ultimately set the town apart from other nascent settlements, and firmly established its preeminence in this semiarid region, was its investment in a water supply: "When residents voted in December 1894 to build and operate a municipally owned water system, they embarked on a third stage of political maturation that carried with it greater public control of the community and an unshakeable confidence in Grand Junction's future" (Underwood 1987, 53). The conservation of water resources continues to be a focal point for future development across most of the intermountain West, and perhaps nowhere is this more apparent than in our next two states of New Mexico and Arizona.

NEW MEXICO

This state represents the southeast quadrant of the New West. From the flat plains along its eastern edge, it's all downhill from here to Texas and the Gulf Coast margin. New Mexico is roughly bisected north to south by the Rio Grande, and most of its larger towns and cities are tied to that river. Because of lingering problems with poverty and economic development limitations, the state has not been able to participate in a transformation to the New West lifestyle in wholesale fashion. Yet there are legendary pockets that have long been considered desirable locations by the wealthy or elite segments of our society, and Santa Fe continues to function in that manner as the de facto capital of the New West. Meanwhile, Albuquerque and its perimeter environs have finally caught on to the idea of sprawl, and the growth once so sought after has now become disadvantageous yet only partially recognized as a force to be reckoned with. Elsewhere, retirement targets have started to emerge in the central and southern parts of the state, wherever mountainous terrain accords more moderate climatic conditions and the requisite recreational and scenic amenities. New Mexico's regional growth is illustrated in figure 3.13.

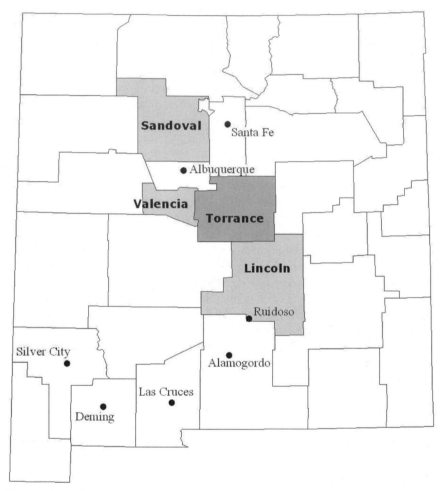

FIGURE 3.13

New Mexico, showing the fastest growing county for the decade 1990–2000 in darkest shading, the next fastest growing counties in lighter shading, and selected towns and cities discussed in text. Data source: U.S. Census Bureau. *Map by Ian Gray, CWU graduate program in resource management.*

Northern New Mexico was occupied by the Spanish long before settlers from the eastern United States tried to make it their home. Upon reaching this region from the colonial core territories of New Spain, those earlier pioneers displaced and/or enslaved the Pueblo peoples who had farmed this high-altitude, arid plateau for perhaps a millennium. Using a combination of agrarian skills adopted from the native population along with their own experience and knowledge, the new arrivals adhered to a cultural ecology based on strong religious faith, a complex system of land grants governing tenure, a livestock ranching system with roots on the Iberian peninsula, and rigidly enforced cooperative efforts to manage and control irrigation water necessary for growing crops. Today their descendants, known as Hispanos to distinguish from the more recent Hispanic immigrants to the United States, still inhabit these lands and endure the trials of sharing the region with Anglos who have come seeking a simpler life and with federal officials who are perceived to have confiscated long-standing rights of usage to the national forests. And, inextricably associated with productive use of the land are water rights, jealously guarded, fought over, and ultimately adjudicated by the state's legal system. This clash of culture and economy has been examined in picaresque, humorously ironic fashion in the literature of John Nichols, especially in a trilogy of novels that includes the highly acclaimed *Milagro Beanfield War* (1974). Other writers have taken a more tranquil view and have documented positive experiences of cultural cooperation and understanding, such as found in Stanley Crawford's *Mayordomo* (1988), which elucidates the social and time-consuming labor demands of making sure an irrigation ditch delivers the right amount of water on schedule.

Albuquerque

The largest city in New Mexico, Albuquerque has been perceived as stagnant or slow growing for so long that its current surge of expansion and far-reaching urban tentacles may come as a surprise to some. And not everyone has caught on to the consequences. As long-time scholar of the city V. B. Price (2003, 146) noted, "At the turn of the century, when many big cities in the West are realizing, belatedly and probably too late, they have to manage their growth, Albuquerque is racing as fast as it can to the developable edges of town, despite threats of severe water shortages." Disregarding a consolidated government policy calling for specific growth management strategies such as urban infill taking precedence over pushing beyond the city's outer perimeter, sprawling new development has begun to carpet the river valley to the north and across the foothills of the Sandia Mountains to the east. Out on West Mesa, well-publicized attempts to do things differently are nothing of the kind, and Price (2003, 153), again, has called into question the outcome of such projects:

> Mariposa development with its seven thousand proposed houses in an "environmentally sensitive planned community" on the outer limits of Rio Rancho near US

550, almost halfway to San Ysidro, touts itself as having learned the necessary lessons about smart growth and new urbanism. And perhaps it has. The only problem is that it amounts to the farthest vanguard of urban sprawl in the history of westside development. It's so far from other houses or any jobs that residents there could end up being stranded in their luxurious sensitivity during an oil crisis as severe as those of 1974 and 1979.

To the south, on the other hand, separate satellite communities like Los Lunas and Belen are now attempting to densify newer development patterns and retain something of their own identity through a more compact urban form. Such was not always the case, however, and abandoned plats with only the barest skeletons of bulldozed roads bladed across the desert (figure 3.14) mark the land and speak of failed schemes on a grand scale. Bounded on the north by Isleta Pueblo and its reservation, and on the south by the Sevilleta National Wildlife Refuge, the vast alluvial fan situated between the river and the Manzano Mountains is so utterly and insanely divided up and parceled out within its own grid of scraped access ways that the map has come to resemble a gigantic maze.

But this network of streets represents a phantasm that most likely will never serve a neighborhood, as a remarkable aerial photograph taken by Jim Wark of one piece of this collapsed venture shows clearly. The photo is published in an insightful new guidebook to the vocabulary of sprawl put together by noted urban scholar and Yale professor Dolores Hayden (2004), who uses this place in New Mexico as an example of an "alligator" or even a "blue-sky" development:

> Sprawl is fueled by developers' tendency to divide lots in many more subdivisions than they ever develop. But raw land can turn into an alligator, an investment producing negative cash flow. "Up to one's ears in alligators," a nineteenth-century phrase, conveys deep trouble. Blue-sky, a related slang term from the early 1900s, refers to extreme speculation. A blue-sky deal is so visionary there is nothing in it except "blue sky and hot air." (Hayden 2004, 18)

Santa Fe

Resting astride a modest but reliable tributary of the upper Rio Grande, at an elevation of nearly 7,000 feet above sea level, the leading exemplar of New West urbanism basks in the clear light and vibrant atmosphere of its natural setting and built environment. Self-consciously proclaiming itself "The City Different," stylish Santa Fe has long enjoyed preeminent status as the leading proponent for the uttermost fashionable genre de vie in the American West. The lavish attention to architectural design, regional cuisine, fine arts, and indigenous traditions permeates nearly all aspects of the city's culture. From its continued focus on a centuries-old civic plaza to the rigidly enforced design controls imposed on all new developments, Santa Fe has determined to maintain its special character.

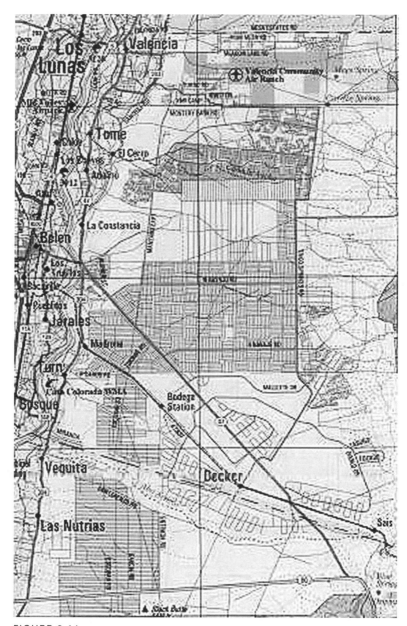

FIGURE 3.14

Extensive grid of platted roads are a ghostly reminder of failed subdivision schemes such as Rio Communities south of Albuquerque. *Source: De-Lorme's New Mexico Atlas and Gazetteer, 2000.*

The historical settlement was founded in 1610, making Santa Fe one of the oldest continuously occupied Euro-American towns in the country. When Spanish conquistadors ventured north from Mexico toward the headwaters of the Rio Grande, they did not discover an untouched wilderness ripe for the taking, however. Indeed, these fortune hunters under the command of Don Pedro de Peralta encountered a sedentary urban civilization of Pueblo dwellers who successfully adapted to a harsh environment through careful horticultural practices and water conservation measures. Except for a dozen or so years following the 1680 Pueblo Revolt, when Santa Fe was again Indian occupied, the town has been controlled and influenced by Spanish colonial traditions from its inception. Although access to rich bottomlands along the river actually stimulated an early form of sprawl, the very center of town at least was planned in accordance with the dictates outlined in the Law of the Indies, and still features a rectangular central plaza surrounded by civic buildings and dominated by the adjacent cathedral.

Local traders quickly established connections to the outside world, largely through the tenuous linkage of the Santa Fe Trail leading northeast to the Missouri River settlements of the Midwest. With the arrival of the telegraph in 1868 and the coming of the Atchison, Topeka, and the Santa Fe Railroad in 1880, both Santa Fe and New Mexico underwent an economic revolution, and this former Spanish territory eventually became part of the United States. With its adobe and old wood timber frame construction style for buildings, the vibrant colors applied to doors and window trim, and the exterior courtyards with their fountains and tranquil gardens, Santa Fe soon became an exotic attraction for the rest of the country. Beginning with the 1912 City Plan that was formulated with the influential Museum of New Mexico's assistance, the stringent codification of amalgamated design elements that had been borrowed from Pueblo and Spanish traditions fixed these local architectural standards for all new construction or remodels (Wilson 1997). These days, "Santa Fe style" has become an overused marketing ploy, lending a fabricated ambience to everything from tract housing to mass-produced interior design motifs (Mather and Woods 1986).

Land use patterns within the town itself have held on to a remarkably compact urban form until fairly recently. The core of the city remains vibrant and continues to function as it has for well over 400 years. Manifold uses compete for prime locations at the heart of the plaza, or in close proximity to it, including commercial, residential, both government and private office space, and public buildings such as libraries, art galleries, and museums, along with tourist facilities like the emblematic La Fonda Hotel. Over the past few decades, however, the standard commercial strip scene has emerged, not only along Cerrillos Road, which is the major highway coming into the city from the south, but also at various key intersections of other main roads.

Affordable housing has been one of Santa Fe's chief problems associated with this area's popularity and continued population growth. Several newer projects have attempted to both increase density and allow for a range of housing options to mesh in with their surroundings. Nava Adé is a residential community of 500 affordable homes that has been developed south of the central business district and is connected to the downtown by public transit. Within this community "the developers preserved the natural landscape and ensured that the project design was compatible with the character of local historic structures" (Schmitz 2003, 121). It is further protected by restrictive covenants, under the guidance of a homeowners association (Nava Adé Hoa 2004). Across town, Second Street Studios is a innovative project designed by Peter Calthorpe, featuring a number of "live-work" units for artists as an alternative start-up space to the city's more expensive and chic addresses such as Canyon Road. Claimed to be "among the first newly constructed live/work projects since the Great Depression," it contains seventy dwelling units within a five-acre site, and "caters to the needs of young artisans and business owners while following smart-growth principles" (Benfield, Terris, and Vorsanger 2001, 61).

While these two projects represent a laudable attempt to maintain and enhance the city's quality of life for a broad spectrum of the population, other housing and recreation options are decidedly limited to only those squarely in the upper-income brackets. To the north and northwest of the city, just beyond the new controversial bypass that facilitates access to this area (especially from the airport at Albuquerque), sprawls a constellation of exclusive housing tracts. Predominant among several higher end subdivisions occupying the northwest edge of Santa Fe, Las Campanas is a master-planned golf course development sprawling across some 4,700 acres of piñon-studded hills approximately ten miles from the center of town. This project was developed by the Lyle Anderson Corporation, which has also executed several golf course subdivisions in Scottsdale, Arizona. Las Campanas features two golf courses, clubhouse and spa, an equestrian center, and more than 1,700 platted residential parcels. During the spring of 2003, bare lots were starting at $375,000, while finished homes were being offered from $1.5 million and up. More than 1,000 lots have already been sold, and a majority of those have been built upon. As a very revealing added note, most dwellings in Las Campanas are second homes.

In what might be viewed as a logical extension of the city's own design code, stringent conditions, covenants, and restrictions (CC&Rs) within the development ensure that structures carefully maintain the neopueblo adobe facade that has become the hallmark of "Santa Fe style." All utilities are underground, and native vegetation cannot be altered. Arterial streets in Las Campanas are designed as parkways and intersect only as overpasses to avoid traffic lights. While main access routes remain open to public use, internal private security personnel diligently monitor visitors, as RK found out when he stopped along the road to take some photographs. The two golf courses have become a contentious issue with many Santa Fe residents, who have been asked repeatedly to conserve water as the population of the region expands. A string of legal challenges was resolved for the time being when developers reached a judicial settlement that guaranteed Las Campanas would receive six million gallons per week for golf course maintenance.

Potential Growth Areas

While it is probably correct to assume that the upper Rio Grande region has been absorbing a good portion of New Mexico's recent population growth, it may also come as a surprise to learn that the two fastest growing counties in the state are Torrance County and adjacent Lincoln County, located south of the Belen-Santa Fe corridor. Torrance County is situated across the Manzano Mountains southeast of Albuquerque and comprises a mixture of Hispano land grants, large ranches with overutilized rangelands, and piñon-juniper studded hillsides that more and more people are finding to be an attractive setting for the house they cannot afford to build over on the other side of the mountains. The high plains grazing grounds seem abandoned, bereft of cattle, and have a sere, burnt-out look, hardly supporting vegetation of any kind, let alone decent forage. Nevertheless, they are being subdivided into smaller parcels and offered for sale, sometimes as "equestrian homesites" or "ranchettes." Much of the area along Highway 41, between Willard, on through Estancia, and into Moriarty, has already been split piecemeal into small holdings and contains an assortment of what appear to be owner-built homes and trailers or other manufactured housing. Properties along here have a derelict appearance, a rundown dwelling with a piece of dusty "pasture"—some with a horse or a few goats, many more empty, where fences seem to do nothing so much as trap stray tumbleweeds. Everywhere there are for-sale signs, such as the one illustrated in figure 3.15, sometimes advertising affordable terms or expressing the lack of limitations on the type of dwelling allowed.

Lincoln County includes the pleasantly low-key county seat of Carrizozo, situated at the base of Sierra Blanca, at close to 12,000 feet above sea level the highest point in the Sacramento Mountains. Nearby is the unobtrusively latent New West lifestyle center of Ruidoso. Public lands recreation opportunities abound in a high enough elevation to make summer weather comfortable, and there are even some winter skiing facilities in the nearby mountains. This region holds appeal not only for the denizens of urban New Mexico, but also for many vacationing Texans, refugees from either El Paso and the cities further east or the barren high plains, who drive up here and seize upon these first real mountains with trees. Ruidoso has a burgeoning arts scene and is also known for its equestrian pursuits, with a racetrack and an official Museum of the Horse. Meanwhile, across the county line to the east, the town of Roswell has attempted to capitalize on homegrown legends of UFO sightings and supposed government cover-ups concerning a captured alien. Commercial sites there have resorted to thematically developing such left-field notions, with extraterrestrial museums and motif-styled restaurants and

FIGURE 3.15
Sign near Moriarty, New Mexico. *Photograph by Robert Kuhlken.*

lodgings. Lending its name to the air of mystery is nearby Bottomless Lakes State Park, while activities that derive from more authentic local culture may be pursued in the pair of off-road vehicle use areas set aside by the Bureau of Land Management. To the south of Carrizozo is Alamagordo, once a key support facility for the atomic weapons program, but now more peacefully regarded as the gateway community for the White Sands National Monument.

The lowland Rio Grande Valley in New Mexico is dominated by Las Cruces, home to New Mexico State University. Already larger than what might be considered an optimum size by those who seek the New West lifestyle, Las Cruces nonetheless could see population growth from retirees who find the cost of living in Arizona too dear. How the city will handle new growth remains to be seen: It can opt for letting developers stake their claims unimpeded by messy regulations or constraints of water scarcity, or it can take a more proactive stance, and creatively shape the future urban form of a true oasis. The goal is not to stop growth but to ensure that it occurs under the guidance of a well-designed plan, and within ecological limitations. For an example of how not to accommodate new growth, the carving up of desert floor into countless rectilinear survey lots is evident toward the west in nearby Deming, where a retirement and seasonal RV grid extends for miles.

But of all the smaller out-of-the-way places in the state that might one day see a spurt of new growth, Silver City must be ranked at the top of the roster. This remote mountain town is in the midst of a profound transformation, from a dirty and disheveled mining hovel to a New West enclave for amenity-driven migrants seeking sunshine, clean air, and a milder climate moderated by relatively high elevation, set amidst abundant public lands offering unlimited recreational pursuits. Historic downtown architecture that has somehow endured decay from age and the ongoing threat of demolition, along with a four-year university and an emerging arts scene, now provide the foundation for a newer community to flourish, one no longer tied to extractive industry, one that is less rural and aligned more closely with urban sensibilities. Paradoxically this has stimulated land development in the surrounding countryside, where some of the first of what will surely prove to be numerous new subdivisions have recently been platted, including the long, slithering perpendicular cul-de-sac design of Apache Mound (figure 3.16).

As the New West makes inroads here, conservation measures addressing scenic and ecological resources are beginning to replace environmental impact statements associated with logging or mining. A symbolic harbinger of things to come can be seen in the Nature Conservancy's Bear Mountain Lodge, an "exquisitely restored 1920s hacienda" where visitors are lured by the promise of exploring the

FIGURE 3.16
The perpendicular cul-de-sac development Apache Mound is a harbinger of things to come around Silver City, New Mexico. *Photograph by Robert Kuhlken.*

Conservancy's nearby preserves, spotting upward of 300 species of birds, and the opportunity to "immerse yourself in one of the Last Great Places on Earth" (Bear Mountain Lodge 2004). Playing the trump card of historical wilderness protection, the lodge's advertising also notes that "America's First Wilderness is outside our back door." This claim refers, of course, to the Gila Wilderness, officially established in 1924 at the insistent urging of Aldo Leopold, patron saint not only of designated wilderness but of scientific wildlife management in this country.

ARIZONA

As a leading target for Sunbelt-bound migration, Arizona has witnessed phenomenal population growth. During the last half of the twentieth century, the majority of these new arrivals clustered in and around the state's two largest urban areas of Phoenix and Tucson. In many ways, the economy of these cities was built upon the business of catering to health and leisure seekers. Tucson was well known for its collection of health spas and guest ranches, where tourists could stay for awhile and sample western living. Many visitors, it turned out, would decide to move back on a permanent basis, perhaps persuaded by wage opportunities associated with the university or the Air Force base. Industrial development in both Phoenix and Tucson meant even more jobs, which required housing for an influx of workers, and so the sprawling residential and commercial matrix spread outward from the downtown areas. Meanwhile, retirement suburbs such as Sun City, northwest of Phoenix, lured an age group that had no need for employment and so became substantial communities almost instantaneously. These two metropolitan regions continue to attract new residents, especially to the more recently formed outermost ring of edge settlements. But there are new-growth regions within Arizona, and several locations that can be identified with New West development patterns (Fig. 3.17).

One area that is experiencing very rapid land use change is the west-central part of the state, from Prescott northeast across the Verde River Valley to Sedona. Here, commercial retail space is quickly swelling, while highways are widened and hundreds of houses are being built simultaneously. In several locales a number of old mining towns have refused to shrivel up and blow away, and contemporary residents instead breathe new life into what was once the old frontier of settlement.

Along the banks of the Colorado River, from Bullhead City downstream to Yuma, a whole series of lower elevation, leisure-oriented settlements have realized a quickening of new development, not only in terms of residential land use but also for industrial parks, warehousing facilities, and commercial establishments. In certain locations, tens of thousands of snowbirds flock together in their RVs avoiding the cold, thereby seasonally changing a relatively sparsely populated summer scene into a de facto urban place during the winter months. This is perhaps most apparent at Quartzsite, where each season up to a million and a half

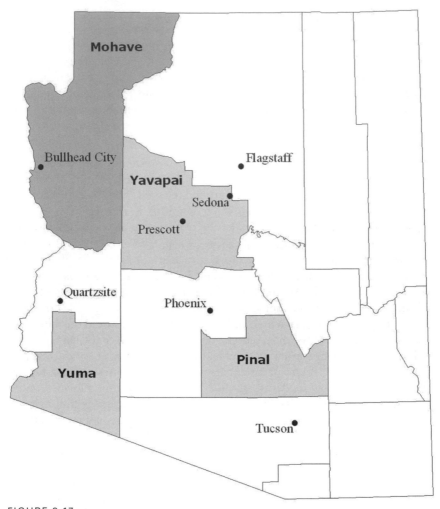

FIGURE 3.17
Arizona, showing the fastest growing county for the decade 1990–2000 in darkest shading, the next fastest growing counties in lighter shading, and selected towns and cities discussed in text. Data source: U.S. Census Bureau. *Map by Ian Gray, CWU graduate program in resource management.*

visitors arrive, a good many of them staying for awhile in their parked campers. From its origins as a modest gem and rockhound show, the winter gathering at Quartzsite has escalated each year, and a carnival atmosphere now prevails during what has become a series of extremely large swap meets where virtually anything might be set out on the tables. One eminent cultural geographer, the late James Parsons (1992, 3), wrote that this place is a "Woodstock for RV'ers . . . who seem convinced that in the winter, when the wagons are circled, this friendly desert encampment is the closest thing there is to Nirvana." In the northern part of the state, recreation destinations including the Grand Canyon and Lake Powell have turned Flagstaff into something of a gateway community, although with a four-year university and expansive public land playgrounds all around, this medium-sized town at a relatively high elevation was already well on its way to becoming a growth magnet for those whose lifestyle rejected the larger cities in the lower desert. We now consider recent developments surrounding those large cities and then take heed of Arizona's newest growth poles.

Phoenix and Tucson

Phoenix rose from the ashes of the Hohokam civilization's irrigated oasis along the Salt River and grew from its new life as a nineteenth-century farming center to become the massive, sprawling city that is now the vivaciously marketed sparkling centerpiece of the so-called Valley of the Sun. With a fierce summer climate offset by the mild winters that many new migrants come in search of, the region has a growth forecast that shows no sign of slowing down. More than three million people now live in the metropolitan region, which encompasses Phoenix and its many satellites, including upscale Scottsdale, tony university town Tempe, and expansive and far-reaching Mesa. Across this desert plain the basic rectilinear grid of neighborhood streets extends outward in all directions with major arterial roads at every mile, intersecting each other at right angles, on and on, mile after mile. Newer subdivisions sport the gated entrance look made popular in southern California, but these amount to nothing special and still contain the same series of limited design tract houses our culture has grown so accustomed to. Unlike Tucson, which now mandates xeriscaping, yards here are planted to heat-tolerant species of grass that often must be flood irrigated, and the transpiration from all that turf leads to a reversal of the newcomer's expectations of dry air that makes high temperatures tolerable. Commercial retail space struggles to keep up with the pace of residential development and ends up occupying just one standard-looking strip mall after another, each vying for the preferred location at arterial intersections. Few outcrops of higher terrain interrupt the flat valley floor, and these are snapped up by the higher end housing schemes, or have been enveloped within yet one more master-planned golf resort. There have been suggestions to do things differently, to fashion designs for new suburban development that would conform more closely to the environmental limitations of local landscape and terrain, but these have not had much of an overall effect (Steiner, McSherry, Brennan, Soden, Yarchin, Green, McCarthy, Spellman, Jennings, and Barr 1999; Gober 2003). The scattered rocky knolls that somehow made it into the realm of public parks and open space are even today contested ground, as evinced by the controversy over urbanization encroaching upon Camelback Mountain (Protas 2003).

Tucson, over the horizon to the southeast, possesses an overall different geographic situation, at a slightly higher elevation than Phoenix and snuggled up against more prominent mountains. And though it shows greater promise as an urban form that may yet learn to live in an arid setting, the development occurring in formerly rural areas that surround the city continue to exhibit pronounced patterns of the same old tired "unsustainable" sprawl. Here, one well might ask if it is so unsustainable, why then does it keep happening? This question becomes even more of a conundrum given the history of local resistance to growth (Logan 1995). For the most part, downtown Tucson is a walkable place, not nearly as automobile dependent as its larger cousin. Commercial space is relatively compact, and there are residential neighborhoods that have remained attractive alternatives to the suburbs. But water supply has been a chronic problem, and concerns over dwindling groundwater sources for Tucson's municipal needs in part led to the construction of the Central Arizona Project's monumental canal from Lake Havasu on the Colorado River across 336 miles of desert to the city. Home to the University of Arizona ("the Wildcats"), Tucson is also known for its aerospace industries and is poised to take on further high-tech industrial possibilities. But even here, in an environment where a densely developed and compact urban oasis ought to be considered the most successful cultural adaptation, the appeal of living in the country persists. With so many people pursuing such a lifestyle, the overwhelming reality of this large-scale urban transformation quickly brings home the message that rural living is but a fleeting dream.

Wildcat developments are not named after the nearby university mascot but for the rapid and stealthy manner in which they appear. Many of these subdivisions are simply rectilinear survey lines quickly drawn on paper, with little or no infrastructural provisions or intended improvements. Some of them may never have applied for a legitimate land division in the first place, let alone ever filed a plat. They represent a sort of fly-by-night style of land hustle that has somehow managed to persist in the furnace of the Sonoran Desert. These wildcat subdivisions are particularly troublesome in the areas of Pima County to the west of Tucson, across the Avra Valley, and in neighboring Pinal County, northwest toward Casa Grande.

They may look nicer, but in terms of their cumulative effects, life is usually no better in the more upscale, deliberately planned developments, all designed according to code. Driveways lead from triple-car garages to lanes and courts within countless subdivisions, which bleed out to a handful of secondary roads that cannot handle the load, creating traffic congestion not just at the morning and evening rush hours but typically all day. At night, those stars in the night sky that people wanted to gaze upon by moving outside of town have been dimmed by accumulated light pollution shining from all the street lamps, illuminated parking lots, and household security fixtures. The sense of community that people crave is nowhere to be found. Shopping is accomplished on the drive home from work, at one of the larger strip malls with its franchised grocery store, or at one of the big box discount stores relatively nearby, though never within walking distance. The chance for neighborly discourse comes by paying a price—either joining as exclusive a country club as you think you can afford, or by staying active in the local homeowners association, whose main reason for being is to enforce the various CC&Rs that keep the development looking so tidy and so nice.

One area where this kind of urban edge development has literally changed things overnight is Oro Valley, some thirty miles north of Tucson. There, at the base of a dramatic eastern backdrop formed by the Santa Catalina Mountains, a multitude of planned subdivisions extend outward from the intersection of Tangerine Road and Highway 77. In an apparent fit of conscience that must have precipitated such a feeble attempt to gravitate toward new urbanist tendencies, a "town center" has already been laid out, and when we visited during the spring of

FIGURE 3.18
Newly constructed street intersection, complete with xeriscaping and sidewalk sculptures, in what is intended to be Oro Valley Town Center, north of Tucson, Arizona. *Photograph by Robert Kuhlken.*

2003, there was an incipient strip mall with only one shop open for business: a national chain drugstore, its identifiable logo and template architecture intact but with its signage adaptively colored turquoise. Behind this building was a ghostly covenant of things to come. Attractive brick-paved sidewalks converge on a street crossing, complete with wheelchair-accessible curb cuts and a set of life-size sculptures celebrating small town community life (figure 3.18).

Stop signs and crosswalk designations await the roving ambler. Park benches beckon to absent passersby. The details of pedestrian life are already in place but there is nobody around. These neourban streets go nowhere and serve no purpose. The single establishment open for business is already oriented to the highway, and as the remainder of the commercial site invariably develops, this lost intersection, so thoughtfully installed beforehand, is destined to become paradoxically but a quaint afterthought hiding behind the storefront facades.

For this entire area is already emphatically automobile oriented, and the way things are going, no amount of densifying will deny that trend. Thousands of dwellings have already been approved within several dozen new developments. While each housing scheme on its own might "make code" in terms of its internal specifications, the overarching reality of all this expansion in disconnected residential land use adds up to the exact same kind of low-density, sprawling suburbia that almost everyone professes they wish to avoid. In terms of appearance, these subdivisions are designed to win the favor of new residents looking to achieve the southwestern image, often termed "pueblo style," or even, with a shameless deference to the paragon, "Santa Fe style." Houses are constructed according to four or five standardized blueprints, and in one particular development, each bearing a conjured-up name based on native plants that, it is hoped, will catch the potential homebuyer's fancy: the "Agave," or the "Mesquite." Most of the separate developments are supplied with one of the requisite infrastructural amenities that win approval but that remain simply cosmetic and largely useless: sidewalks that nobody will ever walk on. Business signs out along Tangerine Road reveal the kinds of things people here spend money on: "Buhrke's Pet Resort" and "Paradise Kennels."

We end our survey of the growth patterns associated with Phoenix and Tucson by briefly examining the circumstances surrounding one of the largest housing developments ever contemplated in Arizona, or anywhere in the West for that matter. It is intended to take up a large swath of desert land in Pinal County, situated between the state's two large metropolitan areas. Osa Ranch is the name of this proposed development that entails subdividing some 22,000 acres into smaller parcels to accommodate 67,000 dwelling units, which would ultimately make it the eighth largest city in the state. This is the brainchild of one George Johnson, an unscrupulous speculator who has racked up an impressive resume of punitive fines and environmental violations from state and federal resource management agencies over actions taken at several other projects he has been associated with in central Arizona (Nelson 2004). Here at La Osa, wildlife officials are worried about the impact on a herd of desert bighorn sheep who depend on native range of the adjacent Ironwood Forest National Monument. The military has expressed concerns that the massive new housing complex could threaten the continuation of helicopter training exercises in the nearby rugged terrain that for the pilots simulates nothing so much as a Middle East war zone. And of course as of yet there is no realistic assessment of how a development this big might impact the region's volatile water resources. But Johnson has gone ahead with his plans anyway, despite never obtaining the necessary county approvals on a zone change request, and has proceeded to blade roads and grade land, removing fragile vegetation in the process and possibly destroying several archaeological sites (McKinnon and Pitzl 2004). It remains to be seen if this so-called La Osa Master Planned Community will ever come to pass.

Flagstaff and the Mogollon Rim

Flagstaff at first glance might seem an ideal candidate for New West transformation, poised to be overwhelmed by hordes of new residents. After all, it has a well-respected four-year university, comfortable summer temperatures moderated by its elevation, and loads of public recreation lands in all directions, including Grand Canyon National Park. It is, indeed, a growing city of about 40,000 sitting pleasantly in the pines at the base of an isolated chain of conic volcanoes considered sacred to the Navajo. But Flagstaff, at over 7,000 feet above sea level, has the misfortune of being situated at slightly too high of an elevation, which creates downright frigid weather during the winter months. And most people moving to Arizona are not interested in embracing the kinds of winter conditions they are hell-bent on leaving behind.

There's just something bleak about the town, a perception not exactly helped by the winds whipping off the Coconino Plateau, or the lonely sound of freight cars noisily being shunted in the stillness of the night. Other than serving as major gateway to the Grand Canyon, Flagstaff has not been able to fully capitalize on tourism, and except for a slight increase in its hardy devotees, will not likely witness a substantial surge of new population growth. As for the Grand Canyon, there are basically two ways to reach the all-too-popular South Rim: first by going north then west, which is the more scenic route, past Sunset Crater, taking a left at Cameron with its truly lovely and architecturally significant trading post, past the Little Colorado overlook, and slipping sideways into the park; or, heading west on either Interstate 40 or Highway 180, then turning north on Route 64, where just before the park boundary "the expectant traveler must pass through Tusayan, a minor blip on the path through the natural landscape . . . a brief settlement that includes a memorabilia shop, a gas station, a landing site for tour helicopters, a McDonald's, and the IMAX Theatre" (Zonn 1990, 1). Tusayan now includes a more upscale motel and restaurant complex along with residential homesites ready and available for owner-built dwellings. But this high-plateau territory on the edge of the "big ditch" has a long way to go before it can gain admission to the New West. South of Flagstaff, the potential for rapid population growth increases dramatically. We now examine typical development patterns taking place in one of the more rapidly changing areas anywhere in the West.

Prescott and Vicinity

Lastly for Arizona, we turn our attention to the most aggressively urbanizing area in the state, Yavapai County, and its identifiably New West communities ranging from Prescott in the south to Sedona in the north. This region presents an attractive environment, especially for those who find Flagstaff too cold and the Sonoran desert locales too hot. From where the northern plateau breaks out into colorful sandstone buttes around Sedona, south across the lush riparian ribbon of the Verde River, up into the rugged mountains where the reinvigorated mining town of Jerome perches like some happy canary that made it out of the shaft, and down again across the treeless grasslands of Prescott Valley and into the granite knobs and lake country around Prescott, represents a richly varied and highly scenic transect of all that amenity-driven migrants find most appealing. Let us begin in the south, with the old territorial capital of Prescott, and proceed to document the current conformation of land use northward to Sedona.

Prescott is perhaps the most livable community in the entire state. It is virtually surrounded by ravishing countryside affording a myriad of recreational opportunities on public land. There is an alternative-minded four-year institute of higher education—Prescott College—that emphasizes outdoor learning and environmental awareness in the curriculum. History is authentic rather than fantasized here, and the town boasts more than 500 properties listed on the National Register. Prescott's pioneer heritage is also reflected in its urban form, the core of which constitutes a classic Courthouse Square, such as found throughout the South and especially in small town Texas. Vibrant businesses line the sides of the four streets facing the courthouse and framing the square, as they have ever since the establishment of the town during the 1860s, when "Whiskey Row" took up an entire block with side-by-side watering holes. These days, a remnant of that particular block hangs on, together with cafes and restaurants joined by the traditional lawyers offices and now art galleries, but, as illustrated in figure 3.19, along these four streets may be found even more of an indication that the town has entered the New West: upscale promotional sales offices for massive new master-planned real estate developments, including Whispering Canyon and Talking Rock Ranch.

Whispering Canyon, as proclaimed on the sales brochure, is being marketed as "Prescott's premiere *(sic)* custom homesite community" and consists of some 900

FIGURE 3.19
Real estate sales offices for competing higher end master-planned developments are prominently situated along the Courthouse Square of Prescott, Arizona. *Photograph by Robert Kuhlken.*

"extraordinary" acres with a planned build-out of 400 single-family dwellings. According to its promotional website, the development "is located just north of Prescott's Historic Downtown District in the beautiful Williamson Valley, which allows you to benefit from the non-city location yet retain all the amenities and prestige of Prescott" (Whispering Canyon 2003). The advertisement emphasizes the natural surroundings of the site as well: "beautifully rugged terrain with numerous rock outcroppings and arroyos—forested with juniper and pinion pine." While it is claimed that more than 40% of the subdivision will "remain dedicated to open space," its overall design resembles conventional tract housing developments. Indeed, the sales information stresses the "pod and cluster" configuration and states that "most homesites are situated on paved cul-de-sac streets to limit traffic and provide greater privacy."

Talking Rock Ranch is even larger, at 3,600 acres, and features a golf course as its centerpiece amenity. Additional facilities include swimming, tennis, a "fitness barn," and a clubhouse, basically making Talking Rock Ranch a very large country club. Hundreds of parcels have been platted, ranging in size from one-half to one-and-one-half acres. Yet there are literally dozens of similar developments in the Prescott vicinity, many of them with private golf courses. This has resulted in a substantial area of land being split up into thousands of newly created lots. While community water and sewer systems are available to some of these subdivisions, many parcels must rely on individual wells and septic tanks. Golf course irrigation alone ought to be a matter of some concern. These are just a few of the examples of the way that Prescott is growing and changing fast. But that momentum has been building for a decade or more, and by at least that long ago one reporter claimed that the area had become contested terrain: "The town of Prescott has metamorphosed into a tranquil valley where California equity barons battle long-time landowners for available space" (Folkart 1994). The scramble for developable land has now encompassed not only the immediate vicinity of Prescott itself but also much of the surrounding area.

Up until recently, the separate municipality of Prescott Valley had been but a sleepy outlier of its larger neighboring jurisdiction. But this place is fully intent on mushrooming, and is currently in the midst of a wholesale makeover. During the decade 1990–2000, the town more than doubled its population, from fewer than 10,000 to more than 20,000. Punching all the right buttons that will attract residents, the local Chamber of Commerce has pushed for new development based on becoming a bedroom community for the cities to the south: "Prescott Valley's proximity to the larger population center of the Greater Phoenix area allows for an easy commute yet allows for the natural relaxation and opportunities for recreation and safe living that today's family craves. . . . Prescott Valley residents cherish their rural lifestyle and scenic vistas" (Prescott Valley Chamber of Commerce 2003, 36). The town has officially embarked on an aggressive approval policy for proposed residential developments. Dozens of named subdivisions have already recorded plats that indicate at least 13,000 dwelling units will soon be added within the community's corporate boundary. This should easily again more than double Prescott Valley's current population of 26,000.

The scale and pace of development is staggering and rivals anything we have seen across the eleven western states. Examples of these developments, whose locations are illustrated in figure 3.20, include Stoneridge, with 3,043 dwelling units on 1,880 acres; Granville, with 3,400 dwelling units planned for 1,243 acres; Viewpoint, with 2,600 dwelling units on 640 acres; and the somewhat less dense Pronghorn Ranch, with 1,440 dwelling units planned for its own adjacent rectangular square mile.

In a scene characteristic of all this instant urbanization, Pronghorn Ranch (figure 3.21) was in the midst of frantically carving out its street pattern and putting up houses when we paid a visit in the spring of 2003. This subdivision's new community center, at the end of a curving boulevard, welcomes prospective home-

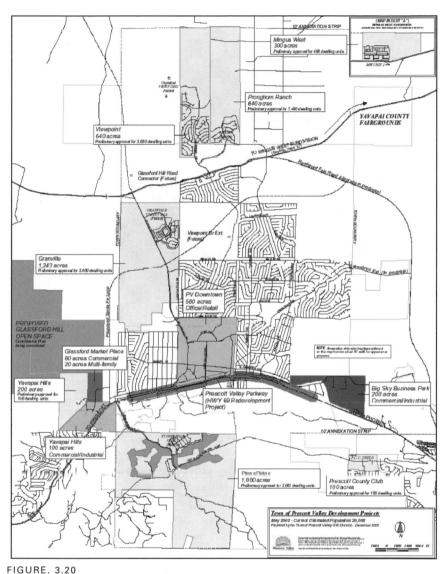

FIGURE. 3.20
Locations of approved subdivisions in Prescott Valley, Arizona.
Source: Town of Prescott Valley web site, "Residential Developments in Prescott Valley": < www.pvaz.net/Services/maps/downloads/ProjectDevelopmentMap.pdf>.

FIGURE 3.21
Statues of pronghorns greet visitors to the sales office of the 640-acre Pronghorn
Ranch subdivision in Prescott Valley, Arizona. *Photograph by Robert Kuhlken.*

buyers with a set of sculptures that ironically serves to commemorate the animal
whose habitat was effectively destroyed and replaced by its namesake human settlement.

But all is not sprawl across this entire valley, for at the center of things, quite
literally, there is a remarkable experiment in progress. The Prescott Valley Town
Center is a 580-acre mixed-use development project designed by renowned new
urbanist proponent Peter Calthorpe. When completed, it will feature five different
use areas: residential units, civic buildings, medical offices, business and technology suites, and a retail-entertainment complex. At the heart of Town Center is a
pedestrian-oriented Main Street with several large structures that will accommodate retail shops on the ground floor and dwelling units on the second floor. Will
such attention to a human-scaled small-town setting make any real difference in
a place that has obviously gone predominantly the other direction? It should be
interesting to see how the Prescott Valley Town Center actually functions as it matures and takes on its assumed role as focal point and central business district for
one of the fastest growing towns in a state that has itself come so utterly to depend
upon the automobile.

To the north, the dispersed settlement pattern of Chino Valley represents a more affordable alternative to Prescott's airs of exclusivity. Housing occurs with less density here, and there is a feeling of elbow room that residents apparently seek to reinforce, primarily through the use of yard fencing and guard dogs. Unlike Prescott, which enjoys topographic diversity and natural arboreal vegetation, in Chino Valley the terrain is for the most part level or consists of gently sloping alluvial fans, and there are few trees beyond the exotic planted Siberian elms and tamarisk. Yet subdivision after subdivision continues to both fill in and push out from the perimeter of the currently built-up area. Houses are generally small, hence the affordability, and there are very few amenities. Streets are often not even accepted by the city or the county as dedicated rights-of-way. In some places, elemental infrastructure such as storm drainage not only appears wholly inadequate, but approximates a "natural disaster" waiting to happen, as depicted in figure 3.22, which shows a new home adjacent to a large arroyo.

Outlying areas surrounding Chino Valley are now attempting to emulate the ranchette model of New West development, but the overall effect is less than promising. Take, for example, the subdivision designated "Haystack Ranches," to the east of the main populated area. The sales advertisement for this particular development has a few photographs that only serve to accentuate the desolate and featureless terrain, along with a diagram of the plat map, indicating seventeen parcels ranging in size from thirty-six to fifty-two acres. The text reads: "Discover

FIGURE 3.22
Model home situated precariously close to an arroyo in Quail Ridge subdivision, Chino Valley, Arizona, where these culverts beneath the street may not be adequate to convey stormflow coming off Sullivan Buttes. *Photograph by Robert Kuhlken.*

this breathtaking ranch property where the deer and antelope roam under peaceful cloud-scaped vistas" (Dusman and Dusman 2003), once again paying homage to displaced ungulates. In a minimalist attempt at restrictive covenants, the particulars declare that "site built homes only" are to be allowed. As an incentive to lure speculative investment seekers, the list also specifies that each parcel may be split, with an overall eight-acre minimum lot size. One of the photographs depicts the entrance monument somewhat artlessly constructed from landscaping cinderblocks and tubular steel panels painted white, the gravel access road, some barbed wire fencing running off to a vanishing point across a forlorn and ever so flat landscape, all set against a distant background of bleak and barren hills. It is little surprise that at the time of our visit, only one complete parcel and one-half of another had been sold.

Just across the brooding hulk of Mingus Mountain to the east, the former copper mining town of Jerome perches on its lofty roost and welcomes the newcomers who have revitalized the little community and saved it from the fate of so many other busted and abandoned mining towns across the region. It has earned a permanent place in the mythology of the New West, for it is the subject of a poignant song written by none other than the late Kate Wolf:

> Drinking early morning coffee, talking with good friends,
> And walking the streets of rough-cut stone,
> She was once a miner's city, now the ghost of a dying town
> But there's a fire burning bright in old Jerome.
> Some have come for fortune, some have come for love,
> Some have come for the things they cannot see.
> Now the grass is green and growing
> Where the gardens once had died,
> And the birds sing in the young ailanthus trees. (Wolf 1983)

To negotiate the hairpin curves of "old Jerome" and gaze at the view from its guardrailed sidewalks overlooking the upper Verde Valley far below is to partake in one of the more sublime prospects around these parts. Despite the legacy of mining that still stains the land, this area has a wealth of recreational and tourism assets, ranging from the prehistoric Indian urban center now protected and managed as Tuzigoot National Monument to the fishing and boating opportunities at nearby Pecks Lake, to the expansive camping and picnicking grounds of Dead Horse Ranch State Park, with its diverse riparian habitats where birdwatching is guaranteed to please. An additional attraction for tourists is the excursion train ride through the Verde Canyon departing from Clarkdale. With land prices currently at a reasonable level, we sense that the Verde River Valley, particularly the centrally positioned town of Cottonwood, will become the next "undiscovered" place to join the ranks of rapidly growing communities across the West.

Further north, Sedona is located some thirty miles south of Flagstaff and is situated at the mouth of scenic Oak Creek Canyon at an elevation of 4,300 feet above sea level. Its latest population count is only twelve thousand, but the town is presently experiencing growing pains (Ringholz 1992). Self-styled capital of the New Age movement, Sedona has become the darling of the well-heeled seeker. Hollywood celebrities such as Shirley Maclaine have helped to foster greater awareness of what is merely an amorphous bundle of borrowed beliefs. Among its garbled attempts at conjuring a mystical response to the postmodern world, this loosely configured quasi-religious philosophy has latched on to certain "power centers" where earth's vortex points are supposed to impart strength and wisdom for those pilgrims expressing the proper reverence. As it turns out, Sedona has been pinpointed by those who know about such things for its potent assemblage of these vortices, which are characteristically embodied in the oddly shaped sandstone buttes or prominent mesa tops that are naturally abundant in this landscape where plateau breaks to lower elevation terrain. There is no denying the powerful beauty contained in these brilliant red and orange formations or the stirring aesthetic response they can generate within the viewer. But to make the case for energy transfer and transmission of power from these identified vortex points is somewhat beyond the scope of our study. As a land use issue, however, there remain several ramifications.

Commercial attention to nurturing New Age sensibilities by Sedona's retail merchants has led to a proliferation of businesses that peddle consciousness-raising wares like beads, incense, and especially crystals, along with service ventures that support pilgrimages to energy centers in the vicinity. A number of tour concessions, one of them using trademark pink jeeps, will be glad to drive you to these places for a fee, and let you derive whatever magnetism you may be inclined to feel once there. Unfortunately, this activity utilizes numerous off-road vehicle tracks, which has contributed to negative environmental impacts upon these ostensibly sacred lands. Helicopter tours offer a less tangibly detrimental aerial perspective, yet are tainted by their own intrusive aura. For an ideal Sedona souvenir, crystals are claimed to help with healing the soul and making sure one stays the course on the journey to enlightenment. As luck would have it, there are quite a few purveyors of these geometrically shaped gems downtown, as well as in the other shopping outlets at the town's highway entrances.

Local merchants certainly have been able to capitalize on the geographic enchantments that are sought after by spiritual adherents. But here in Sedona, New Age meets New West, and the town has become known for its more standard art offerings as well, with paintings and sculptures displayed in almost two dozen galleries. One travel writer asserted that "what Sedona lacks in size as an art center, compared with Santa Fe or Scottsdale, it strives to make up for in higher quality" (Weir 1990, 191). Commercial land use reflects the target clientele. A fanciful shopping complex, called Tlaquepaque, is pleasantly situated beneath the shade of sycamore trees along Oak Creek south of town. It resembles an old pueblo-styled trading post, with adobe walls enclosing courtyards and interior patios amid the gift stores and art galleries. Elsewhere along the entrance highways, standard-looking strip malls predominate, with their typical collection of grocery store anchors, banks, clothing and other specialty shops, and the ubiquitous fast food restaurants, including the only McDonalds anywhere with turquoise arches. To their credit, town officials have instituted strict parking lot landscaping guidelines, along with restrictive design codes that severely limit the size and height of commercial signage.

Residential land use has responded to the mystical enhancements of Sedona, as well as understandably to the more quotidian aspects of a charming small town set in scenic surroundings and circumscribed by recreational public lands. Even without the influence of New Age geography, Sedona would be a desirable place for second-home development or retirement, hence a candidate for rampant growth patterns in the twenty-first century. The town overall has stayed relatively compact, but real estate offerings have pushed the envelope beyond what might be considered affordable housing. As land becomes available for development, roads are snaking their way into alcoves and box canyons, where ever larger homes are creeping up the slopes beneath the lustrous red rimrock. And there are additional hidden charges associated with the spiritual dimension. One house recently advertised for sale at nearly a million dollars included its own kiva and meditation room. It is largely up to local citizens and their town government to decide if effective growth management strategies may be applied to stabilize the disruptive influence of New Age magnetism and keep a perfectly lovely place from becoming overly developed.

CALIFORNIA

Known far and wide as a lifestyle hearth and trendsetter for the nation, this huge state on the edge of the country is nevertheless home to a complex, diverse, and ever-changing population. And largely because of a north-south extent that encompasses nine degrees of latitude, the physical setting of California manifests an equally wide assortment of environments and terrain. Deserts, forests, mountains, and the spectacular Pacific Ocean coastline frame the margins for a natural habitat that has been relentlessly modified by human agency. Stephanie Pincetl (1999) has demonstrated how the state has squandered the riches of its natural bounty through a combination of ineffective land use planning and an inability to reconcile conflicting visions of community and landscape, thereby contributing to a political impasse over resolving issues of environmental conservation and social needs that too often have been at odds. The three massive urban areas along the coast—San Diego, Los Angeles, and San Francisco—have been expanding outward now for more than a century and show little sign of slowing down. As a result, the cultural landscape of California has perhaps to the point of cliché been epitomized as suburban sprawl.

The growth machine has been such a juggernaut for so long that most of the state can hardly be construed as belonging to the New West. Nevertheless, rapid growth within several counties situated amid the foothills of the Sierra Nevada range have recently evinced a pattern of unanticipated development with the same characteristics of many intermountain communities across the western states (Duane 1999). Likewise, a handful of former logging or mining towns have managed to preserve enough historic architecture to keep themselves alive, first through tourism and now by welcoming new migrants, including mortgage refugees from the larger urban areas who are seeking a more quaint and affordable address. At the other end of the economic spectrum, a handful of ski resorts have discovered the riches of all-seasons recreational boosterism, which can quickly become residential in nature. As one of the more attractive college towns in the state, Chico can be viewed as California's representative equivalent of Bozeman, or Fort Collins: a vibrant and livable community that has its cultural life enriched by the presence of a university.

One of the major growth management issues for the Golden State these days involves anticipating and accommodating development pressure in places on the outermost edge of the larger metropolitan areas. With home prices now well out of reach of the average wage earner in the larger cities and immediate surroundings, workers in search of affordable housing are being forced to make longer and longer commutes. Frequently the countryside in between built-up regions has become subject to increasing restrictions on conversion of open space, or else property owners have unrealistically raised the selling price of raw land in a speculative attempt to cash in on demand. The end result of these complex development dynamics can be seen in the new growth of many smaller cities and towns far beyond the periphery of the larger metropolitan areas. Note the fastest growing California counties in figure 3.23.

Many of these municipalities were already large urban places in their own right, but recent in-migration along with natural increase has caused them to swell and rip apart at the seams. This is nowhere more apparent than in the state's agriculturally rich Central Valley. More than a decade ago, William Fulton (1991, 2) wrote that thousands of commuters "now race across the floor of the fertile San Joaquin Valley from their relatively inexpensive homes in Stockton and Modesto to jobs on the edge of the Bay Area in Livermore and Pleasanton." It has only gotten worse, of course, and the drive now begins farther and farther away from work. Consequently, local environments and quality of life degrade on several fronts. There are several areas where sprawl continues gobbling up acre upon acre of what is arguably some of the richest soils and most productive agricultural land on earth, and Fresno, for instance, has become the fastest growing city in all of California.

FIGURE 3.23
California, showing the fastest growing county for the decade 1990–2000 in darkest shading, the next fastest growing counties in lighter shading, and selected towns and cities discussed in text. Data source: U.S. Census Bureau. *Map by Ian Gray, CWU graduate program in resource management.*

Western Sierras

At the rural level, the fastest growing places in the state, according to Census population figures for the decade 1990–2000, include the counties of San Benito, Placer, Calaveras, and Madera. Other nearby counties, while not in the top growth tier, are also experiencing problems associated with new arrivals (Duane 1999). Among these rapidly changing rural communities, Nevada County officials have encountered stiff resistance to local land use planning efforts that seek to envision future conservation opportunities at the landscape scale (Hurley and Walker 2004). Additional areas that have witnessed phenomenal development pressures include many of the smaller towns southeast of Sacramento that find themselves on the route to ski resorts and other mountain recreation targets. Northeast of Sacramento there are growing pains apparent in Auburn and the rest of the Interstate 80 corridor and to the north at Grass Valley, where the late Wallace Stegner once lived and from where that beloved dean of western writers observed the changes that the region was undergoing throughout the broad sweep of its settlement history.

Deep within these mountains, Mammoth Lakes, California, is one of those exceptionally scenic out-of-the-way places that are nevertheless within reach of a weekend commute from the coastal cities. Since the mid-1950s, when the Forest Service first requested bids from developers for a proposed lodge and ski complex, this area has emerged as one of the West's most enjoyable family-oriented ski destinations. At an elevation of 7,000 feet, and a resident population very close to that figure, Mammoth is a small town on the verge of explosive New West development.

Warm summer days turn quickly to brisk evenings, and winter snow storms can be daunting in this remote location on the back side of the Sierras, but the natural alpine beauty and the clean, crisp air scented by ponderosa pines is exhilarating to most lowland Californians. Even so, the resort complex has experienced variable visitation over the years: "By the 1980s Mammoth hosted 1.4 million skiers a year, but several years of anemic snowfall and increased competition from western ski areas such as Vail, Colorado and Park City, Utah pushed visits down to 450,000 by the early 1990s" (Vincent 2005). Declining winter recreation revenues prompted the town to consider plans to diversify its economic base and to attract more full-time and seasonal residents. The eastern Sierra Nevada Mountains hold some of the West's most spectacular glaciated granite terrain, punctuated by sky-blue lakes and picturesque waterfalls. Yosemite National Park to the west is seasonally accessible via Tioga Pass, while Mono Lake is only a few miles to the north along U.S. Highway 395. The area's summer resorts are popular stopping points for wilderness adventurers and those interested in guided trips into the backcountry. The idea, then, was to promote Mammoth both as an upscale alpine residential community and as an easily accessible year-round vacation destination. This strategy simply follows what has proven to be successful at places like Sun Valley and Vail and indicates the same trend in resort transformation from hotel-based to residence-based (Rothman 1998, 247). Ultimately such a change will place greater control in the hands of outside capital and extend rights to those who purchase second homes, resulting in less empowerment for local residents attempting to shape the design of their community.

In 2003, the Intrawest Corporation of Vancouver, Canada, opened the Town Center Village at Mammoth, replicating a European-style, pedestrian-oriented village—similar in design and function to Whistler, B.C.—featuring shops, restaurants, condominiums, and a gondola with direct service to the slopes. The company owns more than 500 condominium units at the site, and there are plans to construct more than 1,000 more over the next few years. The village centerpiece will be a 240-room Westin hotel, an international brand that signals "a very significant step for Mammoth to be recognized as a world-class destination" and, the company claims somewhat more ambitiously, "the renaissance of Mammoth as the premier mountain resort destination in America" (Vincent 2005).

Town Center Village is not the only type of residential development taking place at this location. Higher end custom homes with views of Mammoth Lakes are currently under construction to the southwest of town. Prices for vacant residential lots have been escalating, resulting in homes that generally sell for $300,000 or more. Both the scale and pace of change are unsettling to many local people:

> Mammoth's improvements have alarmed some residents, neighbors and planners who fear the town's charms will be diminished by traffic jams, housing shortages, a higher cost of living, and even possible water shortages. Middle income people fear they soon will be priced out of the area, if they haven't been already. City officials and other boosters acknowledge mixed feelings about the changes in Mammoth, but insist that improvements must be made if it is to catch up with other world-class ski resorts in the West. (Vincent 2005)

But there are also a few unavoidable red flags hoisted by the local environment that should temper the enthusiasm for urban expansion and population increase. Future growth plans across this seismically active zone must take into account some rather unusual hazards beyond the problem of simply being prone to earthquakes, a situation that has become all too familiar for most Californians. Indeed, not only does the Mammoth area have a higher risk for earthquakes than almost anywhere else in the West, but it is susceptible to other potentially more violent events such as volcanic eruptions or steam and gas emissions. Fumaroles are active in the vicinity, but most startling has been the discovery of emissions of ultra-high levels of carbon dioxide that have decimated large areas of the forest:

> First noted in 1990, the areas of tree kill now total about 170 acres in six general areas, including the most visually impressive tree-kill area adjacent to Horseshoe Lake on the south side of Mammoth Mountain. The soil gas in the tree-kill areas is

composed of 20 to 90 percent CO_2; there is less than 1 percent CO_2 in soils outside the tree-kill areas. (United States Geological Survey [USGS] 2005)

Such hazards may well put a damper on further expansion efforts, but at the very least need to be considered when formulating land use plans.

Arcata and Redding

The far northern reaches of the state encompass a physical and a cultural geography that is more connected to the convoluted terrain of the humid Pacific Northwest than to California's arid south or the industrial farm country of the central valley or the dramatic escarpments of the high Sierra. These connections are so pervasive that novelist Ernest Callenbach once included northern California within his fictional northwest domain of Ecotopia. Of the several small towns that increasingly serve as a magnet for those who seek the New West lifestyle, two in particular stand out: Redding and Arcata. With a population now pushing 100,000, Redding is by far the larger of the two and has become one of California's fastest growing medium-sized cities. It is also more advantageously situated along the Interstate 5 corridor, roughly midway between Portland and San Diego. While its downtown still seems forlorn and a bit shabby, there are signs that change is on the way, and there is every indication that Redding may assume greater prominence in the continuing development of New West urbanism. Commissioned by local municipal leaders, a fancy new pedestrian bridge designed by world famous Spanish architect Santiago Calatrava spans the Sacramento River, and its unusual shape and towering Sundial have become a landmark structural showpiece and emblem of civic pride. Opened on the Fourth of July, 2004, the bridge connects the parklands of Turtle Bay with Redding's extensive river trail system.

Recreational facilities on other nearby public lands literally encircle the town, and the large impoundment of Shasta Lake has grown in popularity, particularly among the houseboat crowd. Residential subdivisions in the surrounding area highlight picture-window views of Lassen Peak or Mount Shasta, which itself has been the target of New Age ministrations that have run afoul of more genuine ceremonial tributes by Native American tribes who perceive the mountain as truly sacred. In the last decade, population in the greater Redding area has grown from less than 50,000 to more than 175,000, and the city now serves as the retail commercial and medical service center for all of northern California and southern Oregon.

A much smaller town, with only 15,000 residents, Arcata is over on the north coast, and is well endowed with both natural settings and the people who care about them. The town and surrounding area continues to attract those who espouse an alternative lifestyle of living close to nature and treading lightly on the planet. In 1996, the progressive periodical digest *Utne Reader* declared Arcata to be one of the "Most Enlightened Towns" in the country. Humboldt State University, long known as one of the last holdouts of hippiedom, boasts of having "the largest undergraduate environmental engineering program in the country," and claims of "sending more volunteers per capita to the Peace Corps than any other institution" (Humboldt State University 2005).

A history of gold mining, commercial fishing, and logging has given way to a decidedly New West posture, and much of the town's economy now focuses on the appreciation of natural scenery associated with tourism and recreation. As the southern gateway community for Redwoods National Park, Arcata shares in the potential for even greater transformation with other towns across the West that find themselves positioned to take advantage of that singularly fortunate geography. There are also state and additional federal lands set aside for their amenity values, and grassroots activism has sought to preserve many other local natural areas such as estuaries and marshes.

This entire northern California region seems ready to accept additional migrants, and many areas eagerly anticipate the influx as a way of holding things together in the wake of a downturn in extractive resource economies. But for whatever reason, only a portion of the new retirees and others fleeing the high costs of living in California's main cities are stopping at the top of the state. A good many more, however, are continuing on to the Pacific Northwest. Or perhaps, as Starrs and Wright (1995) have noted, they are moving to Nevada.

NEVADA

At the southern point of this wedge-shaped state lies the fastest growing city in the country. Las Vegas, one of the youngest urban places in the West, is now one of the largest. This place is the absolute antithesis of rural, but it is New West nonetheless. Its rate of growth is nothing short of astounding, and you can literally watch as a thin urban veneer oozes out across the floor of the desert valley. At least one scholar has attempted to depict the singular phenomenon of southern Nevada sprawl machinery at work as an extension of the California lifestyle gone blue-collar (Davis 1995). Others, such as William Howard Kunstler, become harsh critics who delight in taking aim at the obvious social and environmental drawbacks. But it is Hal Rothman (2002) who lends us the most observant and compelling voice to help make sense of what is ultimately a nonsensical urban area and its voracious patterns of expansion. Rothman, a professor of environmental history at the local campus of the University of Nevada (UNLV), has come to view Las Vegas as both a tangible and honest reflection of the dominant national culture and a frightening apocalyptic vision of where the country is heading.

From simple stagecoach stop to gambling and entertainment mecca for a society that seems to thrive on artificial stimulation and glitter, the city proper, and especially its rapidly expanding apron, is now experiencing massive migrations of people intent not just on visiting, but on staying and making a life. Figure 3.24 illustrates the relative growth rates of Nevada counties.

FIGURE. 3.24
Nevada, showing the fastest growing county for the decade 1990–2000 in darkest
shading, the next fastest growing counties in lighter shading, and selected towns and
cities discussed in text. Data source: U.S. Census Bureau. *Map by Ian Gray, CWU
graduate program in resource management.*

Time magazine recently reported that "7,000 people move to Clark County each month" (Stein 2004, 26). As a result, massive new residential and commercial spaces seem to instantly appear almost overnight. Many of the new housing developments responding to this market are in unincorporated areas beyond the municipal boundary, and much of the growth actually has been encouraged outside of city limits by the deliberately ineffectual planning policies of Clark County. Urbanization at this pace and scale becomes a procreative force that shapes metropolitan morphology:

> Along with tourism and gaming, real estate development drove Las Vegas, transformed its look, created its revenues, made its economy, and continued the growth that marked the 1980s and 1990s. Clark County and every municipality in it depended on development dollars to pay their way. Each municipality raised its fees for everything from expediting the approval of planning documents to new sewer hookups to pay for the infrastructure to assess, record, and maybe even manage growth. The county commission granted variance after variance to developers because the impact fees they paid provided a good chunk of the county's budget. Urban sprawl is a fact of life in a city that has nearly doubled in population and physical size in the last decade. New subdivisions emerge so fast that it is impossible to keep up. They spawn business districts of strip malls that seemingly weren't there yesterday. Even the police need maps. New streets and subdivisions open with such regularity that the most recent directory is out of date within weeks of issue. (Rothman 2002, 262–263)

Dwellings are indeed being built so fast that local infrastructure providers cannot keep up. There are even tales of people taking possession of a new home, moving in, and then waiting weeks for electric power to be hooked up. While the entire perimeter of the city is gushing outward, some of the most dramatic landscape transformations are taking place to the northwest of town.

To navigate through this world is to leave the natural environment far, far behind. Rapid suburbanization has resulted in the near complete paving over of the landscape city's northwest perimeter. Any semblance of native life has been scraped clean away, and exotic vegetation mulched with rocks and requiring artificial irrigation has come to establish the normal visual parameters for everything from residential yards to curvilinear collector streets, as illustrated in figure 3.25.

The braided channels of desert washes with their unique riparian zone flora have been replaced by a complete concretization of stream channels and arroyos that often, almost as soon as they are built, become inadequate for handling the runoff from an ever-increasing amount of impervious surface created by all the new development (figure 3.26).

But not all is uncoordinated growth on the city's edge. Summerlin, northwest of Las Vegas, is a 22,500-acre master-planned development started in 1990 by the

FIGURE 3.25
Typical street scene on the northern edges of ever-expanding Las Vegas. *Photograph by Robert Kuhlken.*

FIGURE 3.26
Concrete channels have completely replaced desert washes and riparian vegetation in North Las Vegas. *Photograph by Robert Kuhlken.*

Howard Hughes Corporation. It is organized around thirty individual "villages" with mixed residential, recreational, and commercial uses, including golf courses, business parks, and several very upscale shopping centers along with resort spa hotels. By the end of 2003, Summerlin contained 33,000 dwelling units and held a population of 85,000 and has been designed to house at its build-out, now scheduled for the year 2020, a residential population of more than 160,000. A recent publication by the Urban Land Institute hails Summerlin as "one of America's best-selling master-planned communities" and one that "fosters a sense of community through its 68 parks and extensive trail networks" (Schmitz 2003, 53). But Summerlin is deliberately designed to remain segregated from the urban fabric of the rest of the surrounding sprawl. In many ways it is the epitome of what is about to happen to larger cities across the West, where people want to stay connected to jobs and other economic functions of the larger community, yet wish to stay socially aloof, and are further disinclined to participate in the civic life of the greater polity. Moreover, once inside places such as Summerlin you become enveloped in an utterly standardized monotonous landscape. Adjacent to Summerlin is the retirement mecca Sun City, followed by a pair of new master-planned developments at Lone Mountain.

Even while the city is bursting at the seams along its outermost edges, there are increasing signs that the core has begun to intensify in terms of residential density. Newly constructed multistory condominium towers along the Strip are selling out fast, leaving one writer to wonder if the city "might be developing a real urban center, where people not only party but meet, live, and perhaps form the kind of community Vegas never had" (Stein 2004, 33). New proposals for large developments slated for nearby Henderson profess to embrace New Urbanism, yet without a regionwide commitment and coordination of planning that now remains highly unlikely, these isolated instances of "smart growth" will do little to alleviate the growing problems. Consequently, the Las Vegas metropolitan area already teeters at the shining portal of chaos and inefficiency, and things only promise to get worse.

Other urban areas across the state are also experiencing in-migration, especially around the vicinity of Reno and Carson Valley, which are advantageously situated at the base of the eastern Sierras and just downhill from Tahoe. Playing host to the state's flagship university with its cultural as well as educational offerings, and providing plenty of outlying private lands for low-density development, Reno probably manifests the closest thing Nevada has to the typical patterns of New West transformation taking place in other parts of the region. The entire urbanized area in this corner of the state is now pushing toward a population of 300,000. Elsewhere, the overall scale and effect of new development pales in comparison, although as geographers Starrs and Wright (1995, 424) have noted, "small towns in Nevada witness growth as proportionately confounding as anything happening in Las Vegas, Reno, or Carson City."

Mesquite is situated just south of the Virgin River Canyon as it slices through the upended sedimentary strata of the far northwest corner of Arizona and is less than 100 miles northeast of Las Vegas along Interstate 15. Built on a scattering of farm- and ranchlands, the place was initially conceived as a destination casino-resort complex. Developers of gaming hotels sought to take advantage of the site's border location to intercept enough south-flowing traffic along the interstate highway. But the town is now developing into a retirement-residential community. Building permit applications are presently at an all time high, with infrastructure extensions struggling to keep up with construction. Preferred building sites providing views are most often located on elevated mesas and nearby slopes of the broad alluvial fans or bajadas. But lower level sites at the base of shallow canyons have also become the target of residential development. Never mind the lack of view, such sites experience increased risk potential for being impacted by infrequent, but often catastrophic flood events. With golf course plans afoot, Mesquite seems intent on mimicking the frenzy of development taking place just to the north at St. George.

While most small towns of Nevada hardly evoke growth potential, there are some that nevertheless appear as blips on the edge of the development radar screen. Pahrump, certainly, has already started to bulge as the Las Vegas area's westernmost satellite. Likewise, north of the big city lies Caliente, altogether somnolent now, but perhaps awaiting discovery as an affordable retirement spot. Isolated settlements in the state's interior mainly remain true to their heritage as outposts of the extractive minerals economy. Many of them, such as Austin and Eureka, are historic relics of classic hard rock prospecting. Others, like Tonopah and Ely, continue in their role as modern mining centers. Of all the interior settlements, those positioned along the interstate highways, such as Winnemucca and Elko, may stand the best chance of attracting new development. It's a long shot, to be sure, since geographic isolation and distance from urban amenities are working against them. Extensive rural subdivisions, only partially developed to provide housing for mine workers, are now infilling with retirees and others who don't mind the solitude and lack of amenities (Starrs 1998, 165). Perhaps an example of a much more likely eventuality for these parts would be the Burning Man festival that takes place every Labor Day weekend, a wild "happening" and experiment in ephemeral cityspace that annually interrupts the utter tranquility normally pervading the Black Rock desert playa just north of Gerlach. Which just goes to prove that these days, in this region, almost anything can happen.

OREGON

Oregon has for more than three decades maintained its position as a national leader in formulating comprehensive rational planning solutions for conserving its natural resources and managing land use change related to population growth, so it should stand to reason that urban sprawl is more restrained here, and rural lands are less intensively developed than in other areas of the West. For the most part this is true, although by the time statewide planning initiatives were adopted during the early 1970s, a number of remote locations were already experiencing wholesale division of parcels into smaller lots for speculative marketing, while many towns exercised little control over leapfrog developments that were being built beyond municipal limits in the unincorporated periphery. Areas of special concern include the fertile and productive farmlands of the Willamette Valley, as well as the state's coastal environments, with their critical estuarine resources and dynamic beach and dune systems. Most recently, the November 2004 election has delivered a wake-up call to the state's planning ethic, however, in the form of a passed citizens' referendum that requires local jurisdictions to either pay for lost value caused by zoning regulations or else waive the regulation (see chapter 5). In the next section, following a brief review of the state's urban and suburban geography, we examine in greater detail current land use conditions in the most rapidly

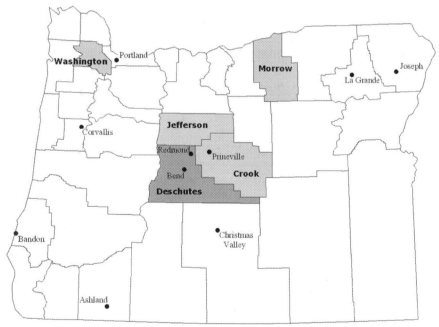

FIGURE 3.27
Oregon, showing the fastest growing county for the decade 1990–2000 in darkest shading, the next fastest growing counties in lighter shading, and selected towns and cities discussed in text. Data source: U.S. Census Bureau. *Map by Ian Gray, CWU graduate program in resource management.*

growing area of the state, central Oregon, where characteristics of the New West are very apparent. Oregon's fast growth counties are illustrated in figure 3.27.

Urban Oregon

The largest urban jurisdiction in the state, Portland, is widely regarded as being one of the most livable cities in the United States. The downtown has been kept vibrant with public spaces and a strong commitment to pedestrian life. A freeway along the riverfront was removed some years ago and a two-mile linear park was installed, with intensive mixed-use developments endorsed at either end. Inner-city parking spaces were intentionally limited and a light rail transit system initiated that continues to be amplified with new lines to the outer suburban zones. Of course, Portland itself is surrounded by a dozen or more smaller satellites, and these discrete incorporated areas have all expanded through annexations over the years to blanket the metropolitan region with adjacent municipal governments. But this entire conurbation of multiple jurisdictions now coordinates its guidance of further development through the elected regional government known as METRO, which also oversees the mass transit systems. Most significantly, the market-driven tendency to develop less expensive real estate at the fringes of the metropolitan area and to sprawl outward from the built-up edge has been reined in by a single urban growth boundary (UGB) for the region, carefully adjusted through time by METRO to allow for expansion of the developable frontier.

Population projections, the adequate provision of public infrastructure and the logic of street and road networks, together with the avoidance of natural hazards or impingement upon important resource lands, largely determine the definition of land areas where development is needed and desired. Using the state-mandated technique of delineating a UGB, potential urban properties are thus separated from those areas to be conserved as rural. A range of different housing options at increasing densities allows more population growth to be accommodated on less land already designated urban, thereby reducing pressures to expand the UGB. Moreover, the Portland area is nationally recognized for its aggressive pursuit of mass transit opportunities, including a successful light rail system known as MAX (Metropolitan Area Express), a downtown pedestrian transit mall for bus connections, and an inner-city streetcar. In terms of land use, METRO has encouraged the linkage of outlying higher density, mixed-use developments with light rail stations. One of the more renowned examples of such so-called transit oriented development (TOD) is the Orenco Station project west of Portland along the western MAX line. On the other side of the urban region, at the east end of the light rail network, the city of Gresham is also creating new urban spaces designed with TOD in mind. Meanwhile, the nearby smaller city of Fairview has emerged as a textbook case of re-inventing the suburbs as pedestrian friendly town centers linked by public transportation options. Here in the Portland metropolitan area the principles of New Urbanism have been fully embraced and have been proven to offer a successful alternative to the same old tired pattern of low-density tract homes, isolated office parks, and endless strip malls that plague most other large cities.

Other urban concentrations in the state include a scattering of Willamette Valley cities extending south (upstream) from Portland to Eugene. The state government's Department of Land Conservation and Development as well as the citizen watchdog group 1000 Friends of Oregon are both keeping a close watch on urban development in this area because of the potential loss of valuable farmland and open space. In the southwest corner of Oregon are the large towns/small cities of Roseburg, Medford, and Grants Pass, all of which were once closely tied to either timber cutting and lumber production or the volatile economics of fruit orchards. Most recently this region has discovered the value of supporting recreational activities on public lands as a community asset. One indication that this area is ripe for development as an amenity-rich outpost is the recent surge in activity at the Rogue Valley International Airport, which registered a record number of passengers last year (Quinn 2005). Meanwhile, there has been increased interest in this particular area, as well as the nearby southwest coast, as a retirement location. Further south, close by the California border, are the locations for what might be considered the only truly New West communities on the Pacific side of the Cascades: the former mining town of Jacksonville, the nearby Shakespearean theatre hamlet of Ashland, and the up and coming golfing mecca of Bandon and nearby settlements on the state's far southwest coast. We first take a closer look at that nouveau coastal geography and then focus on central Oregon.

The Southwest Coast

Nascent New West development has sprung up along the Pacific Coast Highway—U.S. Highway 101—from Brookings to Bandon, Oregon. Small coastal communities on Oregon's far south coast have formed a residential property and destination vacation marketing program that promotes "the Wild Rivers Coast," comprising "101 Miles" of nearly undiscovered scenic shorelines and beaches. But, of course, these lovely and relatively remote communities have previously been discovered by California development corporations searching for opportune recreation and retirement properties. This development corridor, consisting of several picturesque harbor towns, is constrained to a narrow littoral zone by the Pacific Ocean on the west and the steep slopes of the Siskiyou Mountains immediately to the east. Cramped river valleys leading to the coastal zone offer some room for expansion, but federal forest ownership dominates much of the landscape. Highway access to larger inland towns including Grants Pass, Medford, and Roseburg is limited by mountainous terrain to only a few torturous surface routes.

Brookings, on the far southern Oregon coast, is a prototypical example of New West coastal development. The Pacific side of the Siskiyou Range is heavily timbered with Douglas fir, cedar, and redwood; consequently, the timber products industry has been a primary source of employment for coastal communities. However, Brookings is uniquely favored with a climatic characteristic known as the "Brookings Banana Belt" phenomenon. There is a nearly year-long freeze-free season, with an extremely mild winter temperature regime promoting the cultivation of high-value nursery stock, bulbs, and fresh flowers for the cut floral market. While annual rainfall averages more than seventy inches, the seasons are unusually mild for the coastal environment, with many clear and warm winter days, a feature that has not been missed by those interested in promoting development.

Scenic Brookings Harbor, at the mouth of the Chetco River, offers opportunities for recreational boating and sport and commercial fishing. The City of Brookings, with a population of only 6,000, is a mix of quaint tourist-oriented establishments and no-nonsense central business district commerce. A diversified local economy is rapidly expanding, and residential and vacation home developments are presently on the rise. Local recovery has been slow since the economic downturn of the early 1990s and the associated loss of timber products employment. Taking up the slack has been a strong building and commercial resurgence primarily energized by California retirees. The Salmon Run Golf Resort is an example of the type of new development planned for the southern Oregon coast. Salmon Run is a world-class golf destination set in a valley of rushing, forested streams, waterfalls, and ocean views. This high-quality development is the recreational centerpiece for associated residential growth and commercial expansion. The town of Bandon, once known primarily for its cheeses, specialty ice cream, and cranberries, is a new golfing mecca, featuring some of Oregon's most picturesque coastal courses.

Growth is managed by the coordinated comprehensive plans of the City of Brookings and adjacent Curry County. While economic recovery and stability are primary goals for the area, growth impacts are carefully evaluated, and new developments are required to share community development and infrastructure costs. In addition to the review of new developments for compatibility with Oregon's statewide agricultural, forest, and shoreline goals and for mitigating potential environmental impacts, the city has implemented permit development charges that can exceed $10,000 per residential unit.

Central Oregon

We demarcate this region in general by the tri-county area shown in figure 3.27: Deschutes, Jefferson, and Crook Counties, which together constitute the most rapidly growing area in the state. Most of our discussion focuses on Deschutes

County, the state's growth leader, and its three main towns: the recreation mecca of Bend on the high lava plains at the edge of the forest; Sisters, the false-fronted Old West artists haven; and Redmond, which just recently was decreed the fastest growing community in Oregon. Neighboring Crook County, and its county seat of Prineville, offers some interesting alternative insights into the historical processes of land development in remote rural areas, as well as the changing fortunes of a community once utterly dependent on timber supply from federal lands. Jefferson County, with its combination of arid rangeland, irrigated agriculture, and reservoir-focused leisure, was also the scene of a unique religious experiment in what might be termed agrarian urbanism, when followers of Indian guru Bhagwan Shree Rajneesh purchased a large ranch along the isolated John Day River and proceeded to circumvent a number of Oregon's statewide land use guidelines during their rapid albeit brief population build-up. Let us now consider the circumstances of growth in this pivotal region of the New West.

Bend, named for a wide and shallow turn in the Deschutes River, which once allowed wagons to cross, has been a popular vacation destination for many years and has been known throughout the Northwest for its all-seasons recreational opportunities. The town functions as a gateway to the vast national forest holdings composed of pine-clad volcanic landscapes full of sparkling lakes to the south and west, where access is greatly enhanced by Century Drive and the Cascade Lakes Loop Highway, thoroughfares attractively paved with the rich red tone of locally quarried cinder. A series of snow-capped peaks profiles the western skyline, dominated by a trio of clustered volcanoes named the Three Sisters, along with nearby Broken Top, an eroded fragment, and Bachelor Butte, an almost perfectly circular cone. Here, the Forest Service has issued a long-term lease for the operation of a major ski facility, Mount Bachelor. Its several dozen chairlifts radiate out from the center of the mountain like spokes, including one that goes all the way to the summit at just over 9,000 feet above sea level.

Throughout these mountains are numerous lakes, encircled with thick lodgepole pine forests, harboring many public campgrounds and small resorts. Fishing, sailing, motorboating, whitewater rafting, mountain biking, and hiking are just a few of the activities that visitors to this area enjoy, while wilderness trails offer the prospect for finding greater solitude and a chance to truly get away from it all in the backcountry. Winter provides just as many options, with both downhill and cross-country skiing along with inner tubing, ice skating, and snowshoeing all being popular pastimes. To the east of Bend lies the so-called High Desert country, characteristically identified by a vegetation complex primarily consisting of sagebrush, bitterbrush, and juniper. Much of this area is also publicly owned, with National Forest lands southeast of town merging with Bureau of Land Management administration farther east.

There are large blocks of private lands at some distance south of Bend, around the forested community of La Pine, where parcelization has resulted in the creation of hundreds of residential lots, typically of five acres or less. This area is a flat, nearly featureless lava plain with porous soils, supporting an open forest cover of ponderosa pine. The settlement pattern is willy-nilly, with access roads spread in loosely connected grids across the plateau. Master-planned this is not, and the timing and sequence of the residential infill process involving the granting of building permits on preexisting lots is only now revealing the scope of how widespread the development potential is for this area where mobile homes and manufactured housing are much more prevalent than trophy mansions. Many of the residents in the vicinity of La Pine are retired or otherwise living on fixed incomes and generally do not support tax-based infrastructure. Roads tend to be dirt or gravel, resulting in dust during the summer and mud in the winter. There are few urban services beyond basic provision of electricity and telephone, and most of the dwellings are on individual septic tanks for sewage disposal and individual wells for drinking water. This has caused some serious problems with failing septic tanks contributing to groundwater pollution and well contamination. Furthermore, fire protection is universally inadequate, with pumper stations spread too thin and districts strapped for the capital needed to purchase equipment. Many of the residents burn wood in fireplaces and stoves for winter heating, which can add to the danger, although the real hazard comes during the late summer and early fall, when the woods are tinder dry and convective thunderstorms are common. It is a fire-prone environment, heavily laden with fuel, into which a substantial rural population has been injected. This represents more than the creation of a so-called natural hazard; it is, indeed, a recipe for disaster.

By contrast, about halfway between La Pine and Bend is the manicured residential–recreational development known as Sunriver, one of Oregon's first destination resorts. This master-planned golf and condominium complex with integrated commercial retail space represents the epitome of first-generation New West land use patterns. Major construction began in 1978, and the project has expanded in carefully sequenced phases through the years. Recreational facilities now include a pair of eighteen-hole golf courses, swimming pools, an ice rink, stables and bridle trails, and more than two dozen tennis courts. A hotel and conference center forms the centerpiece of the built environment, and there are several restaurants. In terms of size and luxury level, there is a range of dwelling types, from larger stand-alone single-family homes to townhouses and time-share apartment units. There is an overall abundance of common open space, and the various pods of living units are all connected with nearly thirty miles of bike paths and walkways, which also line the perimeters of most fairways on the two golf courses. A grocery store anchors a somewhat standard-looking strip mall, but commercial signage is noticeably absent, and as the arboreal landscaping has matured, the appropriately scaled shopping center is now a very inconspicuous though essential element of the project. Other specialty shops are situated closer to the hotel. Sunriver has been, by most measures, a successful venture, although it hardly needs pointing out that the experience of just being here, let alone buying time here, is not available to everyone.

The City of Bend is a frustrating case of the good, the bad, and the ugly. Situated in what is obviously a drop-dead-good-looking physical setting, the city has had plenty of time to figure out what the future holds but has failed to guide the growth that should have been so easily anticipated. Neither has it arranged to provide urban-level services for what can no longer be considered a small town. There are ongoing and lingering failures. It is reported to be the largest city west of the Mississippi River without a public transit system. Streets have been laid out haphazardly, with little attention to connectivity or logic. Commercial strip zoning along north-south arterial Highway 97 has created one of the longest four-lane retail promenades this side of Las Vegas. By the end of the 1990s, traffic had clogged this stretch so completely that a partially elevated bypass was deemed to be the only plausible fix. As of now, the patient has survived, yet the diet has not changed, and additional commercial land use extends well north of the mall at the Y-junction of Routes 97 and 20.

Residential development now climbs up and over several of the prominent volcanic cones that surround the urban area. Only its public ownership and management as a state park allowed the one named Pilot Butte to escape the same fate and to stave off the rampaging horde of houses popping up out in the sagebrush and junipers east of town, where rapid urbanization has been most dramatic. Following the recent "discovery" of Bend, mainly by retirees and mortgage refugees from California, this outlying area has literally gone from rangeland to urban land use in a few short years. Despite knowledge to the contrary, development patterns typically continue to replicate the same single-family dwelling on a preferred cul-de-sac location within a maze of curvilinear streets. Gas stations and convenience stores commandeer every main intersection, while more sizable structures such as churches, hospitals, and new schools, each with its own extensive parking lot, compete for the larger parcels. Residential subdivisions are embedded within a volatile fire-prone sagebrush-juniper vegetation complex, leading some residents to expect disaster at any time. Lois Gruver, for example, whose house in Bend is "surrounded by juniper trees," keeps a suitcase packed "with pictures of her children and her favorite paintings . . . always ready to sling it into her trunk if flames head toward her home" (Wagner 2004). The relentless sprawl of nouveau Bend is somewhat countered by the compact nature of the city's core, where commercial and residential land use exhibits an attractive mix.

Downtown Bend is blessed by its location astride the Deschutes River, where a low dam has created a winding impoundment known locally as Mirror Pond. An attractive city park incorporates several landscaped acres of riverside access with pedestrian walkways and a footbridge over the water. Older residential neighborhoods surround this public open space. Because recreation in Bend had already become an established alternative to industry, the central business district easily survived the slump in local economy following the closure of the mills, and the pair of parallel one-way couplets now sports the reinvigorated look of a perfectly typical New West downtown. There are sporting goods stores, of course, along with brew pubs and all natural ingredient pizza joints, now joined by trendier restaurants complete with candles and white tablecloths. Art galleries and designer clothing shops are more prevalent than hardware or department stores; indeed, these new specialty shops have now filled the vacuum created when the more traditional downtown establishments moved out to the highway strip.

Just to the south of the city's commercial core is a recently rehabilitated brownfields site where a large lumber mill once provided a mainstay of employment. The Old Mill District has now been redeveloped by transforming these former industrial buildings into commercial retail space, with integrated restaurants and a nearby music amphitheater, cashing in on one of the hottest new crazes in the Pacific Northwest: outdoor concert venues (Kuhlken 2003). The Les Schwab Amphitheater, named after its benefactor, the retail tire king from Prineville, holds approximately 9,000 concertgoers on a grassy lawn along the river. Opened in 2002, during the first few years of operation it has successfully attracted national acts such as Bob Dylan and the Eagles, and has hosted the nationally syndicated radio show "A Prairie Home Companion." Mixed use will be taken a step further when a hotel and condominiums are constructed in the complex. Other new developments elsewhere in the city have also followed the principles of New Urbanism, with high-density residential units built within a pedestrian-friendly setting. Only time will tell if enough of these sorts of projects can be stitched together into a richly textured urban fabric that will constitute a cohesive whole. The natural environment that surrounds the place remains stunning, but that now needs to be matched by the same quality of built environment. It would be one of the real tragedies in the annals of New West land use if Bend simply plods down the pathway of sprawl, ignoring its own potential to become one of the most livable places in the entire eleven-state region.

Redmond is centrally positioned among the other towns of central Oregon and maintains the further advantage of being home to the regional airport, which not only has daily scheduled flights to Portland, but also serves as the training facility for one of the Forest Service's elite smokejumper units that have become a key weapon in staging the initial attack on inevitable wildfires that flare up across the West. Downtown is in the midst of a commercial revival, despite the proliferation of big box stores along the highway strip. Offering a range of more affordable housing than the inflated real estate scene to the south, Redmond has become the fastest growing community in the state. West of town, Eagle Crest, one of the newer and more popular master-planned communities in the region, perches on the basalt rim overlooking the northward-flowing Deschutes River.

Prineville kicked off the region's early development as the first major urban settlement in all of central Oregon and served as the southern terminus for a stagecoach line that ran south from The Dalles. Early economic lifeblood flowed from livestock grazing, and it has been said that the town's ultrawide streets resulted from the requirement that they be able to accommodate the frequent cattle drives that were punched through the center of town. The surrounding grazing lands were also the setting for some of the so-called range wars that would occasionally disturb the peace in the Old West, and a local "sheepshooters association" was active in the Prineville area. After a newly established Ochoco National Forest began "managing" the rich timber lands in the mountains north and east of town, the steady supply of logs turned Prineville into a quintessential Northwest lumber town, with seven separate mills operating around the clock. When the log supply diminished from overcutting and the application of new federal policies requiring sustained yields, the town's economy declined, yet never went totally under, largely because of the Les Schwab Tire Company. The headquarters office, along with a massive recapping/retreading facility, are still located in the town where this local entrepreneur had opened his very first tire store. The firm is now the largest retail tire vendor in the Northwest, with hundreds of locations across a five-state area.

Economically, Prineville has always been both lucky and somewhat stubborn. Its fortunes looked like they might take a turn for the worse during the early decades of the 1900s, when the major railroad trunk line decided not to divert from its more or less straight line route some nineteen miles to the west. Not wishing to be left stranded, city officials started their own railroad, proceeded to lay track along the valley bottoms of the Crooked River, and ultimately connected to the Union Pacific (then Oregon Short Line) mainline near Terrebonne. To this day, the City of Prineville continues to operate the only municipally owned railroad in the country.

These days, Prineville is banking on the notion that livability does not necessarily require industrial development or traditional employment opportunities: "Business decline does not preclude population growth in an era when there are more retired people and greater propensity to live in one place and work and shop in another" (Fuguitt, Brown, and Beale 1989, 65). Former areas of low-budget "sagebrush subdivisions" south of Prineville have been the target of recent infusions of new capital and residential development interests, and county planners have responded with innovative techniques aimed at preserving rural character, such as 200-foot setbacks from edges of cliffs and requiring the use of nonreflective glass in new dwellings, further angled to prevent the projection of a glaring sun image (Zelenka 2003). The town itself has begun to feel the spillover effects of residential real estate prices in nearby Bend that have spiraled beyond affordability. Telecommunications and Internet commerce have largely overcome the disadvantages of remote location and, furthermore, promise to become a potent force in preserving the amenity values that continue to attract people to central Oregon in the first place (Levitt and Pitkin 2002). Meanwhile, a massive "new ur-banist" community is on the drawing board for a former one-thousand-acre ranch on the northwest edge of town, which will decidedly revolutionize the look and feel of the place (Jones 2005). Here, then, amid the echoes of what was sup-posed to be a dying timber town, we see taking shape a prime example of the next generation of New West communities.

WASHINGTON

Finally we come to the northwest corner of this country, where Washington shares with its neighbor to the south a cross-state environmental divide that has stimu-lated intensive urbanization west of the Cascades, while east of the mountains re-mains culturally and ecologically part of the more sparsely populated intermountain West. The far northwestern part of the state is a fascinating world of mountains, islands, and inland waterways ultimately connected to the ocean through the Strait of Juan de Fuca. It is a wet and soggy place much of the year, although certain favored locations such as the town of Sequim, on the Olympic peninsula, or Friday Harbor, situated on one of the ethereal San Juan Islands, do bask in the sunnier and drier climate derived from the rainshadow of the lofty Olympic Mountains. Even though this beautiful world of saltwater and forested archipelago might be viewed as the polar opposite from the land of cowboys and big sky, we feel that this place belongs on a map of the New West in every sense of that word. These amenity-rich landscapes are attracting an unprecedented surge of migration and resultant homebuilding, making San Juan County the second fastest growing county in the state (Rudzitis and Streatfeild 1993). The Olympic mountains are the centerpiece of one of the region's renowned national parks, but even this has so far failed to establish the classic "gateway community" of runaway growth that we have encountered elsewhere in the New West (Howe, McMahon, and Propst 1997). Likewise, just to the east, the North Cascades National Park sits along the Canadian border, an alpine gem high atop the range, with little by way of support services or tourism infrastructure on either side of the park along the one road traversing it. Perhaps this part of the country is still too new, too recently tied to its logging and ranching past.

Environmental conditions in that part of Washington east of the mountains, as in Oregon, are much different from the well-watered west side, and several areas in this part of the state are beginning to show symptoms of landscape alterations more in keeping with those rural and small town settings we have already visited across the West. In terms of cultural geography, however, there are some marked differences between eastern Washington and eastern Oregon. Rather than being a relative population void, there are some good-sized towns and cities, including Spokane, Yakima, Walla Walla, and the so-called Tri-Cities, consisting of three separate but adjoining municipalities of Richland, Kennewick, and Pasco. Spokane, in particular, has been targeted by many new migrants to the region seeking job opportunities and a chance to participate in the New West economic transformation. As a result, much of the surrounding area has been colonized by residential subdivision and attendant commercial sprawl. But Spokane itself has emerged from its historical identity as self-styled capital of a largely artificial regional concept known as the "Inland Empire" (Morrissey 1997). The city continues to explore options for revitalization of the downtown setting beyond its somewhat ineffective first attempt at reinvention during the 1974 Worlds Fair. The undeniable attractions of scenery and outdoor recreational activity are being combined with a new sense of responsibility for fashioning a city as habitable space. As the eminent historical geographer Donald Meinig (1991, 27) wrote: "Spokane is poised between the escapism of Arcadia and the fresh civic possibilities of the New Urbanism."

In another contrast with Oregon, across eastern Washington there is generally much more private land, hence much less public domain available for recreational pursuits. In the southeast corner of the state there is the Palouse, one of the world's premier dryland wheat-growing regions. To the northwest, the expansive industrial-scale Columbia Basin Project has taken on vastly different purposes from its original intent, when Roosevelt tried to reinvigorate the Jeffersonian dream of small yeoman farmers (Macinko 1963). West of the Columbia River, along the fertile Yakima Valley, are thousands of acres of rich farmland, irrigated by the snowmelt held within storage reservoirs high in the Cascades and producing high-value crops such as hops and grapevines. Indeed, the principal connection to the New West is here represented by the trendy custom-label wine producers with their showrooms and estate homes.

On the wet side of the mountains, Clark County is located in the southwestern part of the state where the city of Vancouver is situated across the Columbia River from Portland. Farms and orchards to the north and east of Vancouver have been divided and relentlessly paved over during the last two decades, constituting what is perhaps the worst case of sprawl in the Pacific Northwest. Perhaps it is the geographical juxtaposition with Portland that makes it seems so egregious. Here the state line separates two different philosophical worlds with two different structures of governance and regulation: the coordinated urban growth boundary management system south of the river counterpoised against this nearly-anything-goes private-property-rights theme park north of the river. Many new residents of these unincorporated urban areas might feel they have the best of all worlds: they reside in an expanding laissez-faire landscape where land use regulations are lax and there are no city taxes and services to pay for; but they also live and work in a state without an income tax, yet are able to cross over either of the two bridges into the Portland metropolitan area and practice carefree consumer behavior in a state without a sales tax. No wonder Clark County is the fastest growing county in the state of Washington. Figure 3.28 illustrates Washington's population growth by county.

FIGURE 3.28
Washington, showing the fastest growing county for the decade 1990–2000 in darkest shading, the next fastest growing counties in lighter shading, and selected towns and cities discussed in text. Data source: U.S. Census Bureau. *Map by Ian Gray, CWU graduate program in resource management.*

Pugetopolis

There is a huge urban complex, dubbed by some as "Pugetopolis," stretching along the shores of Puget Sound and its ancillary waterways, from state capital Olympia in the south to Everett, some thirty-five miles north of Seattle. The core of this metropolitan area is dominated by the larger cities of Tacoma and Seattle, around which are clustered outlying satellites, which once served as bedroom or industrial suburbs but are now structurally viable, self-standing, and self-aware: Lakewood, Auburn, Kent, Renton, Bellevue, Redmond, Kirkland, Edmonds, and Lynwood. These incorporated areas form an inner ring of original "edge cities" that were not simply a suburban asylum, but also granted new job opportunities across both the industrial and service sectors of the economy, and in terms of real estate, offered ample office and retail space. Numerous other communities on the perimeter are previously stand-alone small towns now being swallowed up by the urban fabric, such as Bothell, Issaquah, or Puyallup, or else fiercely attempting to hang on to individual identity in the face of increasing land development pressures. These would include places such as Duvall and Carnation, former farming centers situated on the rich bottomlands of the Snoqualmie River basin, and

Maple Valley, in the hilly woodlands of the Cedar River watershed southeast of Seattle. These locations are all within a twenty-mile radius of Seattle and are no more than ten miles from the Interstate 405 beltway. Under those conditions of proximity, there is nothing exceptional about the growth patterns and landscape transformations taking place there. To their credit, jurisdictions such as King County have attempted to install sophisticated growth management techniques, including programs for the purchase of development rights in certain areas where agricultural activities such as dairying result in higher value and return. But for the most part, as with any location in a state where the overall guiding legislation for local planning lacks teeth, cities and counties have allowed development to occur where market demand happens to dictate.

There must be something about the combination of soggy climatic conditions and inevitable expansion of the urban scene in western Washington that would seem to preclude any association with what is normally considered to be "New West." Yet if we examine the far outer perimeter of Pugetopolis, and consider those areas that have only recently come under the blade of the bulldozer, here we see places that represent not so much a new kind of lifestyle, but a new suburban way of living. As such, they might be used as examples of what other places around the West may look forward to in the event their particular pattern of peri-urban growth proceeds beyond its normal pace and spatial reach. Unlike the inner ring of earlier satellites, these are not "edge cities" by any stretch of the imagination, for they have no intention of providing a medley of jobs, abundant commercial retail space, and a wide range of domiciles. For these are primarily massive housing developments, despite all the hype about mixed use and the highly touted traditional small town settings.

The main difference between these new outermost developments and the older suburbs is greater distance from conventional employment opportunities that still require a commute, and for that matter, an even greater reliance on the automobile. As has been the case in similar situations found elsewhere around the country, many of these new developments are aggressively selling the notion of "community" or the idea of "neighborhood," as if in denial of the fact that a longer drive to work might actually preclude the proper functioning of those concepts. The emptiness of these locales during weekday working hours reveals the transparent ploy at marketing nostalgia for a long-lost time when neighbors must have socially engaged each other on a daily basis. Back to a time when the neighborhood grocery not only furnished most necessities but served as a gathering place to exchange greetings and a bit of gossip. While some newer developments often include a limited amount of commercial retail space, residents of these subdivisions not only drive long distances to work, but also must drive to the nearest shopping center for their frequent consumer purchases.

Growth within this second-tier ring in the foothills of the Cascades embodies the prediction expressed by Edward Blakely and Mary Snyder (1997, 14): "expansion of the suburbs is likely to accelerate as development moves ever farther out, supported by and leapfrogging beyond the new economic centers of the edge cities." Here we find the master-planned developments, many of which sport the trappings or assume the outer appearance of new urbanist enclaves, but are decidedly automobile-oriented in their transportation regimes and are exclusionary in the marketing and pricing of their housing options. The result is a renewed commitment to homogeneity rather than diversity among the local population.

To provide a glimpse into the type of development that has become most desirable within the larger urban areas of the Northwest, let us consider Snoqualmie Ridge. Ever since the first model homes went on the market, this 1,340-acre project has been the top-selling new housing location in the entire state of Washington for three years running (2000–2003). It is located atop a rolling plateau to the east of Issaquah, itself one of Seattle's fastest growing edge cities. Snoqualmie Ridge is designed as a mixed-use development, with commercial and office space sharing the plat with well over 2,000 houses in just Phase I alone. Despite the landing of a Philips electronics plant, several office buildings sit empty, and industrial space is way underutilized. Likewise, for all its claims to represent "new urbanism" the token commercial sector of the project manifests less than full occupancy, and even constructed buildings suffer from empty storefronts. Establishments that *are* open for business might be considered marginal or simply target the luxury side of consumer wants, rather than basic needs: a few take-out Asian food joints, manicure parlors and hair stylists, pet grooming, and a Taekwondo academy.

Several custom design builders are featured in the different sectors of the development; one, Crestview Homes, advertises its dwellings with a pitch that perfectly summarizes the New West paradigm: "Nestled in the heart of Snoqualmie Ridge, Crestview offers a retreat to a haven sheltered from the hustle and bustle, while providing convenient access to recreation with breathtaking views." Balancing the built environment, developers claim that "over 40 percent of the community has been set aside as open space, including parks, trails, preserved wetlands and a Jack Nicklaus Signature TPC Golf Course" (Snoqualmie Ridge 2004). This is but one of three master-planned developments in the region under the direction of the Quadrant Corporation, which proudly proclaims its projects as "created for people yet integrated with nature." Critical reading of such transparent discourse is unnecessary, for this is quite obviously the old suburban dream in a newly packaged format, forging the "middle ground" where wilderness and civilization merge, and where residents are presumed to be able to enjoy the best of both worlds. The project's office space advertisement goes one step further, by proclaiming the natural setting as inspirational: "Building at Snoqualmie Ridge Business Park is more than a smart business decision. It is a lifestyle choice. The uncongested roads, clean air and remarkable views make it easy to feel inspired and get to work" (Snoqualmie Ridge 2004).

Following customary nomenclature that is hardly new, office buildings are typically set within "parks"; but here the selling point is the overall natural environment, beyond the confines of the structural complex itself. At this sprawling development in the hills above Seattle, and in countless other projects at the outer edge of the West's ever-expanding urban landscape, scenic amenities are no longer a nice appended luxury but have emphatically become an essential "lifestyle choice."

Kittitas County

Much of the development pressure that is oriented to, or fixated on, New West lifestyles within the state of Washington is currently targeted on Kittitas County, which extends across a diversity of complex terrain, from the subalpine crest of the Cascade Mountains to the desert canyon walls of the Columbia River. This remarkable east-west transect thus results in an unusually wide range of environmental settings that are increasingly being exploited and manipulated by human agency, each in their own peculiar way. Indeed, many of the issues that we have encountered one by one at different locations around the West are all here in one place, and thus Kittitas County, as featured in the political cartoon in figure 3.29, may be seen as a microcosm for New West development patterns and land use issues.

The forested highlands historically have seen coal mining and logging come and go, and are now in the throes of resort creation and recreational subdivision. Irrigated farmland in the Kittitas Valley surrounding Ellensburg is being lost to residential subdivision at an alarming rate, despite de jure agricultural zoning that sets minimum lot size at twenty acres, a basic regulatory control that has been blissfully ignored by local government officials. Many of the fields now undergoing conversion are important components of the local economy that still counts on specialty hay production as an export commodity, primarily for the overseas market in Japan. This trend toward embracing nonfarm development not only will affect the land itself, but also will impact nearly all other elements of the agricultural infrastructure currently in place, representing a major investment in time, energy, and capital. Several irrigation companies and canal delivery systems have been installed over a period of more than a century, ultimately including the federally subsidized Kittitas Reclamation District, completed during the first decades of the twentieth century, which effectively doubled the irrigated land area to its current total of more than 85,000 acres.

Ellensburg is the county seat, a small college town with all the simmering potential of a New West capital city. Its geographic situation is along an ecotone between ponderosa pine forest and semiarid shrub-steppe, and the scenic mountain and desert surroundings hold an almost embarrassing abundance of all-seasons recreational opportunities on public land. Supported now for more than a century by the largess of an irrigated agricultural economy, the town and its environs

FIGURE 3.29
Political cartoon by Jon R. Herman from the Ellensburg *Daily Record.*

have inexorably carved the first turn toward a more amenity-driven cultural ecology. There is a budding arts community, a newly remodeled public library, and out in the vanishing countryside, plenty of privately held lands for large-lot housing developments. Downtown lately has been going through some growth pangs. The compact grid of streets that make up the central business district currently exhibits a high vacancy rate for storefronts that have been abandoned by more conventional retail establishments. But this is a transition period. An eerie quiet simply translates into the calm before the storm, as it is only a matter of time before entrepreneurs with investment savvy find this place. All they need to do is follow the growing number of new residents that have relocated here.

Initially occupied by a dispersed settlement pattern of cattle ranches specializing in beef production, the valley soon took advantage of its location as a second-tier vonThünen dairy zone centered on the growing urban region of Puget Sound, and by the 1930s more than 100 dairies earmarked the Kittitas as a producer of blue-ribbon butter for the trans-Cascadian market. While the dairies have every one disappeared, local farmers have latched on to a cash cow of a different sort. Because it is situated at an elevation of over 1,500 feet above sea level and at a latitudinal position astride the 47th parallel, the Kittitas Valley experiences the cool summers and windy conditions that make it ideal for cultivating timothy, the high-quality forage that fetches strong market prices from Asian buyers. This lucrative hay trade may soon become adversely impacted by land conversions now well underway. As manifested by the sharp increase in the number of building permits being issued for rural dwellings, we are witnessing the break-up of many larger parcels and the creation of a horse lover's suburbia. Retirees along with second-home buyers coming over the mountains from Puget Sound intent on establishing their place in the wide open spaces are being joined by an ever-increasing number of commuters who so far seem willing to make the two-hour drive to the Seattle metropolitan area.

One of the more contentious land use issues to arise in recent memory concerns several proposals to develop large-scale "wind farms" for the commercial generation of electrical energy. Early in 2005, following a series of public hearings by the county Planning Commission, the Board of Commissioners voted to approve one windfarm situated on a barren hillside some distance east of Ellensburg, but denied the application for another that was slated to be placed just north of town in a more densely settled mosaic of farms, ranches, and residential "view lots." Controversy centered on the proximity of the massive turbines to a number of existing dwellings as well as an even greater number of developable properties in the vicinity that were purchased as either a retirement parcel or for residential market speculation. Opposition to the energy projects stemming from a perceived loss in value of these properties caused by siting a wind farm next door is a classic case of NIMBY ("Not in My Backyard").

The so-called upper county is in the midst of undergoing profound change, as a major destination resort breaks ground and implements its master plan. Suncadia is a master-planned golf and residential complex that was pushed through the approval process as a test case for the state's new destination resort land use category, allowing preferential treatment within the overall mandates of the Growth Management Act. The resort's plan to develop fifty-four holes is an ambitious ploy to capture a major share of the golf market for the Puget Sound metropolitan area, whose residents often look to the other side of the mountains for their recreational pursuits, partly because of the low population density and abundant public lands, and partly because there will be less chance for the cloudy skies and rain that so often dampens the western side of the mountains. Associated with the extensive golfing opportunities at Suncadia will be a range of residential housing and time-share condominium choices. Most of the prime lots have already sold out and are now listed on the secondary brokerage market, even before being improved as homesites. Developments at Suncadia, when projected build-out is complete, will result in more than two billion dollars of assessed value, effectively doubling the county's current total assessed value for structural improvements. Then, of course, there is the near-hysterical proliferation of land divisions on surrounding private land holdings, with ever-smaller parcels being offered for sale at inflated prices. In the immediate area of the resort, the real estate speculation game has caught on like the proverbial wildfires that sometimes make a run through these dry woods during late summer and fall. For-sale signs on formerly idle parcels along the edge of Lake Cle Elum, especially, have sprouted up recently in hopes of riding on the coattails of the obvious interest in the nearby resort. The three existing communities in the immediate vicinity are also caught in the crosshairs of imminent change brought about by the process of a major destination resort being created in their midst.

Despite what developers would lead us to believe, the resort's master plan is not being drawn upon a blank slate. Upper Kittitas County was already a settled landscape and is the setting for the former coal mining towns of Roslyn, Ronald, and Cle Elum, historically associated with the Northern Pacific, the first railroad to breach the high Cascade divide. Cle Elum, the larger of the three towns, is a former railroad and coal-loading facility whose downtown main street has come back from its deathbed in hopes of cashing in on resort-related business and the new customers that Suncadia will provide. Up the hill lie Roslyn and Ronald, former coal-mining towns once associated with the Northern Pacific Railway. Diminutive Ronald, whose commercial district consists of a bar and a general store, probably stands to benefit from its location nearest the vast public recreation lands of the Wenatchee National Forest. Roslyn, larger and infinitely more quaint, received its initial brush with New West notoriety when it was chosen to be the outdoor set for the fictional town of Cicely, Alaska, on the popular television series *Northern Exposure*. The national attention and tourism that emerged from that starring role is a classic case of artificiality transforming reality in the representation of place (Hanna 1996). In this particular situation, the irony is that Roslyn was already an intensely interesting place in its own right, both visually and historically. Partly as a result of its media-induced fifteen minutes of fame, many of the town's nineteenth- and early-twentieth-century wood frame vernacular dwellings have been purchased at inflated prices and spruced up by urbanites needing a weekend retreat in the mountains. Having been attracted to old and decrepit in the first place, many of these newly arrived homeowners would like to freeze-frame the town just the way it is and are not looking forward to the changes that the adjacent Suncadia is bound to bring.

Washington's Growth Potential

Among other locations in the only partly aptly named Evergreen State that may encounter a spurt of growth associated with New West lifestyles are several towns along the eastern slopes of the Cascades. Similar in geography and environment to Kittitas County, these places show a marked decrease in rainfall with distance from the Cascade crest, and thus have the sunshine and dry weather that western Washingtonians crave. Premier among them is Chelan, located at one end of the

deep fiord-like, squiggly shaped lake by the same name carved out by earlier gla-
ciers. This area was formerly renowned for fruit production, but the seeds of
Chelan's transformation have been there all along. It is a long drive from the Seattle conurbation—too long for the daily commute—but Lake Chelan is nevertheless a popular destination, and the beauty of this area has long induced a resort
atmosphere. Second homes and vacation cabins have been part of the scene here
for years, but lately there has been a substantial increase in permanently occupied
dwellings, as more and more people withdraw from the urban bustle across the
mountains. Private access to the waterfront commands a high price, especially
considering that nearly all of the land along the upper reaches of the lake is within
national forest ownership. One response to such limited land availability has been
a recent new development pattern entailing the tearing out of orchards on hillsides to create residential view lots.

North of Chelan is another glacial valley, but this one, the Methow, is not
nearly so full of water, save for a small river beloved of the fly-fishing crowd, and
whose flow has been the subject of recent litigation over irrigation withdrawals
damaging these fisheries. The main town in the Methow is Winthrop, described
by one regional outdoor writer as a "Western-kitsch town that began its 'civilized'
life as a trading outpost for trappers and miners, then reverted largely into a
mecca for polar-fleece-clad hikers, skiers, mountain bikers, anglers, and campers"
(Judd 2003, 111). As if the false-fronted Old West buildings and wood plank sidewalks were not enough, the town now boasts an annual Rhythm & Blues Festival
that attracts national talent and is held outdoors during one weekend each summer (Kuhlken 2003). Here then, in one tiny community, are many of the attributes that are most pronounced in the New West paradigm. In this place we can see
historical settlement of the frontier and displacement of native populations, subsequent engagement with natural resource exploitation schemes targeting tangible goods for export and marketing in the world economy, and finally a shift
toward nonconsumptive appreciation of recreational amenities and landscape
scenery, with a dash of imported culture thrown in for good measure.

To the south of Chelan, tucked into the narrow bottomlands at the confluence
of Icicle Creek and the Wenatchee River, is the faux-Alpine municipality of Leavenworth. Formerly a lumber town along the mainline of the Great Northern railway where the tracks begin their steep ascent toward Stevens Pass, town officials
came up with a plan to reinvigorate the local economy after the mills lost steam.
Using the spurious architectural motif of a Bavarian village, Leavenworth has
transformed itself into a service-oriented destination for those tourists who have
grown accustomed to themed entertainment. By code, all commercial buildings
and signage must present a generic Swiss or German mountain-style appearance.
Even familiar retail franchises such as Safeway and McDonalds must modify their
own trademark look and adhere to the design guidelines of Leavenworth (T. Price
1997). Such posing goes a few steps beyond even the adamant creation of Santa

Fe's amalgamated design standards and calls into question the idea of locational authenticity and whether that really matters, after all.

Privately owned parcels in the vicinity of Leavenworth command top dollar, especially waterfront properties along the shores of popular Lake Wenatchee, where vacation homes have tightly hemmed in the northern shoreline frontage. Meanwhile, several narrow stream valleys that converge upon the town hold promise for future intensive developments. One recent land use proposal has been controversial and highly unusual. Plans have been drawn up by two University of Washington scientists for a high-tech laboratory to be buried deep inside a nearby mountain, which will be used for studying solar neutrinos and other astronomical problems in the physics of stellar bodies. While locals do not pretend to understand the specific research frontier operating here, they don't much like the idea, either (Partridge 2004). But this sort of thing, so understated and unexpected, is emblematic of the land use issues that will continue to face communities across the New West.

And so we have arrived at the eleventh hour on our clockface sweep across the eleven western states. We have noted growth trends that are reshaping both urban and rural areas alike, and have provided examples of typical development patterns that are appearing as new forms on the landscape, and which help to define the regional identity of the New West. We have seen how growth has overwhelmed some locations, and appears to have bypassed others. Our survey has touched on places that never saw it coming along with places that very well should have. A few rural counties would seem to have emerged from the nineteenth century directly into the twenty-first, skipping past a hundred years of what has constituted elsewhere a more or less organic pace of historical development. We have seen how small towns have become the new darlings of the region, as well they ought to be, and a select group of these, illustrated in figure 3.30, may be referred to as the capital cities of the New West.

Some of these places, such as Santa Fe and Prescott, have been at center stage before, or have been in the forefront of economic surges for some time and are now simply witnessing a contemporary renewal of energies. Others, such as Bend or St. George, have arrived more suddenly. As residential use subdivides and converts more and more traditional resource lands, and the alchemy of commercial expansion transforms historical and unique landscapes into an identical series of homogeneous consumer theme parks filled with national corporate franchises, we might well ask: What has been the response on the part of state and local governments? Whither planning in the New West? In a region that has undergone such a colonial history, you might think that people would jump at the chance to set their own course. But the story is never that simple or easy to tell. The next chapter looks at the range of response mechanisms available as the various states, their towns and cities, and their rural counties wrestle with the dilemmas inherent in managing growth.

FIGURE 3.30
Principal cities of the New West. *Map by Ian Gray, CWU graduate program in resource management.*

REFERENCES

Albrecht, Don. Recreational and Tourism Development vs. the Decline of Agriculture in Southern Utah. In *Small Town and Rural Economic Development*, edited by Peter Schaeffer and Scott Loveridge, pp. 107–113. Westport, Conn.: Praeger, 2000.

American Electronics Association (AEA). Boise Metro Area is Nation's Second Fastest Growing Small Cybercity. 2000. <www.aeanet.org/PressRoom/idmk_cc_boise.asp>. [accessed 15 July 2004]

Amundson, Michael. Yellowcake to Singletrack: Culture, Community, and Identity in Moab, Utah. In *Imagining the Big Open: Nature, Identity, and Play in the New West*, edited by Liza Nicholas, Elaine Bapis, and Thomas Harvey, pp. 151–162. Salt Lake City: University of Utah Press, 2004.

Barth, Gunther. *Instant Cities: Urbanization and the Rise of San Francisco and Denver.* Albuquerque: University of New Mexico Press, 1988.

Baxter Meadows. Baxter Meadows Development. 2004. <www.baxtermeadows.com>. [accessed 1 November 2004]

Bear Mountain Lodge. <http://www.bearmountainlodge.com>. [accessed October 2004]

Benfield, F. Kaid, Jutka Terris, and Nancy Vorsanger. *Solving Sprawl: Models of Smart Growth in Communities across America.* New York: Natural Resources Defense Council, 2001.

Berger, Alan. *Reclaiming the American West.* New York: Princeton Architectural Press, 2002.

Blakely, Edward, and Mary Snyder. *Fortress America: Gated Communities in the United States.* Washington, D.C.: Brookings Institution Press, 1997.

Boag, Peter. Mountain, Plain, Desert, River: The Snake River Region as a Western Crossroads. In *Many Wests: Place, Culture, and Regional Identity*, edited by David M. Wrobel and Michael C. Steiner, pp. 175–203. Lawrence: University Press of Kansas, 1997.

Boone, Rebecca. The Rich and Famous Are Taking a Toll on Small Idaho Town. *Seattle Times*, October 20, 2002, p. B4.

Booth, Douglas. *Searching for Paradise: Economic Development and Environmental Change in the Mountain West.* Lanham, Md.: Rowman & Littlefield, 2002.

Brosnan, Kathleen B. *Uniting Mountain and Plain: Cities, Law, and Environmental Change along the Front Range.* Albuquerque: University of New Mexico Press, 2002.

Brown, Ralph. A Southwestern Oasis: The Roswell Region, New Mexico. *Geographical Review* 26 (1936):610–619.

Buffalo, Wyoming Chamber of Commerce. 2004. <www.buffalowyo.com>. [accessed 10 July 2004]

Choate, Alan. Sonju Industrial Earns Long-Term Boeing Contracts. *Daily Inter Lake,* April 25, 2004. <www.dailyinterlake.com>. [accessed 12 July 2004]

Church, Lisa. Luxury Looms Over Moab. *High Country News* 33, no. 6 (March 26, 2001).

———. Wrecking Homes for Open Space: Philanthropist Jennifer Spears. *High Country News* 36, no. 7 (April 12, 2004).

Compas, Eric D. Land Ownership Changes on the Upper Yellowstone River Valley, Montana: A Geographic Analysis. Unpublished master's thesis, University of Missouri, 2001.

Concrete Log Systems. News. 2004. <www.concretelogs.com/news.htm>. [accessed 19 July 2004]

Consensus Planning. Rathdrum Prairie Implementation Project. 2004. <www.consensusplanning.com>. [accessed 17 July 2004]

Crawford, Stanley. *Mayordomo: Chronicle of an Acequia in Northern New Mexico.* Albuquerque: University of New Mexico Press, 1988.

Culver, Lawrence. From "Last of the Old West" to First of the New West: Tourism and Transformation in Jackson Hole, Wyoming. In *Imagining the Big Open: Nature, Identity, and Play in the New West,* edited by Liza Nicholas, Elaine Bapis, and Thomas Harvey, pp. 163–180. Salt Lake City: University of Utah Press, 2004.

Davis, Mike. House of Cards: Las Vegas: Too Many People in the Wrong Place, Celebrating Waste as a Way of Life. *Sierra* 80, no. 6 (1995):36–43.

Decker, Peter. *Old Fences, New Neighbors.* Tucson: University of Arizona Press, 1998.

Duane, Timothy P. *Shaping the Sierra: Nature, Culture, and Conflict in the Changing West.* Berkeley: University of California Press, 1999.

Duerksen, Christopher J., and James van Hemert. *True West: Authentic Development Patterns for Small Towns and Rural Areas.* Washington, D.C.: Planners Press, 2003.

Dusman, Dick, and Judy Dusman. Homes and Land of Prescott, Arizona and Surrounding Area 8, no. 11 (Spring 2003):62.

Feller, Wende. Urban Impostures: How Two Neighborhoods Reframed Suburban Sprawl as a New Urbanist Paradise without Changing a Thing. In *Suburban Sprawl: Culture, Theory, and Politics,* edited by Matthew J. Lindstrom and Hugh Bartling, pp. 49–63. Lanham, Md.: Rowman & Littlefield, 2003.

Fiege, Mark *Irrigated Eden: The Making of an Agricultural Landscape in the American West.* Seattle: University of Washington Press, 1999.

Fitzsimmons, Jill. Faux Log Homes. *Missoulan,* July 2, 2004. <missoulan.com/articles/2004/07/02/business/bus01.txt>. [accessed 19 November 2004]

Flores, Dan L. Agriculture, Mountain Ecology, and the Land Ethic: Phases of the Environmental History of Utah. In *Working the Range: Essays on the History of Western*

Land Management and the Environment, edited by John R. Wunder, pp. 157–186. Westport, Conn.: Greenwood Press, 1985.

Folkart, Burt. Frontier Town Makes Way for New Pioneers. *The Los Angeles Times,* June 6, 1994, p. A5.

Folk of the Wood. Gibson Acoustic Guitars. 2004. <www.folkofthewood.com/page1946htm>. [accessed 10 August 2004]

Ford, Kristina. *Planning Small Town America.* Chicago: American Planning Association, 1990.

Francaviglia, R. *The Mormon Landscape: Existence, Creation, and Perception of a Unique Image of the American West.* New York: AMS Press, 1978.

Fuguitt, Glenn, David Brown, and Calvin Beale. *Rural and Small Town America.* New York: Russell Sage Foundation, 1989.

Fulton, William. *Guide to California Planning.* Point Arena: Solano Press, 1991.

Gibson Montana. Gibson Montana Factory Tour. 2004. <http://montana.gibson.com>. [accessed 10 July 2004]

Gober, Patricia. Beyond the Suburbs: Urban Growth in Metropolitan Phoenix, 1960 to 2040. Paper presented at the annual meeting of the Association of American Geographers, New Orleans, 2003.

Gordon, Greg. Wyoming Says "No" to More Wells. *The Denver Post,* July 5, 2004.

Hanna, Stephen P. Is It Roslyn or Is It Cicely? Representation and the Ambiguity of Place. *Urban Geography* 17 (1996):633–649.

Hayden, Dolores. *A Field Guide to Sprawl.* New York: W.W. Norton & Company, 2004.

Heenan, David A. *The New Corporate Frontier: The Big Move to Small Town, U.S.A.* New York: McGraw-Hill, 1991.

Hostetler, Jeff. Yellowstone Drifter. 2004. <www.outsidebozeman.com/magazine>.

Howard, Joseph K. The Coeur d'Alene: Vulnerable Valley. In *Rocky Mountain Cities,* edited by Ray West Jr., pp. 55–77. New York: W.W. Norton & Company, 1949.

Howe, Jim, Ed McMahon, and Luther Propst. *Balancing Nature and Commerce in Gateway Communities.* Washington, D.C.: Island Press, 1997.

Humboldt State University. The Humboldt Experience. 2005. <www.humboldt.edu/~humboldt/experience/>.

Hurley, Patrick, and Peter Walker. Whose Vision? Conspiracy Theory and Land-use Planning in Nevada County, California. *Environment and Planning A* 36 (2004):1529–1547.

Idaho Smart Growth. Regional News. 2003. <www.idahosmartgrowth.org/favorite.htm>. [accessed 10 January 2004]

Inman, Katherine, Donald McLeod, and Dale Menkhaus. Rural Land Use and Sales Preferences in a Wyoming County. *Land Economics* 78, no. 1 (2002):72–87.

Jackson, Devon. Driven by Nature. *Southwest Art* 34, no. 1 (2004):88–91.

Jackson, Richard H. Mormon Perception and Settlement. *Annals of the Association of American Geographers* 68 (1978):317–34.

——. Mormon Wests: The Creation and Evolution of an American Region. In *Western Places, American Myths: How We Think About the West,* edited by Gary J. Hausladen, pp. 135–165. Reno: University of Nevada Press, 2003.

Jones, Randall A. Interview with Project Manager for Brooks Resources Corporation, March 25, 2005.

Judd, Ron. *Camping! Washington,* 2nd ed. Seattle: Sasquatch Books, 2003.

Kachina Springs. 2003. <www.splitrockinc.com/kachina.html> [accessed 15 July 2004]

Kemmis, Daniel. Imagining a Democratic West. *High Country News* 36, no. 7 (April 12, 2004):7–10.

Kuhlken, Robert. Louie Louie Land: Music Geography of the Pacific Northwest. In *The Sounds of People and Places: A Geography of American Music from Country to Classical and Blues to Bop,* 4th edition, edited by George Carney, pp. 277–312. Lanham, Md.: Rowman & Littlefield, 2003.

LaCense Montana. About the Ranch. 2004. <www.lacensemontana.com/ranch.html>. [accessed 11 July 2004]

Leach, Nicky. Enchanted Torrey. *Sunset* 205, no. 1 (July 2000):40.

Leaver, Jennifer J. Where Old West Meets New West: Confronting Conservation, Conflict and Change on Utah's Last Frontier. Unpublished master's thesis, Oregon State University, 2001.

Levitt, James N., and John R. Pitkin. Internet Use in a High-Growth, Amenity-Rich Region. In *Conservation in the Internet Age,* edited by James N. Levitt, pp. 99–122. Washington, D.C.: Island Press, 2002.

Loftus, Bill. *Idaho Handbook,* 2nd ed. Chico, Calif.: Moon Publications, 1994.

Logan, Michael. *Fighting Sprawl and City Hall: Resistance to Urban Growth in the Southwest.* Tucson: University of Arizona Press, 1995.

Logcrafters. 2004. <www.logcrafters.com>. [accessed 20 July 2004]

MacGregor, Carol L. The Cultural Life of Boise, Idaho, 1950–2000. In *The American West in 2000: Essays in Honor of Gerald D. Nash,* edited by Richard W. Etulain and Ferenc M. Szasz, pp. 85–104. Albuquerque: University of New Mexico Press, 2003.

Macinko, George. The Columbia Basin Project: Expectations, Realizations, Implications. *Geographical Review* 53(1963):185–199.

Mather, Christine, and Sharon Woods. *Santa Fe Style.* New York: Rizzoli, 1986.

Matthews, Anne. *Where the Buffalo Roam: Restoring America's Great Plains,* 2nd ed. Chicago: University of Chicago Press, 2002.

McKenzie, Evan. *Privatopia: Homeowner Associations and the Rise of Residential Private Government.* New Haven: Yale University Press, 1994.

McKinnon, Shaun, and Mary Jo Pitzl. Proposed 60,000-home Development under Fire in Pinal County. *The Arizona Republic,* January 29, 2004.

Meinig, D. The Mormon Culture Region: Strategies and Patterns in the Geography of the American West, 1847–1964. *Annals of the Association of American Geographers* 55 (1965):191–220.

———. Spokane and the Inland Empire: Historical Geographic Systems and a Sense of Place. In *Spokane and the Inland Empire: An Interior Pacific Northwest Anthology,* edited by David H. Stratton, pp. 1–31. Pullman: Washington State University Press, 1991.

Meloy, Ellen. *The Last Cheater's Waltz: Beauty and Violence in the Desert Southwest.* New York: Henry Holt, 1999.

———. *The Anthropology of Turquoise: Meditations on Landscape, Art, and Spirit.* New York: Pantheon Books, 2002.

Morgan, Dale. Salt Lake City: City of the Saints. In *Rocky Mountain Cities,* edited by Ray West Jr., pp. 179–207. New York: W.W. Norton & Company, 1949.

Morrissey, Katherine G. *Mental Territories: Mapping the Inland Empire.* Ithaca: Cornell University Press, 1997.

Nava Adé Hoa. Nava Adé Homeowners Association. 2004. <www.navaade.org>. [accessed 15 July 2004]

Nelson, Robert. Big Bad Developer. *Phoenix New Times,* January 1, 2004.

Nichols, John. *The Milagro Beanfield War.* New York: Holt, Rinehart and Winston, 1974.

Parsons, James. Quartzsite, Arizona: A Woodstock for RV'ers." *Focus* 42, no. 3 (1992):1–3.

Partridge, Michelle. Science Plan Divides Leavenworth. *Ellensburg Daily Record,* May 10, 2004, pp. A1, 8.

Penner, Andrew. Old Works Golf Course: Vintage Nicklaus in Historic Anaconda. 2004. <www.golf-gear-review.com/article-display/633.html>. [accessed 15 July 2004]

Pickering, James. *This Blue Hollow: Estes Park, the Early Years, 1859–1915.* Boulder: University Press of Colorado, 1999.

Pincetl, Stephanie S. *Transforming California: A Political History of Land Use and Development.* Baltimore: Johns Hopkins University Press, 1999.

Popper, F. J., and D. E. Popper. Great Plains: Checkered Past, Hopeful Future. *Forum for Applied Research & Public Policy* 9, no. 4 (1994):89–100.

Prescott Valley Chamber of Commerce. *Prescott Valley, Arizona Village Profile.* Prescott
Valley, AZ: Prescott Valley Chamber of Commerce, 2003.

Price, Ted. *Miracle Town: Creating America's Bavarian Village in Leavenworth, Washington.*
Vancouver, Wash.: Price & Rodgers, 1997.

Price, V. B. *Albuquerque: A City at the End of the World.* Albuquerque: University of New
Mexico Press, 2003.

Protas, Josh. The Straw That Broke the Camel's Back: Preservation of an Urban Mountain
Landscape. In *Suburban Sprawl: Culture, Theory, and Politics,* edited by Matthew J.
Lindstrom and Hugh Bartling, pp. 177–203. Lanham, Md.: Rowman & Littlefield, 2003.

Quinn, Beth. Medford Airport Growing into Southern Oregon Hub. *The Sunday
Oregonian,* January 23, 2005, p. A13.

Redlands Mesa. Redlands Mesa Homes. 2005. <www.redlandsmesa.com>. [accessed 15
August 2005]

Riebsame, William. Subdividing the Rockies: Ranchland Conversion in the New West. In
Under the Blade: The Conversion of Agricultural Landscapes, edited by Richard K. Olson
and Thomas A. Lyson, pp. 398–409. Boulder, Colo.: Westview Press, 1999.

Ringholz, Raye. *Little Town Blues: Voices from the Changing West.* Salt Lake City: Peregrine
Smith Books, 1992.

———. *Paradise Paved: The Challenge of Growth in the New West.* Salt Lake City:
University of Utah Press, 1996.

Rohleder, Anna. Montana. 2000. *Forbes Magazine* <www.forbes.com/2000/12/13/
ppmontana.html>. [accessed 30 June 2004]

Romme, William. Creating Pseudo-Rural Landscapes in the Mountain West. In *Placing
Nature: Culture and Landscape Ecology,* edited by Joan Nassauer, pp. 140–161.
Washington, D.C.: Island Press, 1997.

Rothman, Hal K. *Devil's Bargains: Tourism in the Twentieth-Century American West.*
Lawrence: University Press of Kansas, 1998.

———. Tourism as Colonial Economy: Power and Place in Western Tourism. In *Power
and Place in the North American West,* edited by Richard White and John Findlay, pp.
177–203. Seattle: University of Washington Press, 1999.

———. *Neon Metropolis: How Las Vegas Started the Twenty-first Century.* New York:
Routledge, 2002.

Rothman, Hal K., and Mike Davis, eds. *The Grit Beneath the Glitter: Tales from the Real
Las Vegas.* Berkeley: University of California Press, 2002.

Rudzitis, Gundars, and Rosemary Streatfeild. The Importance of Amenities and Attitudes:
A Washington Example. *Journal of Environmental Systems* 22 (1993): 269–277.

Scharff, Virginia. *Twenty Thousand Roads: Women, Movement, and the West.* Berkeley: University of California Press, 2003.

Schmitz, Adrienne. *The New Shape of Suburbia: Trends in Residential Development.* Washington, D.C.: Urban Land Institute, 2003.

Schneider, Wolf. My World: A Visit with Expressionist Marshall Noice in Downtown Kalispell, MT. *Southwest Art* 34, no. 2 (2004):120–121.

Seely, Kimberly. Jackson Hole. *Town and Country Travel* (Spring 2004):59–60.

Smutny, Gayla. Legislative Support for Growth Management in the Rocky Mountains: An Exploration of Attitudes in Idaho. *Journal of the American Planning Association* 64 (1998):311–323.

Snoqualmie Ridge. Snoqualmie Ridge Master Planned Community. 2004. <www.sridge.com>.

Soja, Edward. Inside Exopolis: Scenes from Orange County. In *Variations on a Theme Park: The New American City and the End of Public Space,* edited by Michael Sorkin, pp. 94–122. New York: The Noonday Press, 1992.

Spencer, J. E. House Types of Southern Utah. *Geographical Review* 35 (1945):444–457.

Starrs, Paul F. *Let the Cowboy Ride: Cattle Ranching in the American West.* Baltimore: Johns Hopkins University Press, 1998.

Starrs, Paul, and John B. Wright. Great Basin Growth and the Withering of California's Pacific Idyll. *Geographical Review* 85 (1995):417–435.

Stein, Joel. The Strip is Back. *Time* 164, no. 4 (July 26, 2004):22–34.

Steiner, Frederick, Laurel McSherry, Dean Brennan, Mark Soden, Joe Yarchin, Douglas Green, James McCarthy, Catherine Spellman, John Jennings, and Kirsten Barr. Concepts for Alternative Suburban Planning in the Northern Phoenix Area. *Journal of the American Planning Association* 65 (1999):207–222.

Taylor, Kevin. Rathdrum Prairie Is Disappearing Fast. Spokane *Spokesman-Review,* June 21, 2004.

Theobald, David. M. Fragmentation by Inholdings and Exurban Development. In *Forest Fragmentation in the Southern Rocky Mountains,* edited by Richard L. Knight, Frederick W. Smith, Steven W. Buskirk, William H. Romme, and William L. Baker, pp. 155–174. Boulder: University Press of Colorado, 2000.

Timberline Furniture. Timberline Group, Log Furniture. 2004. <www.timberlinefurniture.com>.

Trahant, Mark. New West Grows, But Same Old Questions Persist. *Seattle Times.* Thursday, June 1, 2000, p. A2 <archives.seattletimes.nwsource.com>. [accessed 15 July 2004]

Underwood, Kathleen. *Town Building on the Colorado Frontier*. Albuquerque: University of New Mexico Press, 1987.

United States Bureau of the Census. Census of Population. 2000. <www.census.gov/>. [accessed 10 January 2005]

United States Geological Survey (USGS). Carbon Dioxide and Helium Discharge from Mammoth Mountain. United States Geological Survey, Long Valley Observatory. 2005. <lvo.wr.usgs.gov/CO2.html>. [accessed 4 January 2005]

Vincent, Roger. Major Resort Hotel to Rise in Mammoth Lakes. *Los Angeles Times,* January 6, 2005, Business Section. <losangelestimes.com>. [accessed 14 January 2004]

Wagner, Angie. West Sees Mild Start to Wildfire Season. *Daily Record* (Ellensburg, Washington), July 21, 2004, p. A1.

Wasatch Front Regional Council. Programs and Products. 2004. <www.wfrc.org/programs/programs.html>. [accessed 1 June 2004]

Weber, Carolyn. Flying High: A Former Airport Site Takes Off as a First-class New Urbanist Development. *Builder,* May 2003.

Weir, Bill. *Arizona Traveler's Handbook,* 3rd ed. Chico, Calif.: Moon Publications, 1990.

Wells, Merle. *Boise: An Illustrated History.* Woodland Hills, Calif.: Windsor Publications, 1982.

Whispering Canyon. Whispering Canyon. 2003. <www.whisperingcanyonaz.com/location.html>. [accessed 15 July 2004]

Wilson, Chris. *The Myth of Santa Fe: Creating a Modern Regional Tradition.* Albuquerque: University of New Mexico Press, 1997.

Wilson, Chris. *The Myth of Santa Fe: Creating a Modern Regional Tradition.* Albuquerque: University of New Mexico Press, 1997.

Wiltsie, Meredith, and William Wyckoff. Reinventing Red Lodge: The Making of a New Western Landscape, 1884–2000. In *Imagining the Big Open: Nature, Identity, and Play in the New West,* edited by Liza Nicholas, Elaine Bapis, and Thomas Harvey, pp. 131–150. Salt Lake City: University of Utah Press, 2003.

Wolf, Kate. Old Jerome, a song from the album *The Wind Blows Wild.* Montgomery, Ala.: Rhino Label, 1983.

Wyckoff, William. Postindustrial Butte. *Geographical Review* 85 (1995):478–496.

———. *Creating Colorado: The Making of a Western American Landscape, 1860–1940.* New Haven: Yale University Press, 1999.

Zelenka, William. Interview with Bill Zelenka, Crook County Planning Director, July 9, 2003.

Zonn, Leo. Tusayan, the Traveler, and the IMAX Theatre: An Introduction to Place Images in Media. In *Place Images in Media: Portrayal, Experience, and Meaning,* edited by Leo Zonn, pp. 1–5. Lanham, Md.: Rowman & Littlefield, 1990.

4

Convergent Problems, Divergent Solutions

Across the West we have observed a set of common land use issues related to community growth and rural land use change. Strong differences of opinion exist with regard to these issues, and to the related role of land use planning and growth management as a means for resolving them. One side of the growth issue is strongly concerned about maintaining the qualities and values of small town and rural lifestyles, protecting the scenic qualities and the health and natural beauty of the environment, and limiting encroachment and partitioning that might threaten the continuation of traditional land uses. A second prevailing land use theme seeks to constrain limits on free enterprise in the land market, to protect property values from restrictive government planning programs, to encourage public investments for improving access and infrastructure and promoting the growth of the local economy to encourage broader tax base support for community services. This description represents a very simplified version of two sides of the growth issue; they appear incompatible, but one set is not necessarily exclusive of the other. While advocates of both sides express strongly partisan views, there is common ground, and this is the pragmatic vision of progress in the New West: to achieve continued economic progress and prosperity, to protect land rights, and to protect the existence of traditional land uses and a cultural and natural resource heritage that uniquely characterizes the West.

To many people, growth represents progress, but others are concerned with the changes it brings to community character and the partitioning of nearby resource lands. The benefits include increased land values, enhanced economic development opportunities, employment, commercial services, public services, and, in general, greater financial stability for the community. Others observe that community growth, especially rapid, unplanned growth, may result in adverse consequences to established community character and livability, and may lead to larger government, the reallocation of water rights, partitioning of crop and range lands, higher property and service taxes, and, importantly, reduced control of traditional community decision making to outside investors and development corporations.

In reality, most fast-growth communities experience many of the benefits and consequences related to land use changes. Commonly, the increased demand for large buildable residential lots results in the conversion of agricultural, range, or timber lands. Water supplies throughout the West are naturally limited, and increased demand for surface and groundwater may result in conflicts among uses for fish and wildlife, agricultural irrigation, and urban and recreation uses. Large-scale, low-density land developments may compromise seasonal wildlife and waterfowl migrations and constrain traditional hunting and fishing access. Road building, site clearing, and home construction often diminish scenic views and the aesthetics of natural landscapes. Commercial expansion and shopping malls developed to satisfy urban amenity demands result in traffic congestion and the use of former resource lands and open spaces as paved parking surfaces. Communities must also consider the financial impacts related to the costs and benefits of growth. Tax bases are broadened by growth but care must be used to ensure that they balance the capital improvement budgets to construct and maintain schools, and streets, and to expand and extend water supply services, waste water treatment, and more.

Institutional responses to these issues vary with an individual community vision as interpreted by representative local government and within the land use planning laws and procedures of each state. However, the experience of communities across the West has shown that without a clearly stated community vision, reasonable planning goals and policies, and a rational approach to land use decision making, the consequences of growth may rapidly compromise the benefits.

Community planning goals commonly include two sets of objectives. The first set generally relates to growth management as a societal responsibility: to maintain quality of life, to protect health and safety, to promote governmental fiscal responsibility, and to sustain natural resource lands and protect scenic amenities. The intent of a second set is to protect property rights, to provide affordable and adequate housing, to provide expanded public facilities to accommodate new residents, to facilitate the orderly geographic expansion of a range of land uses, and to efficiently provide services and accommodate the growth of the local economy according to a commonly held vision.

At the outset, these two sets of objectives may appear incompatible. The records of local land use hearings chronicle heated debates over the absolute right of landowners, not government, to make free enterprise decisions about the location, type, density, and design of land uses. On the other hand, those who support the right of representative government to develop rules for land use insist that growth and development must reflect the priorities of the community not just the individual.

Each community must resolve this apparent enigma as it moves toward a pragmatic vision of land use in the West: to balance property rights with government responsibilities, to achieve managed growth according to clearly defined objectives, to promote economic development and enterprise consistent with community values, and to sustain the cultural and natural resource heritage that uniquely characterizes the geography of the community and the region.

While there are common land use and resource issues that transcend state boundaries, there is no regionwide agreement on a model approach with which to achieve land use objectives. Land use planning law, local planning procedures, and growth management strategies vary from state to state and with each locality. The regionwide variation in planning law, structures, and procedures is observed to be the constitutional domain of individual states, delegated to local government as the right to community self-determination. Local plan development and approval by elected officials representing the community interest is inviolate, even where statewide planning goals and standards govern a broader comprehensive planning program.

The American Planning Association (APA), through its "Smart Growth" initiative, has offered a template for local land use planning in the West, but the program has been only variably successful at best. State legislatures and local governments have selectively adopted some of APA's growth management protocol, but there appears to be only mild enthusiasm for enactment of the total package, perhaps reflecting the region's extreme range of views concerning government's role in shaping the private use of land.

The American Planning Association's *Planning Communities for the 21st Century* (APA 2002) offers its professional members, local governments, and state legislatures model legislation and compelling rationale for land use planning as a growth management strategy. The model legislation is designed to establish the legal basis for state and local governments to enact more rigorous institutional growth management regulations and controls. The fact is, much of the local land use planning across the West is conducted under enabling legislation originally enacted in the 1920s, giving local governments the basic authority to plan and zone (APA 2002). This enabling legislation gives local governments broad agency to conduct planning activities in their local interest. Existing enabling legislation generally allows local governments to adopt comprehensive planning, growth management, and other innovative planning techniques to achieve community goals as long as they are rationally applied and there is a compelling community interest to be served.

Rapid, unexpected growth during the late 1980s and 1990s began to challenge the traditional land planning procedures and regulatory authority of local governments, prompting heated debates over "the community interest" to be served by greater institutional involvement and control of land use by comprehensive planning and growth management. One side of the issue advocates stronger growth management and resource lands protection to maintain livability and protection of scenic and resource lands; the other side questions the need for government intervention into the land market, advocates greater protection of private property rights, and demands government compensation for reductions in land values due to planning and zoning regulations. In many areas of the West, the strong difference of views concerning institutional land controls has required candidates for city and county commission seats to take "pro–land use planning" or "anti–land use planning" positions. Even those who favor a greater institutional role in land planning express indignation over the use of "out-of-town expert consultants" who draw up local comprehensive plans. Local control advocates express outright anger toward "activists" and national membership advocate groups who appear to inject their particular social theories and philosophies into state and local land use legislation.

As mentioned previously, efforts to reform or enact stronger land use planning and management legislation to help local communities to manage growth have been variably received. In Montana, Idaho, New Mexico, Nevada, Wyoming, and Utah there has been only limited acceptance of statewide growth management legislation beyond the original enabling provisions.

Rapid growth in western Montana has dramatically affected land use in the scenic valleys of the Rocky Mountains. Rural subdivisions and planned residential–recreation communities are common from Missoula County south into Ravalli County in the Bitterroot Valley. Livingston, the northern gateway to the Yellowstone country, has attracted residential subdivisions and commercial development related to outdoor adventure and recreation. Red Lodge, en route to the eastern Yellowstone gateway, offers a dramatic view of the Absaroka Range, and farms and ranches have been partitioned to make use of ridge top home sites offering spectacular vistas. Kalispell, Polson, Whitefish, and the natural terraces overlooking Flathead Lake have exemplary residential appeal due to scenic and recreational opportunities. Bozeman, a traditional, comfortable regional center and university town, now serves as the nucleus for growth in the greater Gallatin Basin. Traditional urban centers such as Great Falls, Billings, and Helena show important population increases, but the most dramatic residential growth is occurring in the adjacent rural locales where estate homes and golf course–related residential developments are being constructed on parcels carved out of existing farm and ranch lands.

The plains of eastern Montana, in contrast, show generally declining populations. The issue for rural development there is generally stated as, "How can we attract growth and diversify our local economy, sustain local employment, achieve community stability and maintain basic commercial and government services?"

Clearly, growth management and livability mean different things to Montanans, depending where they live.

A 2001 report by the American Planning Association's Smart Growth Coalition cited an opinion survey conducted by the Montana Realtors Association in which 49% of Montanans believed that government should do less to manage growth (45% believed government should do more). Montana traditionally favors a populist rather than an institutional approach to land use decisions, adhering to the concept that the individual property owner, rather than a professional planning staff, should control the use of private land (APA 2002). In 1999, the Montana legislature authorized local governments to adopt growth policies and to coordinate zoning, subdivision, and annexation applications in accordance with adopted policies. Growth management policies are optional, but if local governments adopt stronger policies, they are required to establish schedules for the review of subdivision plats assuring land developers a timely, reasonable, and consistent plan evaluation and permit process (APA 2002).

A good deal of discretionary control over land use decisions and site planning is authorized to groups of individual property owners and to homeowner associations under small district zoning and subdivision ordinances known as Special Zoning Districts. Pending appropriate health and subdivision review permits, an association of landowners may develop and submit their own community plans directly to county commissioners with regard to land use changes, land divisions, lot sizes, and roads and infrastructure improvements. Elected officials directly approve most land use actions whereas local planning officials are given little administrative discretion outside the enforcement of explicit regulations governing building permits, zoning, and subdivision actions.

With the exception of Missoula, where city and county planning is a combined activity, adjoining jurisdictions are not required to coordinate land use planning. Consequently, institutional planning is largely reactive in nature rather than proactive, comprehensive, or long term. Rapid growth is occurring throughout Missoula County, and an example of one such area is French Town, initially developed as a rural irrigated small farm and orchard tract in western Missoula County. The area is presently developing as a patchwork of low-density rural subdivisions within reasonable commuting distance of Missoula. The subdivisions have been individually approved under the Special Zoning District, but there is little in the way of a coordinated plan for the larger area. Particular land use issues include the need for utility services planning and distribution, water resource allocation, potential health problems resulting from groundwater and stream contamination, and costs related to the improvement and maintenance of county highway access to outlying subdivisions (Worley 2004).

Land planning with a transactional approach characterizes Idaho's growth management strategy (APA 2002). The Local Land Use Planning Act of 1975 was a response to particularly rapid growth in the Boise, Ketchum, and Coeur d' Alene areas. Loss of prime farmlands, water resource allocation problems, transportation systems planning, and deteriorating air quality are identified as particular issues consequent to rapid, unplanned growth. The Act authorizes local governments to revise and update comprehensive plans and to manage growth with contemporary regulatory means, including development impact fees, transfer of development density rights, performance agreements, and regional assessments of large-scale planned developments. In 2000, the state authorized voluntary mediation as an alternative to court proceedings as a means for resolving some types of land use disputes between private landowners and local governments.

Economic development planning for rural communities and resolving the resource and financial impacts of rural subdivisions, planned unit developments, and destination resorts are important issues in New Mexico. Impacts of rapid growth relate to local financing of capital improvements, cultural and scenic resource values, and, importantly, the use of limited water resources. A regional approach to land planning was adopted in 1967 and was revised in the mid 1990s, but planning still maintains a regional, cooperative, theme. Growth management has been implemented with development fees, and regional housing impact studies bring rural governments together to evaluate the costs and benefits of growth proposals. Most rapid growth has occurred along the Interstate 25 corridor in the middle Rio Grande Valley. South of Albuquerque, the development of large rural subdivisions such as Rio Rancho on farm and ranch lands has resulted in increased legal disputes over water rights and water rights purchases and transfers.

Nevada's growth in population has increased at five times the national average and includes the nation's fastest growing metropolitan area. Community growth is highly localized, however, as build-out is constrained in many areas by adjoining federal lands, totaling nearly 83% of the state. Since many of Nevada's growth-related land use problems occur at the private–public land interface, the State Land Use Planning Agency, within the Division of State Lands, provides technical planning assistance to rural local governments and represents state lands interests on a variety of priority issues. Examples of rural planning issues include local federal collaborative planning agreements for public lands access, source water agreements, abandoned mine reclamation, and wild land and urban interface planning (Nevada Division of State Lands [NDSL] 2004).

Nevada has had very good success translating quality of life and environmental sustainability into land use and environmental policy at the regional planning level. The Tahoe Regional Planning Compact and the Tahoe Regional Planning Agency were formed in 1985 to protect the natural scenic beauty of the Tahoe Basin and to preserve the unique water quality of Lake Tahoe. Special consideration was given to water quality issues by implementing strict sewage water treatment requirements, controlling surface runoff, establishing shoreline greenways and state parks, and limiting the location and amount of development.

The regional model was adopted in a slightly different form in 1999 to create the Southern Nevada Regional Planning Coalition to serve Clark County and the municipalities of North Las Vegas, Las Vegas, Henderson, and Boulder City. A similar regional planning association exists for local governments in the Carson City-Truckee Valley-Reno area (NDSL 2004).

Aside from the unique regional compacts and fine tuning to improve infrastructure planning and administrative issues, comprehensive community planning in Nevada is highly pragmatic and not designed to significantly constrain growth. Nevada is a strongly free-enterprise state, and the objective of most communities is to accommodate growth where it is reasonable to do so. The regional approach, however, allows for coordinated jurisdictional policy with which to address rapid housing and commercial construction and the associated issues related to the provision of water, sanitation, transportation, parks and recreation facilities, police and fire protection services, and water and air pollution control measures.

Wyoming is the nation's least populated state, but exceptional growth of commercial and residential development related to recreation and tourism has occurred in Teton County and the Jackson area. Casper has seen dramatic growth as a regional commercial and residential center. It boasts the Natrona International Airport and several newly developed high-value subdivisions surrounding a world-class golf course reclaimed from a former oil refinery site. Sheridan and the neighboring small towns of Storey and Big Horn on the eastern slopes of the Big Horn Mountains offer spectacular views of some of the West's most rugged scenery. Thirty-acre home sites pattern the ridge tops of partitioned livestock ranches and grain farms. A new PGA golf course at Big Horn has been constructed on several hundred acres of formerly irrigated cropland. The Powder Horn golf course and its associated residential subdivisions have dramatically increased the local population and shifted Sheridan's growth to the southwest where more croplands are now offered as home sites.

The conversion of farm and ranch land to rural residential sites is also problematic in the highly productive agricultural lands of the Niobrara Valley and in the vicinity of Cheyenne, Rawlins, and Laramie. Conservation of agricultural lands and the preservation of seasonal wildlife migration sites and cultural and scenic resources are important land use issues to the citizens of Wyoming, and regional advisory alliances of local governments have been formed to assist and support one another in the review of large-scale developments.

While local governments across the state welcome community growth, some have enacted prime agricultural land protection ordinances. Of special concern is the protection of the limited amount of private ranch and farmlands in the Jackson Hole region where most of Wyoming's population growth has occurred and where economic demand for land conversion is strongest. While a great deal of the Teton–Snake River Valley is presently federally owned and managed, the Jackson area is Wyoming's fastest growing commercial, residential, and recreational industry location.

Employment related to large-scale fossil fuel exploration in the 1980s rapidly declined and with it the economic mainstay of former boom town communities such as Rock Springs, Newcastle, and Gillette. Rural counties across the state lost population as land speculation for mineral and fuel reserves subsided and energy companies reduced exploration and development. However, a recent resurgence in energy demand has once again sparked a renewed exploration interest for methane gas as fossil fuel prices have dramatically increased in recent years (De-Clue 2004). The need for planning has once again presented itself, to address the runaway demand for new industrial and associated residential developments in some areas. Prices for livestock and grains have continued to fluctuate, leaving ranchers with large tracts of grazing land and little financial diversity. There is a strong economic temptation, in the proper geographic locations, to partition some of the best view sites into residential parcels.

Wyoming state statutes require cities and counties to adopt land use plans, but implementation ordinances are voluntary. Zoning, however, is the only statutorily sanctioned implementation technique. The evaluation and approval of large-scale rural, isolated residential and resort destination projects are technically and financially daunting to local governments and have been addressed by the statewide Land Use Planning Act administered by the Wyoming State Land Use Commission. Beyond its role of adopting state land use goals and a state land use plan, the commission is also responsible for rural "at-large" development evaluations where the location and scope of development may be of more than local significance and could possibly result in environmental or personal property damage (APA 2002).

Utah passed a Municipal and County Land Use Planning and Management Act in 1992 and a Quality Growth Act in 1999. Together, these measures address rapid-growth issues by allowing local governments to voluntarily address several community objectives through land use planning. The goals include the provision of safe and affordable housing, efficient land use through jurisdictionally coordinated infrastructure planning and annexation policy, and farmland conservation. The state also has developed a local government planning grant program to help effectuate these objectives (APA 2002).

Rapid growth in the Salt Lake Metro Area, Ogden, and the Bear River Valley prompted the immediate need for coordinated land planning in the form of agricultural land protection and annexation policies, and infrastructure planning and financing. State authorized agricultural districts may be formed to protect land and water from residential development, and local jurisdictions may adopt exclusive agricultural zoning. Park City's growth prior to and after the 2000 Winter

Olympics required growth management policies to brake runaway land speculation and a flood of annexation proposals. Open space acquisitions and infrastructure controls have been used in an attempt to maintain quality of life and scenic resource values. In addition to legislating growth management strategies, Park City is working to solve a problem common to Western communities: limited water supplies. With the assistance of the Army Corps of Engineers (COE), Park City has embarked on a mined-land reclamation project to remove arsenic from the Spiro Tunnel water source, offering a potentially important supplement to the area's limited water supply (COE 2004). On the western face of the Wasatch Front, the state's Envision Utah program has proposed a series of new transit-oriented town centers that will be much more compact and pedestrian-friendly than the existing urban fabric.

Along the I-15 corridor in southwest Utah's Virgin River Valley, rapid growth is occurring in the communities of St. George and Cedar City. Only recently have these areas begun to grow with an influx of former California residents seeking a low-stress environment with reasonable land and housing prices. The communities are small, the climate is moderate, and the scenic amenities are much greater than that of Las Vegas some three hours to the west. The spectacular recreation lands of Zion, Bryce Canyon, and the North Rim of the Grand Canyon are only a few hours distant. The immense potential for growth and land use change in this development corridor signals the need for community planning as well as a Department of Community Building and Development.

Arizona, Colorado, Oregon, Washington, and California are among the western states that prominently utilize land use legislation to manage growth for social and environmental purposes. Each state has its own set of specific reasons for authorizing land use legislation, and there is no consistent model for implementing growth management programs. However, these states go beyond the basic land use planning enabling legislation most states enacted during the 1920s. Each of these states has developed a strong mandate to manage growth for its own particular purposes.

"Livability" is high on the list of purposes for managing growth. As previously described, livability in the New West has two distinct meanings. One commonly accepted definition relates to quality of life aspirations: the preservation of natural scenic values and maintenance of traditional community characteristics as well as the assurance of high-quality education and health and safety services. Another view of livability is a bit more basic. For many areas in the rural West, livability relates to advancing the local economy, the opportunity for a diverse range of employment and wage levels, adequate and affordable housing, as well as the provision of a quality educational, health, and public services. Public opinion surveys arranged by state associations of realtors across the West indicate that economic stability and economic progress are overwhelmingly preferred to runaway land speculation. Affordable housing opportunities are just as important as high-value home sites, and employment opportunity means more than just providing services for the affluent (National Association of Realtors [NAR] 2004).

A second purpose is to manage the cost of growth. Efficiency in the provision of transportation, sewage, water, and other basic services generally translates to lower overall costs for infrastructure improvements, and logically to lower cost of government and property tax rates. Managing the cost of growth may include the assessment of impact fees, capital improvement costs, and development and facilities charges.

Protection and conservation of resource lands, including farmlands, commercial forest lands, and critical watersheds, is still another rationale for promoting growth management legislation. Coordination of land development policies between municipalities and county governments; annexation based on local referenda, urban growth boundaries, and infilling and urban land redevelopment; resource lands tax deferral; and right-to-farm legislation are all management techniques designed to reduce land speculation and land conversion. While each state approaches land management issues differently from their respective legislative standpoints, they are responding with a commonality of purpose.

The Phoenix Metropolitan area has recorded some of the fastest growth in the nation, adding more than one million residents during the decade of the 1990s. But the initial impetus for the review of rural developments began in the mid 1960s. As demand escalated for Sunbelt retirement property, land development schemes quickly responded. Some of the developments were legitimate real estate opportunities; some were not. The rapid growth of isolated, residential subdivisions became a state administrative concern on the basis of social and environmental impacts. In some cases, rural residential land sale schemes offered low-cost desert parcels without improvements or water supply, sometimes with little possibility of residential occupation. A Governor's Commission on Arizona's Environment was formed to evaluate rural and exurban land development, relative to compliance with environmental impact guidelines. Land uses requiring impact statements generally include mining operations, large-scale land clearing for agricultural developments, large-scale residential developments, and energy production facilities.

On a statewide basis, growth management became a focus of Arizona's community planning with the passage of two "Growing Smarter" Acts passed in 2000. Under this legislation, large cities and fast-growth communities must address the issue with voter-approved comprehensive plans that designate new growth zones and include incentives for infill and redevelopment districts. Communities also must evaluate the impacts of new growth on water resource supply and infrastructure financing. The state-authorized communities and counties to enact development impact fees provided they have a capital development plan to rationally guide the use of the funds (APA 2002).

Landowner protections accompanied the Arizona legislation, prohibiting local governments from designating private lands as open space, recreation, conservation, or exclusive agriculture zones without owner approval. Further, local decision making on rezoning requests, large subdivision applications, and the rationale for impact assessment fees is now open to greater citizen review.

Colorado experienced nearly three times the national average for population growth during the decade of the 1990s. Land use changes have been most apparent in communities offering Rocky Mountain scenic and recreation amenities, and on rural agricultural lands within commuting distance from Denver and other communities along the I-25 corridor. Colorado public opinion polls indicate that loss of open space, water marketing, the conversion of agricultural lands, and the spread of rural subdivisions across scenic landscapes are major concerns. However, voters have indicated that government controls on private property and land use must be rigorously rationalized (APA 2002).

Individual communities and counties across Colorado have shown the ability to innovate and have developed their own growth management strategies designed to address specific growth issues of local concern. The state legislature has followed up on local initiatives by addressing growth management with comprehensive statutes and by developing funding programs for local land use planning. Local growth management strategies include: spatial and temporal timing of infrastructure improvements and extensions, jurisdictional coordination for development planning, development impact fees, minimum rural lot size zoning, rural development and water rights coordination plans, open space purchases and transfers, and tax incentives for conservation easements (APA 2002).

California has more people and land area and perhaps more complex fast-growth–related land use and resource issues than the other western states. Indeed, a separate book could be written to cover California's issues alone (Fulton 1991). Statewide planning emerged as an unresolved issue during the early 1960s:

> Under Governor Pat Brown, the state Planning Office produced no statewide planning document, and the Governor's Commission on Metropolitan Problems restricted its scope of study to urban California. There was no comprehensive structure that could develop policy to address the urban and rural transformations that were taking place. Out of frustration with the state's inaction in the face of frenetic and seemingly unlimited subdivision construction, California Tomorrow, a nonprofit educational institution, in 1962 published a plan called California, Going, Going . . . , whose opening statement said that "although the dough looks good, the cake is not rising, and the reason is simple: nobody wrote out a recipe . . . in other words, there is in California a serious, progressively disastrous lack of coordinated land planning and development." The document advocated a sweeping reorganization of government to enhance more efficient central planning, based on a broad vision informed by scientific knowledge. (Pincetl 1999, 152–153)

Although this call for rational planning on a regional basis across the state was never answered, California law now requires that incorporated cities and counties develop a "comprehensive, long term plan for physical development." The locally developed and adopted General Plan must address a set of seven basic issues: Land Use, Circulation, Housing, Conservation, Open Space, Noise Assessment, and Safety. Each issue serves as a plan element (State of California 2004). In addition, California has a "Little NEPA" procedure, with environmental impact statement requirements for developments or reconstruction of certain agricultural, industrial, transportation, and large-scale urban development projects (Burchell, Listokin, Dolphin, Newton, and Foxley 1994).

The Land Use element addresses the location and intensity of a full range of land uses extending current land use into the future, based on statistical assessments, projections, and geographic rationale. The Circulation element lays out a capital improvements plan for transportation and public utilities scheduling. Housing addresses current stocks and future needs by housing types, location, and affordability. The Conservation element evaluates the need to balance conservation and development of undeveloped resource lands in light of the physical attributes of soils, water, and minerals. The preservation of undeveloped lands with unique natural features, outdoor recreation potential, and productive agricultural lands is addressed in the Open Space element. Noise is at the top of the list of most land use incompatibility complaints and forms a separate element of required comprehensive plans. Finally, important public safety concerns require site-specific location information on the risks of flooding, seismic and geological hazards, and wildfire.

In addition, where appropriate, local jurisdictions must incorporate specific state requirements of the California Coastal Act, Surface Mining and Reclamation Act, the Alquist-Priolo Special Studies Zone Act (earthquake hazards and hazardous materials), and the California Environmental Quality (CEQ) Act. The California Environmental Quality Act figures prominently in local growth management considerations. The local planning department is designated as the lead agency responsible for evaluating the "significance" of environmental impacts resulting from land use development projects. Major land use change resulting from development projects must be evaluated by an Environmental Impact Review; in essence a fact-finding study that considers the nature of the project, a discussion of the potential impacts to air, water, habitat, wildlife and other issues included in the CEQ list of potential impacts. The local jurisdiction in approving a project must base its decision on the facts of the situation, the potential impacts, a discussion of alternatives, and appropriate mitigation strategies (State of California 2004).

Washington enacted a Growth Management Act (GMA) in 1990 and requires all cities and counties to plan for future growth while protecting natural resources. The approach to planning has a strong environmental quality theme, with major development projects requiring environmental impact statements. The range of planning activity is statutorily defined by the State Environmental Policy Act, the Forest Practices Act, and the Clean Water and Clean Air Acts, all structurally woven into Washington's land use planning efforts. Local governments must identify and classify resource lands, and adopt development regulations to protect forest and agricultural lands as well as critical natural areas such as wetlands, wildlife habitat, and aquifer recharge areas. Washington's fastest growing cities and counties are required to establish Urban Growth Areas as special overlay zones with development regulations to conserve resource lands, manage water supply, and schedule infrastructure improvements for a twenty-year build-out period (Washington State CTED 2004).

Recently, agricultural lands protection has become a land use issue of prime concern to Washington's growth management policy. The GMA requires local governments to identify and designate "agricultural areas that are not already characterized by urban growth and that have long-term significance for the commercial production of food or other agricultural products" (GMA 1990). Farmers in Chelan, King, Lewis, and Yakima Counties have called for improvements to agricultural land protection policy due to the growth of incompatible land uses such as residential subdivisions, increasingly permitted in close proximity to commercial farms. Concerned with their right to farm, agricultural growers face increasing complaints and threats of lawsuits from residential neighbors objecting to use of pesticides, farm machinery noise, and odors. Farmer–homeowner land use conflicts and the threat of lawsuits have made farm operations financing more difficult, and for arid land agriculture, the inability to obtain new water rights and loss of water rights for temporary nonuse is of critical concern (Washington State CTED 2004).

Oregon has one of the nation's most highly structured statewide land planning and growth management programs. The program seeks to coordinate land use planning among federal, state, and local governments covering issues that range from community development standards to rural and resource lands conservation. Environmental, economic, and livability concerns are at the heart of the program. The intent is to manage growth in such a way as to encourage the majority of residential, commercial, and industrial land uses to develop within urban settings and to protect Oregon's rural farm, forest, and shore lands from low density residential encroachment (Land Conservation and Development Commission [LCDC] 2004).

The land use program is coordinated statewide by a central administrative authority, but planning is conducted according to locally designed and approved comprehensive plans. There are nineteen statewide planning standards, referred to as Planning Goals, that set the scope of requirements for each local comprehensive planning program. The intent is to balance conservation and development issues, thus the administrative title given to the state's planning authority: Land Conservation and Development Commission.

The planning standards have a geographic context. Jurisdictions within the coastal zone deal with special conservation and development issues related to ocean, shoreline, and estuary environments. Jurisdictions adjacent to the Willamette River are responsible for development restrictions within the river's Greenway. Cities and counties within the Columbia River Gorge must address growth management requirements designed to preserve unique cultural, resource, and landscape values.

Each local planning jurisdiction is required to address a ubiquitous set of natural resources and development goals designed to protect quality agricultural and forest lands from conversion to intensive uses, to designate overlay zones for important watersheds and wetlands, and to identify floodways and landslide hazards to reduce potential damage from natural disasters.

Growth management strategies are implemented by geographically separating resource lands from urban growth. Coordinated planning of urban growth boundaries with rural exclusive farm and forest zones is commonly used to limit urban build-out to areas either presently served by utility infrastructures or previously developed as low-density residential subdivisions. Development goals within urbanized areas reflect socially responsible and environmentally conscious objectives. Communities are required to conduct efficient infrastructure planning to support a broad range of projected urban development, including economic development zones for industrial and commercial expansion, and a range of housing types at densities and market prices.

While the initial intent of the land use planning program remains unchanged, the state legislature (often with urging from the courts) has amended the statewide planning program over time. Legal issues related to jurisdictional responsibility, due process requirements, administrative procedures, and land use definitions have been addressed and clarified. The benefits of Oregon's land use planning program have been weighed against its financial and social costs in several ballot referenda; yet the program still stands. Studies suggest that the land use program has not appreciably slowed the rate of growth; however, the majority of new development has been contained within the system of orderly urban growth boundaries rather than sprawled across the agricultural landscape (Knaap and Nelson 1992).

Charges have been leveled that Oregon's economic development has been severely constrained by land use controls and environmental laws, while others complain that Oregon's resource lands have not been adequately protected and livability has been compromised by weak enforcement of growth management legislation. Data from the 2003 statewide review of land use decisions in farm and forest zones indicates that the number of approved nonfarm dwellings in exclusive farm zones in 2003 was only slightly greater than the number approved a decade ago (257 dwellings in 2003; 225 dwellings in 1994). In exclusive forest zones, only 327 dwellings were approved in 2003, whereas 456 were approved in

1994 (Department of Land Conservation and Development [DLCD] 2004). Popular perceptions of the land use program are highly variable, but generally there is more support for the program by urban residents and rural communities within the Willamette Valley, and appreciably less in the coastal and eastern regions of the state.

Implementing the program in 1973 posed significant legal, administrative, and financial challenges to state and local governments. Two new state administrative agencies were formed: The Land Conservation and Development Commission is a decision-making board appointed by the governor for the purpose of representing a broad range of geographic and professional interests. The state administrative agency, the Department of Land Conservation and Development, is made up of legal and professional planning staff.

There are considerable organizational and budgetary considerations related to establishing and maintaining a program similar to the Oregon model. Oregon follows the rational planning paradigm for policy development and decision making, requiring that zoning and other implementing ordinances be consistent with a locally adopted comprehensive plan and appropriate state goals. All land use decisions must be based on legally defensible facts and information. A good deal of initial expense and effort is required to develop and maintain public support for planning, and to accumulate extensive data bases to support background research on an extensive list of cultural, demographic, natural resource, economic, and social planning issues.

Operational comprehensive plans were common in many Oregon communities prior to the adoption of the statewide planning program, but these local plans were largely abandoned as the new legislation was implemented. City and county governments were now required, not merely granted, the opportunity to create comprehensive land use plans. Further, specific planning issues were to be addressed, new formats to be followed, and strict procedural requirements to be met. Professional planning consultants worked with local staff to develop extensive up-to-date databases and to create information with which to address each comprehensive planning goal (Rohse 1987).

However, this land use planning model required a rigorous adherence to distilling the facts into policies that addressed the many goals. Few planning professionals, whether they were consultants or local staff, had confidence that their final package would meet the test of the state's official plan acknowledgment process. The very first community plan submitted was lauded for its timely completion and heralded as a remarkable success. It was not the acme of plans, however, and the state evaluation procedure became much more critical thereafter. Many local plans were submitted for approval, only to be turned down; some more than once. More than one Oregon county temporarily refused to take part in the process after being told that their planning efforts didn't make the grade.

Planners learned by trial and error. Legal challenges continually changed the rules of the game. A flood of administrative rules attempted to interpret and clarify the issues. Citizen interest and participation started, stopped, waxed, and waned. Nongovernmental advocacy organizations, both pro and con, stirred the pot. Progress toward developing acceptable community plans was much slower than expected. State funding to support the local planning effort was appropriated by the legislature to finance greater-than-expected local planning costs. Incrementally, the professional learning curve improved, and in most cases the attitude between locally elected officials and the state planning agency grew more cooperative. Most importantly, local comprehensive plans proved to be highly useful as a means for rationalizing growth management decisions and representing Oregon's broader resource lands interests.

Oregon presently faces a major challenge to its statewide planning program in the form of a new law proposed by statewide referendum that seeks to protect property owners from land use restrictions that are thought to adversely affect real estate values. The ballot measure calls for local governments to compensate property owners who file a claim for any loss in value attributable to land use planning. In lieu of compensation, local government will have the option of canceling the planning and zoning ordinance that applies. This law will directly conflict with existing state laws that require local governments to implement statewide planning standards or face legal and financial penalties. A new law that calls for some citizens to be compensated for government actions that only regulate, but do not "take," property could create an inequality among citizens—a condition prohibited by constitutional law. A full discussion of this amendment and its political background is presented in the next chapter.

REFERENCES

American Planning Association (APA). *State of the States: Planning Communities for the 21st Century.* Washington, D.C.: APA, 2002.

Bollens, Scott A. State Growth Management: Intergovernmental Frameworks and Policy Objectives. *Journal of the American Planning Association* 58, no. (1992):4.

Burchell, Robert W., David Listokin, William R. Dolphin, Lawrence Newton, and Susan Foxley. *Development Impact Assessment Handbook.* Washington, D.C.: Urban Land Institute, 1994.

DeClue, Corey. Personal communication with author. Casper, Wyo.: Worthington, Lenhart and Carpenter, Inc. Geotechnical Engineers, GPS Survey Branch, 20 October 2004.

Department of Land Conservation and Development (DLCD). *2003 Report on Land Use Decisions in Farm and Forest Zones.* Salem: Oregon Department of Land Conservation and Development, 2004.

Fulton, William J. *Guide to California Planning.* Point Arena, Calif.: Solano Press, 1991.

Growth Management Act (GMA). *Washington State Law (Chapter 36.70A RCW).* Olympia, Wash.: 1990.

Knaap, Garrit, and Arthur C. Nelson. *The Regulated Landscape: Lessons on State Land Use Planning from Oregon.* Cambridge, Mass.: Lincoln Institute of Land Policy, 1992.

Land Conservation and Development (LCDC). Statewide Goals and Guidelines, 2004. <www. LCDC.or.gov>. [accessed June 2004]

National Association of Realtors (NAR). Public Policy Analysis and Tracking: State Issues Clearinghouse. Chicago, Ill.: NAR, 2004.

Nevada Division of State Lands (NDSL). 2004. <www.lands.nv.gov/program/slupa/hml>. [accessed April 2004]

Pincetl, Stephanie S. *Transforming California: A Political History of Land Use and Development.* Baltimore: Johns Hopkins University Press, 1999.

Rohse, Mitch. *Land Use Planning in Oregon: A No-Nonsense Handbook in Plain English.* Corvallis: Oregon State University Press, 1987.

Smutny, Gayla. Legislative Support for Growth Management in the Rocky Mountains. *Journal of the American Planning Association* 64 (1998):311–323.

State of California. *A Citizen's Guide to Planning.* Sacramento: State of California, Governor's Office of Planning and Research, 2004.

U.S. Army Corp of Engineers (COE). *Restoration of Abandoned Mine Sites, Western Region.* Washington, D.C.: COE, 2004.

Washington State Department of Community, Trade and Economic Development (CTED), Growth Management Services. *Designation of Agricultural Lands in Chelan, King, Lewis and Yakima Counties.* Olympia: Washington State Department of Community, Trade and Economic Development, Growth Management Services, 2004.

Worley, Tim. Personal communication with author. Missoula, Mont.: Land Use Planning and Development Department, City and County of Missoula, Montana, 10 August 2004.

The Takings Issue as a Challenge to Growth Management

The recent demand for high-value home sites in the western United States has been exceptional and consequently property values have also increased proportionate to that demand. Rural tracts suitable for partitioning into small acreage residential view sites generally have the greatest speculative value. The subdivision of farms and ranches and the reallocation of traditional water rights to accommodate new residential and recreation development has become a common land use practice. To prevent the fragmentation of commercially viable farms, timber lands, ranches, and shore lands, the state of Oregon nearly thirty years ago legislated its own unique form of local land use planning based on a set of consistent statewide goals and policies. The principal purpose has been to assure an orderly community development process and to establish reasoned procedures with regard to the conversion of important resource lands. However, a fundamental challenge to Oregon's nationally acknowledged and highly regarded land use planning program is presently underway. The challenge comes in the way of a state statute amendment that requires state and/or local governments to pay compensation to property owners whose use of the land has been restricted and thereby theoretically reduced in value. Alternatively, in lieu of compensation, local governments may forego the enforcement of land use regulations and restrictions that negatively affect the value of an individual's property.

Oregon's growth management strategies, purposely designed to slow the conversion of crop, range, timber lands, and lands of natural and scenic value, have necessarily had the consequential effect of reducing the potential value of some individual properties while increasing the values of others. Land use planning and the enforcement tool zoning designate specific geographic areas appropriate for a range of compatible uses according to goals, policies, and procedures approved by local representative governments. A limited range of acceptable uses and specific site restrictions in any designated zone may consequently reduce the list of land uses and the potential development actions envisioned by an individual property owner. In a strong land market, properties designated for residential, commercial, and industrial land uses are most likely to benefit, but those lands zoned for low-intensity use or that are restricted to natural resource uses generally have lower market value relative to others. Oregon's exceptional land market reflects many of the factors driving new growth and development across the West. The direct voter initiative is a legal tradition frequently used by Oregon voters to initiate legal change. This process side-steps the state legislature by deciding amendments to the state constitution and state laws based on a popular ballot. The issue of land use planning and its relation to property values forced a showdown at the Oregon Ballot Box Corral in election years 2000 and 2004. Since Oregon is a national trendsetter for land use legislation, the outcome of these elections may well influence the future character of land use planning as it evolves across the West.

The issue of "taking" is at the core of the latest challenge to land use planning in Oregon. A taking is an action of government that results in confiscation, condemnation, or the use of eminent domain to take title or to preclude all substantial beneficial or economically viable uses of the land. The authors of a constitutional amendment for election year 2000 and a state statute change in 2004 consider any action by local government that results in a reduction of the fair market value of land to be an infringement of property rights so egregious as to require compensation. In lieu of monetary compensation, local governments may choose to modify, remove, or not enforce the land use regulation at issue.

Initiative Petitioners in 2004 sponsored *Measure 37, entitled: Governments Must Pay Owners, Or Forgo Enforcement, When Certain Land Use Restrictions Reduce Property Value.* In the November 2, 2004, General Election, Ballot Measure 37 overwhelmingly passed. Nearly 61% of Oregon voters statewide, and a majority of voters in thirty-five of Oregon's thirty-six counties, favored the proposed law requiring state and local governments either to compensate landowners suffering reduced land value due to planning regulations or, alternatively, to waive the limiting regulations. The measure was supported by rural and urban voters alike, indicating that the argument for "fairness" and against excessive bureaucratic regulation was an effective appeal.

In 2005, Oregon's economy is doing well, employment and income from manufacturing, construction, and industry are steadily growing, but leading up to the general election the state had been slow to recover from the downturn of the late 1990s. The sponsors of Measure 37 reinforced the perception that economic development opportunities had been lost due to statewide land use and environmental regulations that limited local governments' ability to innovatively work with property owners to effectuate positive land development changes. A similar measure to amend the Oregon Constitution was approved by voters in the 2000

General Election, but it was subsequently overturned on procedural grounds by the Oregon Supreme Court. The passage of the 2004 ballot initiative is important to the future character of land use planning in Oregon, and it will likely have an impact on the future of land use planning across the West. Advocates of the "Wise Use" property rights movement considered the passage of Measure 7 in the 2000 General Election a clear moral, if not legal, victory for their positions relative to property rights. The passage of Measure 37, a revised "Son of Measure 7," further served to energize the group's initiatives in other western states.

BACKGROUND

The U.S. Constitution under the Fifth Amendment and the Oregon Constitution under Article I both prohibit the taking of private property by government without just compensation. Measure 7, a 2000 Oregon General Election Ballot Initiative, sought to amend the Oregon Constitution to require just compensation specifically for "a reduction in property value" claimed by the owner to have resulted from government action—in effect revising the constitutional meaning of taking. Introduced by signature petition, Measure 7 received a majority vote of the people in the 2000 General Election. The measure was immediately appealed on procedural grounds, namely, that one measure may not attempt to amend more than one substantive portion of the constitution. An injunction was granted to prevent the amendment from becoming law, pending appeals. The ballot measure subsequently was overturned by the Oregon Supreme Court in September 2002 on the grounds that the measure violated procedural standards for constitutional amendments. The measure, as interpreted by the Court, not only addressed the land use compensation issue; it also sought to regulate "freedom of expression" by defining pornography and excluding "adult shops" as legitimate land uses.

The Oregon Supreme Court, in its decision, did not address the root issue of the question raised by the ballot petitioners: Beyond the strict legal definition of taking (government confiscation, physical invasion, or transfer of property title to the government), should a private landowner be compensated for a "partial taking" such as a reduction in land value claimed to be the result of land use regulation or other government action? The issues raised by this proposal are of great importance to the future of Oregon's statewide land use program, recognized nationally as a rational approach to preserving agricultural lands and environmental quality.

A chief difference in the two initiatives, however, lies in the approach that is taken to affect a legal change of planning procedure. Whereas Measure 7 attempted to amend the Oregon Constitution, Measure 37 amends the state statute related to statewide land use planning. Oregon Revised Statute 197 (ORS 197) legally codifies Senate Bill 100, passed by the legislature in 1973 to create the Land Conservation and Development Commission, whose purpose is to "prescribe planning goals and objectives to be applied by state agencies, cities, counties and special districts throughout the state" (ORS 197. 225). Further, the law established the creation of an administrative agency, the Department of Land Conservation and Development, and appropriated a sum of money to begin the statewide planning process.

Proponents and opponents have advocated their respective views in often heated, emotional debates. Information that might add to a rational discussion of the issue is generally lacking, however. While this chapter is certainly not intended to be a legal treatise, it is intended as a discussion of a classic land use regulation dilemma: Can government act responsibly to assure the health, safety, and welfare of the people by managing land use to achieve reasonable social and environmental goals—and at the same time respect and protect constitutional land rights? A dramatic change in the definition of taking and the requirement for a government-sponsored compensation program related to land values could significantly alter state and local budget priorities, affecting land use planning programs in Oregon and thereby the geography of land and resource use.

The text of Measure 37 explicitly requires state and local governments to pay immediate compensation (after a 180-day review period) to a landowner for any governmental action that reduces the fair market value of their property, or to forego any land use regulation that does so. The measure was purportedly introduced to control what the proponents viewed as a growing disregard for private property rights by local and state land use planning agencies. The measure requires compensation to repair the loss of property value resulting from land use regulations such as local zoning, urban growth boundaries, capital improvement plans, and environmental regulations required to meet state-mandated comprehensive planning laws. Federal environmental and safety regulations would remain unaffected by the law. Present constitutional protections require compensation for government actions that relate to restricting all use of the land, by condemnation and physical invasion (the outright use of the land by government), and for the transfer of private property titles to the government. However, there is no existing requirement or formula for compensating landowners for a partial taking defined as a reduction in property value.

LAND USE PLANNING AND PROPERTY VALUES

In the United States, private property is recognized as a basis for providing livelihood, a source of income, investment, and savings, and a form of personal property of financial worth to be mortgaged, transferred, rented, leased, sold, or inherited. As a form of personal wealth, it is one of the responsibilities of government to protect the owner's interests in land by assuring legal certainty to property title. Classified as personal material wealth, real property is subject to taxation, and forms one of the primary funding sources for local governments.

The private property owner may envision the potential use of a parcel of land by evaluating the alternatives in light of geographic, economic, personal, and other circumstances. But, in addition, the use of the property is dependent on social and institutional variables such as property regulations, deed restrictions, easements, property covenants, and other legal constraints contained in state, local, and perhaps federal land laws.

There are substantive legal limits to government restrictions on the use of private lands, beyond which regulation becomes so severe as to result in all loss of use. In such cases, the remedy for this "taking of all use" is monetary compensation. Eminent domain is a power of government that allows the taking of private property for public use. This power was not intended to be used arbitrarily, but rather to be used sparingly and for compelling public purposes. Its use results in the loss of all private rights and obligations to the property and the consequent transfer of land title to the government. The public purpose to be served must be clearly stated, and there must be a connection between the use of this power and the appropriate exercise of government responsibilities. Except in the case of a clear national or local emergency, the public interest alone is generally not a sufficient reason to confiscate land without due process (Rose 1979). Public easements, often used for locating utility routes, generally result in a small portion of property to be taken for right-of-way purposes. Both these measures are considered confiscation, and compensation must be paid relative to the market value of the specific property taken.

As the sponsors of Measure 37 point out, there are other costs and burdens on private property owners not covered by condemnation or eminent domain proceedings. Land use planning restricts the use of land by zoning and other regulations without compensating the owner for value lost. It is the landowner who must contest the government's actions, the landowner who bears the costs of appellate fees, and the landowner who has an imperfect set of rights while the legal proceedings continue for months and sometimes years of appeals.

Intending to accomplish the greatest social good, comprehensive land use planning and its implementing tools zoning and capital improvement programming naturally result in greater land use opportunities for some property owners, and less for others. There is intrinsic spatial discrimination involved in this process: some properties will be designated for high-density uses and others for lower density uses; some lands are zoned to protect the right to farm, or to allow the continuation of existing ecological functions. But by state law, land use decisions on density and development priorities, like the local comprehensive plans that control them, may not be arbitrary, must be constructed with factual rationale, and finally, they must be enacted and supported by elected community officials. Those investing in land should inform themselves of community growth priorities and regulations before making purchases. Landowners should understand their particular geographic situation, develop insight to land use issues that affect them, participate in the local hearings process to advocate their views, and finally, utilize appeals procedures when a decision affecting their property appears unreasonable, biased, or arbitrary.

Land value is tied to a long list of land resource attributes that include location; parcel size and shape; natural landform features; water, mineral, and timber resources; access; deed restrictions; on-site improvements; and surrounding land uses. The list also includes positive and negative social and economic consequences of government intervention into the land market such as taxes, regulations, permits, and development costs. Some property owners will see increased land values as the result of high-density zoning or government investment in improved transportation services and other infrastructure improvements. Elsewhere, property values may be stabilized by exclusive farm zones, protecting the right to farm by reducing the tax burden on traditional farmland. When land use planning works effectively, alternatives for the use of land are not arbitrary but governed by rationale based on social, economic, and natural resource information and effectuated by fair and reasonable procedures. The point here is that government actions constrain land use alternatives, but there are many attributes and considerations that determine land value, ultimately including the price a willing buyer might pay a willing seller.

Real property consists of land improvements such as buildings, vegetation, subsurface minerals, and, depending on state laws, sometimes water. The rights of a landowner may extend physically to the use of the soil, the subsurface materials, and the air above the property. The principal considerations that contribute values to real property include the makeup of the physical and biological material of the earth at the site, the volume or size of the site, in some instances aesthetics and viewscapes, and the location of the site—its spatial relationship to other land parcels and land uses in the immediate vicinity or local region (Platt 2004). Real property value interpreted as "market value" is a time-dependent measure of the worth of the land parcel because conditions change over time: Accessibility may improve; surrounding land uses may change in intensity and type of use; new laws, rules, and regulations apply; materials or minerals may become technologically viable; and important to land in the West, water resource allocations appurtenant to the land parcel may greatly increase in value. The market for land has to do with the supply and demand for particular property attributes at a point in time. Land appraisers use a list of factors and characteristics to determine the value of a parcel. The list most often includes location, the size and shape of the parcel, the type and quality of site improvements, indications of inherent natural biological or soil productivity, zoning designation, access, deed restrictions, easements, restrictive covenants, the types and characteristics of surrounding land uses, and importantly, the recent selling prices of similar properties (Appraisal Institute 2004).

Landowners favoring Measure 37 are overwhelmingly concerned with time-related market value changes and what they view as the adverse consequences of land use restrictions introduced to reduce the development alternatives available to them. However, there appears to be little complaint about government intervention that subsequently results in property value increases. The measure does not address what should be done with any added value or with any monetary windfall attributable to government land use actions; the concern is simply with reductions in land value. The profits realized from land valuation may contribute to the local economy; they may be reinvested in the community and eventually taxed to be redistributed in some way by government, but it is unlikely that the profits from the windfalls will be redistributed to those locally experiencing the "wipeouts."

On the issue of compensation, the courts have, in numerous cases, defined what constitutes a taking. Under the government power of eminent domain, private property may be acquired for public use. The exercise of this power in the public interest "results in extinguishing all rights of the landowner to a specific parcel of land" (Rose 1979, 421). The owner of the property is therefore compensated directly for the loss of private property at fair market value. Federal courts have generally ruled that "uses of land may be regulated by use of the police power to support basic issues of health and safety; that particular land uses may be restricted to certain locations to lessen the nuisance they pose to the general population, and to support local objectives extending to the conservation and protection of existing natural and resource lands" (Rose 1979, 76). The courts have also found that "some diminished property value is tolerable if government can show that the land use actions are in the public interest, are not arbitrary, and alternative uses and some reasonable value of the land remains" (Rose 1979, 76).

However, several state constitutions include provisions that appear to require local governments to tread very lightly on private property rights. The wording in these provisions do not tolerate diminished property value and require governments to make "just compensation for property taken, injured or destroyed by them" (Rose 1979, 421; referring to Kentucky Constitution, Art. 242). This theory of "compensatory regulation" argues that any injury to ownership rights, including the loss of potential uses, and market value are unfair burdens imposed on a specific set of owners and therefore represent a "taking in fact" (Bosselman, Callies, and Banta 1973).

Measure 37 requires local and state governments to pay compensation to landowners when the land's fair market value is in any way reduced by government action, thus introducing a fundamental difference to the interpretation of what constitutes a "taking of private property," linking it directly to either nonenforcement of land use laws or compensation as a remedy for reduced property value. By law, Measure 37 excepts from compensation particular land uses and regulations, such as: "commonly and historically recognized public nuisances, public health and safety regulations, regulations required to comply with federal law, and regulations restricting or prohibiting the use of a property for the purpose of selling pornography or performing nude dancing" (Oregon Ballot Measure 37, Oregon Voter's Guide [OVG] September 2004, 107).

The authors of the measure state that their intent is to redress the loss of property values due to government action by compensating landowners for a negative change in market value. The measure may have been founded on the legal principle of separable rights of "interest," meaning value and use. The point of this theory is that damage to the legal rights of interest (value and use) is just as important as damage to "physical" rights—the outright government occupation or confiscation of real property assets. The theory apparently used here is that harm to the property owner comes by way of an "injury" or "damage" to these legal rights by government action, and therefore the "damaged rights" should be "repaired" by monetary compensation.

The wording of Measure 37 provides no insight into the legal theory employed in its design; it simply declares that its provisions will be so, therefore, the legal rationale is only speculative. Similarly, the full implications and impacts on property owners and taxpayers and to state and local governments are unknown or only poorly understood, but the estimated administrative cost to state government is likely to range from $18 to $44 million per year and from $46 to $300 million per year for local governments. No new revenue sources to pay the compensation fees or administrative costs are identified (OVG September 2004, 103).

Attorneys might argue the legal issues related to takings and its implications to land use planning: What about the root issue of the amendment; what constitutes a taking? Can property values be "injured" or "damaged" and still constitute a taking? What is the line between regulation and seizure? Can there be such a thing as "partial seizure" or partial taking? Does the amendment contradict or confuse the intent of Article 1 of the Oregon Constitution, which is designed to address the issue of just compensation? Does the amendment seek to do away with the need to bring lawsuits known as "inverse condemnations" and to directly require government to make compensation as though the property had been taken by condemnation? Should compensation be paid for the potential adverse effects on land values of all government permits, and all other regulatory actions related to the use of land, water, forests, wildlife, and other material resources of the land?

Since "fair market value" is a temporary measure of worth and fluctuates over time as physical resources are used, degraded, and altered, and as technical, social, and economic issues change, how can compensation for changes in value be linked to a variable that by its very nature changes over time? Is it possible to fairly and accurately determine the amount of monetary compensation to a landowner when the fair market value of the property is claimed to be reduced solely by government land use regulation?

BACKGROUND TO MEASURE 7,
ELECTION YEAR 2000; THE PROPONENT'S VIEW

In the 2000 General Election supporters of Measure 7, a proposed amendment to the Oregon Constitution, overwhelmingly cited the fairness issue: "If the government takes your land, they should pay you for it and they shouldn't tie you up in red tape and outrageous fees just so you can have your day in court. . . . Simple, understandable, and fair. That's what Measure 7 is all about" (Moshofsky, comments in support of Measure 7, OVG 2000, 101).

> It's not fair to require individual property owners to bear burdens that the general public should bear. Also its not good policy for government to be able to confiscate private property without paying for it. . . . Measure 7 simply makes it clear that government must compensate property owners when regulations take away the right to use their property to provide public benefits. Unfortunately, some government regulators believe they can take away up to 95% of the use and value of private property without compensating the owner. (Nims, comments in support of Measure 7, OVG 2000, 102)

> Measure 7 sets-up a straightforward process to require government to pay land owners when its laws or regulations cause a drop in market value to their private property. Presently the Oregon Constitution states that state government must pay if it "takes" the title to private lands for the public's benefit. Today, however, "takings" law is so convoluted that there is little hope of compensation when government regulations cause a reduction in the value of private property. (Hays, comments in support of Measure 7, OVG 2000, 103)

> Although the Constitution is clear that government shall compensate property owners when it takes private property, government has made the process nearly impossible for individual property owners to receive compensation. . . . Measure 7 is about fairness, common sense, and protecting private property rights. (Johnston, comments in support of Measure 7, OVG 2000, 102)

SOME ARGUMENTS IN FAVOR OF
A REVISED MEASURE 7; MEASURE 37, 2004

The supporters of Measure 37 again appeal to the fairness issue, citing many examples of bureaucratic disregard for individual landowners; a tedious, burdensome, and costly appeals process; and economic concerns that small businesses are discouraged in Oregon because they must unfairly bear the costs of litigation to overcome unreasonable "application," "impact," and "development fees." One of the strongest appeals to fairness is that the continuous proliferation of land use rules and regulations adversely affects certainty in land investments. In this regard the Measure requires local governments to recognize the "grandfather clause": to allow the landowner to use the property for a use legally permitted at the time the owner acquired the property.

I have had everything taken from me—I purchased my property in Portland over ten years ago. At the time I purchased the property it was approximately 3.47 acres of land that could be used for industrial or commercial development—My parcel is not developed. Sometime in 1993, the City of Portland began slowly—encroaching on my property using easements, zoning and environmental overlays, taking away my ability to use my land—Only one-half acre is actually usable.—To make matters worse the city requires —wetland mitigation. As a result, it will be impossible for me to do anything on my property except to leave it in its "natural state." (Pruitt, OVG September 2004, 113)

I own 8.32 acres in Colton, Oregon. I've owned this property since 1965 and have always paid my taxes with the idea that in my senior years this property would provide me with a comfortable retirement. . . . All of the other parcels surrounding my property are 2-5 acres in size. My property has the typical urban services . . . access and fire protection. . . . There is simply no compelling reason why my property should not be divided. Measure 37 will restore the rights of Oregonians, rights that were taken away by an unfair, unbalanced system (Wilcox, OVG September 2004, 115)

Measure 37 is needed to help the environment and the economy. Measure 37 reduces costly litigation . . . too often, well intentioned politicians create new laws and regulations which make it harder for us to use our land and stay in business. Rather than helping the environment, these regulations hurt the environment. . . . Unlike most industries we make our living from the land. As a result we have taken a keen interest in preserving our property and being good stewards of the land so that we can provide the public with quality Oregon grown beef. Measure 37 protects our property rights, protects our investments and makes sure that politicians think about the impact of new regulations on all Oregonians, including property owners. (Oregon Cattlemen's Association, OVG September 2004, 110)

It doesn't take a rocket scientist to figure out what happens to property taxes when government regulations lower the value of property—the tax revenues go down. Imagine what would happen if the government restored just a fraction of what it took each year. When state or local governments pass new regulations that lower property values, everyone loses. . . . On the other hand, when state or local governments give property owners freedom to use their property every one wins. Property owners realize investment. Cities and counties have a new source of revenue. Jobs are created. And the remaining taxpayers aren't asked to support higher and higher tax increases. (Taxpayer Association of Oregon, OVG September 2004, 117)

Measure 37 gives landowners the right to immediately submit a compensation claim "if a local government passes or enforces a regulation that restricts the use of private real property, and the restriction has the effect of reducing the value of a property upon which the restriction is imposed" (OVG September 2004, 103).

Compensation may also be claimed for actions that require landowner expenditures to meet environmental, ecological, and cultural resource standards set by state and local government. A reduction in "fair market value" is defined as "the difference in the fair market value of the property before and after application of the regulation" (OVG September 2004, 103). The measure does not indicate how the compensation revenues will be raised, administered, or delivered.

EXAMPLE ARGUMENTS OF THOSE WHO OPPOSE MEASURE 37

Opponents of Measure 37 point out that the referendum disregards existing constitutional safeguards and legal precedent relative to the takings issue and that it has the potential to render ineffective local comprehensive land use planning and state laws related to resource management, environmental quality, and public safety. They also point out that if monetary compensation is required to remedy the "injury" or "damage" to property rights alleged by potentially thousands of landowners, the taxpayers of the state and individual local governments will shoulder a great financial burden. This amendment could conceivably be interpreted to include property value reductions resulting from regulations and restrictions that in the distant past may have had some bearing on land value, greatly increasing the financial impact of the measure.

Opponents of the earlier referendum issue, Measure 7, cited potentially negative effects on Oregon's environment, lifestyle, economy, and social processes:

[I]t [the amendment] can take decision making away from citizens and put it in the hands of lawyers. No longer will communities or citizens in our neighborhoods be allowed to participate in the process of determining land use or how nearby properties are developed and utilized. Those decisions could be made through money-driven claims of self serving individuals." (Bosak, argument against Measure 7, OVG September 2000, 101)

Measure 7 could overturn local zoning laws, opening up stream corridors to unregulated development. This will limit access to Oregon's best steelhead rivers and harm fish habitat. Limits on logging and development along streams could be overturned. . . . Rules insuring instream flows for fish could not be enforced. (Ritchie, argument against Measure 7, OVG September 2000, 102)

Compensating land owners for theoretical profits will make it too expensive to enforce responsible land use that protects aquatic habitat and Oregon's salmon. . . . Measure 7 would very likely thwart efforts to prevent development in hazardous areas prone to erosion, landslides, and flooding. And it could eliminate our ability to prevent land owners from destroying the natural shoreline by 'armoring' it with sheets of concrete and rip-rap. (Hoeflich, argument against Measure 7, OVG September 2000, 104)

Measure 7 would force taxpayers to pay hundreds of millions of dollars to developers and speculators—or simply to stop enforcing the laws that protect our farm and forest land from being covered with subdivisions. (Parsons, argument against Measure 7, OVG, September 2000, 106)

Measure 37 is so poorly written it will put many farmers out of business by increasing taxes and rolling back the safeguards that protect Oregon's farmland from overdevelopment. As farmers, we are property owners who work on the land every day. We deal with government and all its processes and procedures. We can't afford the additional layers of paperwork, bureaucracy, lawsuits and costs associated with Measure 37. (Marion County Farm Bureau, OVG, September 2004, 119)

Measure 37 will lead to non-enforcement of land use laws. Oregon's land use system has been regarded as a model across the country for over thirty years. . . . Measure 37 will undoubtedly lead to non-enforcement of our land use laws, it seeks to undo all that we have accomplished and we become one of the those "other" states. Land use regulation preserves Oregon for all Oregonians. (League of Women Voters, OVG, September 2004, 121)

We oppose Measure 37 because it will cost taxpayers $344 million in administrative costs alone. Measure 37 does nothing to protect neighborhoods from the harmful effects of development. Measure 37 will undermine our right to participate in local decisions that affect our neighborhoods. (Southeast UPLIFT Neighborhood Program, OVG, September 2004, 122)

Our story is a true Oregon success story. Oregon's farmland preservation laws have helped to protect the land we rely on to grow, make and market some to the world's best wines. We've created an industry that employs thousands of Oregonians and pumps millions of dollars into our state and local economies . . . tourists come from around the world to visit us, taste our wines and enjoy the beauty of our state. Measure 37 puts our economic success story at risk. . . . Our businesses and our lands can't afford more legal uncertainties and ambiguities. . . . Measure 37 will lead to more lawsuits and litigation. There are no limits to the number of claims and lawsuits that can be filed under Measure 37. (Lemelson, Oregon Wine Growers Association, OVG, September 2004, 124)

Nurseries in Oregon are mostly small, owner-operated farms, but our industry is making a big contribution to our state's prosperity. Oregon's fast growing nursery industry is now the largest contributor to our state's $3.5 billion agricultural economy. . . . Unlike other agricultural commodities, most of Oregon's nursery products are grown in counties that also have large urban populations. By protecting our land base from uncontrolled urban sprawl, Oregon's land use and farmland protection laws have enabled nurseries to flourish, even in the face of rapid population growth. (Park, OVG, September 2004, 126)

In the 2000 General Election, Measure 7 received a majority vote in thirty-four of Oregon's thirty-six counties, indicating substantial popular agreement with the spirit of the amendment. Local governments, faced with the continuing legal responsibility to meet state land use and environmental laws, to issue development permits, and to follow capital implementation schedules, sought legal relief from the impending measure. The League of Oregon Cities offered a model ordinance that allowed local governments to waive specific regulations contested by landowners on the basis of property value damage, thereby avoiding a compensation case. The consequence of this type of ordinance, which effectively allowed local governments to disregard state land use laws, was to ensure that the legal group 1000 Friends of Oregon would sue any government agency found to violate existing state land use statutes. In an effort to discourage compensation applications, some local governments instituted filing fees that asked as much as $1,000 from landowners who wished to apply for compensation.

A December 7, 2000, ruling by a Marion County, Oregon Circuit Court judge resulted in an injunction, putting a hold on the implementation of the amendment and thereby giving government agencies a period of relief while the courts sought to determine if the amendment, as opponents charged, was unconstitutional. The primary legal challenge was not based on substantive arguments about takings or on the impacts of the amendment to existing land use law. The arguments against the amendment focused on the procedural issues of how the state constitution of Oregon can or cannot be amended. Legal precedent has shown that ballot initiatives that seek to amend the Oregon Constitution must address only one issue at a time.

The Oregon Supreme Court Rules Measure 7 Invalid

The Oregon Supreme Court ruled on October 4, 2002, that Measure 7 approved on the November 2000 ballot contained two separate changes to the Oregon Constitution. The Court cited its previous interpretation that an initiative may only introduce one constitutional change at a time. Thus the entire measure was deemed to be void because of a procedural flaw. The chief focus of the measure was to monetarily compensate landowners for government actions that reduce the value of property, but the measure also set forth a specific condition that certain types of properties would be excluded from compensation, even if damaged by regulation—explicitly those properties dealing with adult entertainment, such as adult shops and adult video stores. Therefore, the Court interpreted one section of the amendment to be directed at the constitutional right of property and another directed at the constitutional guarantee to the right of free expression.

The decision had nothing to do with the substantive land use issues of takings legislation. Oregon's land use laws were little affected in the 2000–2002 interim because of the court injunction delaying the enactment of Measure 7 until court appeals were concluded.

Proponents of Measure 37 point to the fact that 54% of voters in the 2000 election approved Measure 7 and that the newly revised version offers local government a similar alternative to the Model Land Use Ordinance proposed by the League of Oregon Cities in 2001 to avoid paying compensation. That alternative is to "take no action" on the enforcement of planning regulations affecting property values (League of Oregon Cities 2004).

Opponents concede that this measure serves as a reminder to government land use agencies to maintain a fair, reasonable, and responsible balance between the objectives of land and resource conservation and the legal rights of landowners. However, the implications of this measure go beyond a simple reminder to government bureaucrats; at stake is the future of a rational, goal-oriented, citizen-based process for land planning. While some property owners have been harmed, and their pleas for local bureaucratic reform should be responsibly investigated, there is no legal precedent to support compensation, nor to abandon land use planning as a legitimate tool of representative government. Following the vote on Measure 7 in the 2000 General Election, the Oregon legislature did not act to substantially amend planning procedures or to enhance the public perception of fairness in the land use planning process. It appears at this point that the popular approval of Ballot Measure 37 served as the compelling rationale for amending the legislative purposes and processes of land use planning in Oregon.

At this date in mid-2005, one can only speculate on the impacts to Oregon's land use planning program. The process of implementing ballot measures is slow and legally complicated, especially where statutes related to land use may be contradictory. The relatively slow interpretation and reaction time, however, allows for the investigation of proposals to reasonably deal with this issue. Since no funds were budgeted by state or local governments to pay compensation claims, none have been paid. Instead, claims have been negotiated, and planning regulations have been waived only on a claimant-by-claimant basis rather than as "blanket waivers." Typical claims involve long-term owners of property who, at the time of purchase, bought land zoned for development under local comprehensive plans. Subsequently, the local government comprehensive plans and zoning designations were changed to meet resource lands goals required by state land use laws, thereby replacing the local development zone designations with more restrictive agricultural or forest use designations. Where claims have been upheld, generally the landowners have been awarded the right to use the land as it was zoned at the time of original purchase, pending all applicable original limitations and restrictions (LCDC 2005). In rural communities surrounding the Portland metropolitan area alone, there are nearly 14,000 acres of land for which compensation claims are pending and must be dealt with in a timely manner by payment, waiver, or some as yet to be determined innovative solution (Hallyburton 2005).

It is likely that Oregonians did not vote to destroy the environment, to do away with resource lands protections, to enrich land speculators, or to extort taxpayers. Possibly the voters wished to draw a line at what they perceived to be unreasonable limits on property rights or to encourage workable local solutions to local development issues. Livability is one of Oregon's primary aspirations, and agricultural lands remain a key component in Oregon's economy. Property owners who feel they have a case for compensation related to issues found in local comprehensive plans and enforcement ordinances must file applications with local governments. Those who are potentially affected by state planning laws will file with the Department of Land Conservation and Development. All appeals will go to the courts (LCDC 2005). A new set of detailed Administrative Rules and Regulations will likely be required to carry out the amended law. More speculation here, however: legislative study might include a critical review of traditional zoning as it applies to Oregon planning purposes and perhaps more flexibility for local land use development negotiation, and greater use of local development analysis techniques, impact assessment, and mitigation studies. Finally, there are legal challenges pending that seek to overturn this law. The legal advocacy group 1000 Friends of Oregon considers the law to violate constitutional protections against special privilege by granting some people immunity from community zoning, but not others. Some may receive compensation should they apply for it, and others in similar situations who do not apply will not benefit equally. Additionally, 1000 Friends is concerned that local communities with no budgeted funding for compensation claims may be forced to make "back room deals" with property owners, thus violating procedural safeguards of fair and open hearings. This position reasons that the essential constitutional guarantees of fair treatment and equality are compromised by this statutory amendment. There is also an urgent need to revisit the legal issues defining taking, and specifically to address the effects on property values resulting from economic, technological, geographic, environmental, and institutional changes over time.

REFERENCES

1000 Friends of Oregon. *Measure 37, 2004.* <www.friends.org./issues/m37.html>. [accessed January 2005]

Appraisal Institute. *Property Evaluation Checklist,* 2004. <www.appraisalinstitue.org.pdf>. [accessed January 2005]

Bosselman, F., D. Callies, and J. Banta. *The Taking Issue.* Washington, D.C.: U.S. Government Printing Office, 1973.

Hallyburton, Rob. Personal communication with author. Manager, Community Services Division, Oregon Department of Land Conservation and Development. Salem, Ore.: 10 May 2005.

LCDC. *Final Staff Reports* 2005. <www.oregon.gov/lcd/m37finalstaffreports.shtml>. [accessed 20 August 2005]

League of Oregon Cities. *Measure 7, 2000 General Election,* 2004. <www.orcities.org/currentIssues>. [accessed January 2004]

Official Oregon Voter's Guide (OVG) to the 2000 General Election, Measure 7. Salem, Ore.: Oregon Secretary of State, September 2000.

Official Oregon Voter's Guide (OVG) to the 2004 General Election, Measure 37. Salem, Ore.: Oregon Secretary of State, September 2004.

Oregon Revised Statutes 197.225. *Preparation and Adoption of State-wide Planning Goals and Guidelines.* Salem, Ore.: Oregon Revised Statutes Annotated.

Oregon State Bar (OSB). *Continuing Legal Education Series: Land Use,* chapter 2, George M. Platt, "Constitutional Issues," and chapter 10, Orval H. Etter, "Zoning." Salem, Ore.: Oregon State Bar Association, 1976.

Platt, Rutherford. *Land Use and Society: Geography, Law and Public Policy,* rev. ed. Washington, D.C.: Island Press, 2004.

Rose, Jerome G. *Legal Foundations of Land Use Planning: Textbook/Casebook and Materials on Planning Law.* New Brunswick, N.J.: Rutgers, Center for Urban Policy Research, 1979.

Statesman Journal. High Court Throws Out Measure on Land Rights. *Statesman Journal,* October 5, 2002, pp. 1, 2A.

A Rational Model for Comprehensive Land Use Planning

To this point we have discussed and analyzed the character and patterns of growth in the New West. We made the point earlier that this growth is spatially uneven; it is strongly biased toward rapidly growing region-dominating cities and suburbs. Overwhelmingly, the population of the West must be defined as urban. During the last decade, however, a concurrent growth trend has emerged, and it is characterized by a renewed interest in small towns and rural land development. We observe this pattern at the outer edges of cities as diverse as Seattle, Denver, Tucson, and Las Vegas. Increasingly, the trends in rural growth indicate exceptional percentage increases in population growth and housing development in areas formerly considered too isolated or possessing only marginal settlement potential. These trends are characterized by a movement toward several key regions throughout the eleven western states. Aside from the obvious ski towns and trendy hot spots, a "most favored status" can be assigned to growth in the interstate corridors previously described, and to the regions of Southwest Colorado, Central Arizona, Southwestern Utah, Western Montana, Central Oregon, and West-Central New Mexico. These are the regions where small towns will become much larger, and where rural resource lands will inevitably be carved up and subdivided. This is the settlement pattern that has come to epitomize the New West.

In these areas development pressure leading to runaway growth is a foregone conclusion. Demographic projections for the western states indicate that population migration from California alone will total more than four million before the year 2020 (U.S. Bureau of Census 1995). How well that growth will be managed depends on statewide legislation that favors local comprehensive planning, citizen support for managed growth, and the political will of elected officials to balance the opportunities for growth with the need to maintain local environmental amenities, small-town character, and livability.

Economic choices for the use of land at selected locations will change with increased demand, likely promoting disputes regarding both the use of private lands and common resources for different purposes. Resolving these issues will require respect for traditions and environments, a philosophy of cooperation, and community institutions suited to achieving shared goals. As we noted in chapter 2, many communities throughout the West have found it necessary to adopt a new "Code of the West" for educating new residents about local customs and practices related to the traditions of agriculture and ranching. This modern-day version of the old nineteenth-century code of conduct, unwritten but understood by all, is meant to instill in newcomers a respect for the values, people, institutions, and resources of the area (see appendix).

Clearly, there is a compelling need for citizen-supported land and resource planning in the West. The people who have come to live in the West, whether for traditional economic pursuits or as New West entrepreneurs or retirees, should understand the value of building support for local land use planning and for encouraging innovative state and regional cooperative and collaborative alliances for understanding and regulating the impacts of development on rural lands and resources.

Larger cities and towns generally have well-organized planning departments, but small communities and rural areas often have only a modest program if they have one at all. Many small communities that would benefit most from land use planning are at a disadvantage when faced with new growth and are woefully unprepared to evaluate the impacts of proposed development or to provide an organized structure for decision making. In light of the land use and resource issues we present in this book, elected representatives of local governments across the West should determine the need for improved planning in their jurisdictions and factually justify this choice by citing the important public interests to be served. Local citizens should participate in the development of a vision for future land use. Elected officials with the help of legal and planning professionals should adopt a framework for decision making and adopt growth management policies relevant to their local land use objectives.

THE RURAL AND SMALL-TOWN PLANNER AS SUPERHERO

Unlike larger communities, where a city or county planning staff may consist of many individuals, each with specific and mutually exclusive functions, the small towns and rapidly changing counties of the New West may not even have a planner on the payroll at all. If there is a planner, even a newly hired one, that person is then expected to have a broad understanding of manifold topics, and both in the initial conceptualizing and eventual implementation of tasks must be a skilled generalist who needs to wear many hats. This notion of local planner as superhero has been expressed most cogently by Lapping, Daniels, and Keller (1989, 19):

> The planner has a diverse and demanding role to play in a rural setting. Belonging to a small planning staff, the planner, whether in a county, regional, or small-town office, will have to become knowledgeable about a variety of issues affecting the planning area. Such issues may include farming, forestry, natural areas, water, toxic waste, economic development, land markets, housing, the elderly, mining, and government programs, among others. This knowledge is essential for drafting and updating comprehensive plans, zoning and subdivision regulations, and capital improvements plans.

It is little wonder that most job descriptions for rural and small-town planners typically call for an educational background in geography rather than the more narrowly defined field of urban and regional planning. That much broader discipline encourages training and experience in gathering information from a wide range of disparate sources, covering both the physical and human conditions of a given place. Moreover, many of the concerns and issues traditionally addressed by urban planning are out of scale and out of synch with what is going on out in the countryside.

People skills are likewise of utmost importance, since the planner as an individual must be able to successfully coordinate activities with any number of other municipal or governmental offices. He or she must maintain cordial and mutually supportive relationships with local elected officials, not only for obvious reasons of job security, but because any land use regulations that must be enacted or tinkered with will have to be legally adopted in a public vote by county commissioners or members of the town council. In that respect, the planner must also be a public relations expert, and "must be able to demonstrate the value of planning . . . [as] a way to anticipate change and establish contingency strategies for a community" (Lapping et al. 1989, 20). Furthermore, it is not only land use problems that will need to be addressed by the local planner. Social programs often fall through the cracks in budget allocations, and these along with standard economic development strategies frequently require grantsmanship and other fundraising acumen.

Local residents must be assured that planning is being undertaken for their benefit and advantage, and with their continued welfare in mind. They must be willing to claim the local planner as "their planner" who is working for them, and who is there to help bring about their vision of the community's future. In this regard, citizen involvement during every stage of planning becomes not merely an effective strategy but something that is absolutely essential to the overall success of a planning program. Any effort to educate the public about the benefits of planning not only must demystify the process but also must seek to define what has become the jargon of planning in terms that are understandable to the layperson. The lexicon is replete with obscure vocabulary that is nevertheless sometimes unavoidable in the legal landscape negotiated by planners. But local planners must strive to make these terms and concepts accessible to the general public, and here, something as simple as a set of pamphlets can go a long way: "a much desired and appreciated service is the preparation of small publications related to such topics as property acquisition, zoning, subdivision, and appeals of local land use decisions" (Lapping et al. 1989, 66). Planners might also avail themselves of every opportunity to speak to the public about local and regional issues, especially concerning growth and development and the changes that are becoming increasingly apparent within a community. These talks would best be delivered in an informal setting or as part of a strictly informational workshop rather than in the heated and often confrontational arena of a public hearing. Such educational outreach efforts ought not to be considered optional tasks to undertake only when there is time, but as essential elements of the planning process.

CRITICAL PLANNING ISSUES IN THE NEW WEST

Based on our understanding of current trends, and taking into account the ongoing land use transformations that we examined in chapters 2 and 3, we offer the following as a set of common issues that need to be addressed through the process of community and rural land use planning:

- Loss of local and regional character, traditions, and lifestyles
- Conversion of open space, scenic landscapes, and amenity lands to more intensive uses
- Development in arid and semi-arid areas dependent on limited water resources
- Intensive development in potentially hazardous landscapes
- Conversion of crop, timber, and grazing resource lands to residential uses
- Large-scale development of destination resorts and isolated rural subdivisions
- Lack of affordable housing, employment opportunities, and public services in both rural areas and fast-growing amenity communities

Land use changes related to New West development represent unprecedented challenges for communities caught between their supportive role of maintaining local traditions and lifestyles, on the one hand, and accommodating new residents and pursuing different economic directions, on the other. Local and regional identity, traditions, and lifestyles are challenged as new residents seek to alter the existing types and patterns of housing, commerce, retail establishments, industry, or transportation services. The comprehensive plan explains the guiding rationale, the community vision, with regard to sustaining the "defining features and characteristics" of the area. It sets forth a systematic and democratic approach for logical decision making with regard to the adopted policies toward growth and development. The "community interest" in land use may change over time, but the comprehensive planning process provides a means to systematically take stock of changing sentiments and conditions and to prepare alternative policy choices in a timely manner.

The conversion of scenic landscapes to intensive uses, such as housing developments, is common in natural amenity areas. Outstanding views, appreciated by locals and visitors alike, are often compromised by new home construction in the midst of these unique landscapes. Growth controls can be locally legislated to restrict building on steep slopes, to control road building and access, and to limit the provision of water and sewer services to specific elevations. The rationale for designating "critical view areas" should be made in the comprehensive plan with provisions for arranging cooperative agreements that benefit landowners and the larger public interest. Such agreements might include the trading of open space in critical view areas for greater development densities or other incentives in less observable sites. Other alternatives might involve the purchase of important landscape features by private or public land trusts. Importantly, the comprehensive planning process provides the information services, the institutional framework, and the forum for formulating alternatives to the loss of defining natural landscapes.

The loss of farm, timber, and rangelands either incrementally or by wholesale land conversion for destination resorts and planned residential developments has become a prominent rural land use issue. As we describe in the next few pages, regional associations of governments, soil and water conservation districts, and nongovernmental cooperative organizations can assist county governments in evaluating the impacts of development on commercial farm and forest activity, and on water resources, critical habitat, and other natural features.

Local needs for housing, employment, and community services are addressed in a comprehensive plan by setting community priorities for specific types of land use; offering information on geographic, social, and economic advantages; and providing suitable infrastructure and incentives for appropriate development. The comprehensive plan not only becomes the guidebook for achieving specific community goals, but it offers compelling rationale for soliciting financial support from private and public development interests. To prevent the exclusion of lower income residents in areas of rapidly escalating housing prices, a housing goal related to construction permits might authorize specific development incentives to encourage a range of housing choices and locations.

Community growth is unquestionably beneficial to the social and economic future of the New West. But there are important considerations to be made with regard to its nature, timing, and location. Local property owners conducting commercial farming and ranching operations understandably have an interest in promoting land use policies compatible with the continuation of their enterprises.

There are intrinsic geographic variables involved in farm production, for example, that cannot be easily reconstituted or reclaimed once land use changes occur. Land use conversions that result in fewer agricultural producers or reduced farm acreage adversely affect the economic structure for those remaining. Rapid increases in the prices of land and water due to heightened demand result in increased taxes and add to the costs of operation. High-value specialty crops have revolutionized the agricultural economy in many areas of the West, but annual crop price variability requires that costs related to complying with environmental regulations and local property tax rates remain consistent with production costs. Wine grapes, nursery stock, berries, fresh flowers, variety fruits, and market vegetables are but a few of the high-demand products that have invigorated a renewed interest in the farming tradition. To succeed, these capital intensive farm uses require access to water, preferential farmland taxation rates, the assurance of support services, and compatibility with neighboring properties.

The types of land conversions occurring in isolated rural areas are problematic in that they are often characterized by large acreage purchases of farmland for the construction of golf courses and associated high-value residential sites or for destination resorts with high-density seasonal residency. The new residents often consider existing farming practices to be nuisances. Water use conflicts arise with water rights purchases and transfers from traditional farm use and declining water resource quality and quantity. Gated roads deny access to streams and public lands and the opportunities for traditional outdoor recreation are lost. In general, growth in rural areas brings concerns for changes to quality of life, livability, and traditional community character.

On the other hand, individual rural landowners who see growth as an opportunity for financial gain may strongly disagree with what they perceive as local government interference regarding the use of their property and restrictions on property rights. Land is a natural resource, but it is also a commodity, a form of investment whose value varies with the uses to which it may be put. Therefore, a degree of land use "certainty" is important to all property owners, and the potential for greater land use intensity is most often preferred by investors.

The attribute of certainty is provided by community planning objectives, policies, and standards, and the rules that govern planning operations: the constitutional right to due process, open hearings, and appeals processes. Agreed-upon community plans prevent arbitrary institutional decisions or capricious changes in land use restrictions and regulations. The value of investment property is protected by land use or density designations and traditional land uses benefit from property tax protection and right-to-farm provisions. The challenge to local governments will be to accept the responsibility to develop the legal structures, organization, and procedures to facilitate local growth objectives; to conscientiously review land planning impacts on property values; to protect traditional economic interests; and to resolve the settlement conflicts on the New West's land use frontier.

Land use planning offers a representative, institutional approach to organizing community goals, priorities, aspirations, and visions for new development. It sets forth procedures to make land use decisions and to resolve land use conflicts in a fair and consistent manner. To be accepted and to be effective, planning must have broad citizen support, and it must be relevant to local interests. Our view of a reasonable land use planning strategy for the New West will have these basic features:

- Guiding policy must be developed and effectuated at the local government level by elected officials to have legitimacy.
- Landownership rights must be protected by constitutional standards of due process, open hearings, and timely appeals.
- Development proposals should be dealt with in a timely manner, and decisions should be made considering the nature of the proposal, appropriate planning policies and regulations, all legal issues involved, the conditions of the site, and the impacts to the surrounding area.
- Cooperation and coordination among local government jurisdictions focusing on resource lands, water resource allocation, and unique landscape and cultural features should extend to adjacent rural planning areas, and the effort should be supported with legal and financial assistance from state governments.
- On a rational, factual basis rather than a political one, the federal government should assist rural western communities experiencing declining populations by offering planning and infrastructure grants to stabilize growth and to improve economic development consistent with local land use opportunities and priorities. The planning grants should be allocated through the structure of existing communities, regional associations, and cooperative councils of government. The grants should assist in financing federally mandated housing, education, transportation, environmental, health, and safety standards.

The land use planning procedure we propose for the issues facing the West is the rational planning model. This is the accepted institutional planning paradigm—factually based, democratically developed with the help of citizen involvement, articulated and organized by planning practitioners, and approved and implemented by representative local government. The rational plan supports its decision-making procedures by drawing on an extensive geographically organized information base—facts about the land: legal, environmental, social, economic—to develop and effectuate a community vision for the future. Many jurisdictions have realized the advantages of using a computerized geographic information system (GIS) for storing, organizing, analyzing, and mapping these data. Maps generated by GIS are also helpful in educating the public and in soliciting the citizen participation necessary to the planning process (Huxhold and Levinsohn 1995).

In the rational planning model, land use and land management decisions are fiscally evaluated utilizing cost-benefit accounting procedures to evaluate the budgetary impacts of public investments and the long-term revenues to be realized by land development projects. After considering the facts of a proposal and reviewing both the impacts and benefits, a clear rationale can be made for a decision. As a rule, community-wide decisions are made according to a comprehensive set of issue-oriented policies, without bias, by connecting the facts of the situation to the appropriate policies, regulations, and requirements (Alexander 1986).

Due process is the legal hallmark of the rational planning model as it provides a decision-making structure to arrive at conclusions based on the facts of a specific land use case as they apply to a set of appropriate legal requirements (Alexander 1986). The days when land use planning deals were made in the "back room," behind closed doors, by the local power elite are over. The constitutional right to due process provides for transparent decision making and the assurance that open and fair hearings accompany decisions related to major land use changes or issues of community wide interest. The features of due process include: the right to a fair hearing conducted by responsible and accountable community representatives; notice that a hearing will be held; an opportunity to be heard—by those seeking to present evidence and testimony both in favor and in opposition to a particular land use action. The record of the proceedings includes the ultimate decision rendered along with the rationale for it. Finally there is the opportunity for appeal based on reasonable grounds and a timely appeals process.

RURAL PLANNING COOPERATIVES, COMPACTS, AND ASSOCIATIONS

The rational planning model is adaptable to both community and rural planning issues. Rural planning for large areas with low-density populations often requires the cooperation of two or more governmental jurisdictions and most commonly consists of agreements among adjacent cities, towns, and counties. The City and County of Missoula Planning and Development Department is a good example of a relatively simple cooperative planning arrangement. A clear understanding of administrative responsibilities and rules of accountability to each set of elected officials is a necessary feature of such cooperative arrangements, but they offer an efficient use of professional planning and engineering talent, accounting and record keeping, office space, and shared technology. Most important to the rational planning model is the shared use of technological geographic mapping and engineering information services to support decision making and project implementation.

Regional associations of governments and nongovernmental rural cooperatives are also reasonably common across the West. The organizational structure and purpose for regional associations varies with local priority issues. However, formulating cooperative arrangements between private enterprise and public institutions for solving regional problems is a common objective of these organizations. In this regard, a primary function of these organizations is to assist local governments and rural areas by serving as a forum for rationalizing priorities for the use of local, state, and federal funding for projects of regional importance.

Under unique geographic circumstances, a set of common land use and resource issues may extend across state boundaries requiring congressional approval for the creation of bistate compacts. Whereas cooperative arrangements for city-county planning and regional cooperative associations are reasonably common throughout the West, multijurisdictional, bistate agreements such as those exemplified by the Columbia River Gorge National Scenic Area Act (CGC), and the Lake Tahoe Regional Planning Compact, are unique.

The Tahoe Regional Planning Authority (TRPA) operates as a bistate, multijurisdictional agency approved by the U.S. Congress. The Authority is responsible for land use and watershed management within the Lake Tahoe Basin shared by California and Nevada. The objective of the regional compact is to protect the water quality of Lake Tahoe by regulating land use, and controlling runoff and pollution into the lake and its tributary rivers and streams. The Authority is also responsible for monitoring the lake's water quality, enforcing water quality standards, developing a regional management plan and recommending amendments in accordance with water quality findings (TRPC, 1980).

Land use management responsibilities for more than forty miles of the Columbia River corridor are cooperatively shared among two states, six counties, thirteen urban areas, two national forests, and the Bureau of Land Management (BLM), under the authority of the Columbia Gorge National Scenic Area Commission formed in 1986. Incorporated communities in Oregon and Washington retain jurisdictional planning and management authority relative to each state's statutes, but a common set of management rules, intended to preserve scenic beauty and cultural values and to sustain the natural resource amenities of this unique geographic area, apply to unincorporated areas. Federal lands are managed for low-impact recreation use and low intensity timber harvest practices. Residential growth and economic development are expected to take place within existing communities, whereas special management areas allow only low-intensity uses or low-visibility site development on private lands (CGC, P.L. 99-663, 1986).

Regional planning councils are also reasonably common throughout the West, with various planning missions that include economic development planning; securing funding for social, medical, and financial assistance services; and the coordination of a range of federal and state programs for local areas. Increasingly, these councils and associations of governments deal with land and resource issues of importance to their regions. The Uintah Basin Association of Governments in Utah, for example, deals with a diverse set of natural resource, economic, and human resource issues. It serves as a common forum of information exchange among its member jurisdictions and reviews and coordinates state and federal programs pertaining to local government affairs (National Association of Regional Councils [NARC] 2004). The Bear Paw Development Corporation of Northern Montana is a private nonprofit organization whose primary mission is to improve regional economic conditions by coordinating community economic development planning. Bear Paw represents five rural counties and two Native American tribal reservations (NARC 2004). The group is independent of state and federal agencies, and uses its nongovernmental status as a "third party" to negotiate agreements and coordinate and effectuate development project planning between local governments and private entrepreneurs. The Community Planning Association for South West Idaho serves Ada and Canyon Counties and towns and cities of the Boise and Treasure Valley region. Land use and transportation issues are at the top of planning concerns as the association attempts to deal with the consequences of rapid growth and its impacts on agricultural land conversion and air quality (NARC 2004). In summary, the key features of the regional association structure include a technical side: statistical and information services with which to address regionwide issues ranging from economic development to environmental quality. On the social and political side, the associations offer a catalyst for building regional agreements and a forum for local representatives to discuss issues, develop consensus, and set regional priorities.

COMPONENTS OF A LOCAL COMMUNITY PLAN

Comprehensive land use planning is the most commonly used program by local governments to develop a democratically responsible approach to achieving community goals and preserving local character. The local comprehensive plan is made up of several primary elements, but future land use is perhaps the most visible and critically important part of a comprehensive plan, literally as well as figuratively. The future land use planning element should be in map form, clearly marked and illustrated. It should be publicly displayed and referred to as a consistent guide to community growth. The plan thematically displays the patterns of land uses resulting from comprehensive planning efforts. The challenge inherent in the future plan is to bridge the transition from existing land use patterns with those planned for the future. This challenge should not be understated, because most conflicts arise with regard to differences between existing rules and those proposed to achieve future land use (Kelly and Becker 2000). In this regard, future land use patterns should be based on compatibility to reduce conflicts, to protect economic viability, and to enhance livability. The rules and regulations guiding the transition should be perceived as legally correct, fair, and reasonable. Achieving a viable plan relies on the support of citizens and their elected representatives as well as the use of correct, factual information and workable, credible decision-making procedures and implementing ordinances.

In addition to the future plan element, the comprehensive plan is composed of several elements that rationally support it and logically coordinate scheduling and implementation. These planning elements typically include guiding principles and plans for physical development, social advancement, economic advantage, public improvements, citizen participation, and implementation programs. Each of these elements is vitally important, but perhaps most critical to success of the future-oriented concept is the handling of the citizen participation and implementation elements.

Without citizen understanding of, and visible support for, local planning objectives, there is little to sustain community decision making other than the existence of cold, hard rules and regulations. The adoption of a universal list of objectives and standard implementation tools copied from somewhere else not only lacks creativity, it often results in citizen apathy, or worse, hostility toward planning. Certainly, all the state and federal statute requirements, building codes, health and safety regulations, environmental laws, and government responsibilities must follow explicit guidelines, but each community should set its own goals and priorities for development and select appropriate implementation procedures.

Public improvement and capital investment scheduling programs serve to provide timely, efficient, and functional connections to related uses. As we saw in chapter 2, many of the old reasons for separating different uses are no longer valid. The principles of "New Urbanism" offer an effective and powerful alternative to what many now consider to be the obsolete mode of Euclidean zoning. The future demand for different types and densities of community land uses—residential, commercial, industrial, and institutional—is a function of the existing development infrastructure and projections of population and demographics, employment, and economic growth. In concert with the growth policies of the area, adequate land should be available to maintain a stable land market. One of the unanticipated consequences of rapid growth is the greatly increased economic demand for a limited amount of residential land, often resulting in problems of unaffordable housing for local residents. Pro-active land use planning can track actual market conditions and openly discuss proposals and alternatives for community response in a public forum.

Across the West, preservation of wildlife habitat, riparian and wetland corridors, natural resource lands, and scenic features have become of greater public importance. In this regard, complex natural resource information is required to validate local and regional physical and resource program elements for future plans. This is especially critical for planning the future of rural undeveloped lands. Ever since Ian McHarg (1969) first established a method for land suitability analysis using his composite overlay technique in the groundbreaking publication *Design with Nature*, planners have realized that one of the more important responsibilities they are shouldered with is a careful inventory of an area's natural features, including critical wildlife habitat, open space, and scenic properties,

along with wetlands and floodplains, steep slopes, and other potentially hazardous sites where development should be avoided. Methodological advances along
these same lines have been outlined and spelled out in a host of various publications (Marsh 2005; Wheeler 2004; Aberley 1994; Steiner 1991; Simonds 1978).

The use of geographic information mapping systems allows for visual and statistical comparisons on a parcel-by-parcel basis. GIS technology for area-specific
inventory and mapping of natural features, prime farm and forest land, and natural hazards, and for projecting build-out trends has become a necessary tool for
rural as well as urban planning (Maguire, Goodchild, and Rhind 1991).

Transportation routes, sewer lines, and water supply significantly affect future
land use. While most communities provide infrastructure services in response to
demand, a proactive planning strategy would make infrastructure services a lead
feature of any future land use plan, rather than following incremental, random
patterns of new development. This same reasoning applies to the extension and
improvements to rural roads and infrastructure. Improved state and county access
routes have not only improved agricultural commodity transportation, but they
have benefited the low-density residential land market as well. A "development capacity analysis" is useful for anticipating the potential growth of neighborhoods
and serving as a rational guide to capital improvements for roads, gas and electric
utilities, water, and sewage disposal. To have relevance, a development capacity
analysis should be based on an area-by-area analysis of economic, social, and
landscape factors that present realistic opportunities and constraints to development (Todd 1985; De Chira and Koppelman 1984).

Landscape limitations such as elevated, hard rock terrain, excessive slopes, av-
alanche and land slide hazard, flood risks, seasonal wildfire hazard, and groundwater depletion or contamination, considered in the physical planning program
element, are examples of public health and safety that represent constraints to development. It may be economically unreasonable to improve the capacity or to extend services to particular areas based on cost factors. Socially relevant factors are
those that may contribute to the continuation of traditional farming and ranching. Relatively low development capacity is required for the continuation of commercially viable farming in areas of prime cropland, highly productive soils, and
areas with intensive farming infrastructure (Marsh 2005).

The development capacity analysis also provides the rationale for establishing
a geographic transition zone known as the "urban growth boundary (UGB)." The
UGB is the geographic zone of transition between existing city limits and unincorporated rural lands. Generally speaking, the UGB serves to constrain intensive
residential, commercial, and industrial land uses to existing developed areas
where public services can be reasonably provided (Land Conservation and Development Commission [LCDC] 2004). Annexations may be used to formally recognize the need to increase the levels and types of services within the growth
boundary transition area. Rural land uses such as forestry, agriculture, and other

locally important low-intensity uses are designated for areas outside the bound-ary. Coordination among infrastructure providers, especially city-county cooper-ation, is a critical aspect of this planning strategy. Strict adherence to predictable scheduling of improvements is an essential feature of any meaningful future land use planning effort.

In the New West, future plans must take into account the opportunities and challenges offered by large-scale developments such as destination resorts and planned resort communities. It is important to develop policies and procedures that can help with decisions in anticipation of large-scale land developments. There are numerous anecdotes about the "investment broker" from Manhattan who takes his first trip to Montana's Bitterroot Valley, is struck by nature's grandeur, proclaims that it is the perfect place for a destination resort, and pays a very large sum of money for a tract of farm- and ranchland. Once the new owners arrive, they admire the natural wonders, but immediately set to work on "needed improvements"—such as extending the runway of the local airport to accommo-date jet aircraft, requesting local road and drainage improvements, restricting pub-lic access, and fencing off stream corridors. If the vision of a resort-oriented community is agreed to be in the public interest, planning policy can do much to encourage that trend by strategic capital improvements programming and plan-ning for land uses that are compatible with resort activities. If the community vi-sion is otherwise, planning efforts should reflect those priorities.

The West has its share of abandoned industrial or resource-processing sites that adversely affect future land use. Contaminated lands resulting from environ-mental pollution at mine and mineral processing sites, petroleum refineries, and waste storage facilities were until recently considered to be nondevelopable. Statu-tory liability for absolute, mandatory cleanup of the site passed to all future own-ers under the federal Comprehensive Environmental Response, Compensation and Liability Act. However, Congress has since amended the law to focus on the practical removal, containment, and restriction of flows of contaminants from the sites. Under "brown fields" amendments, relief from liability has been granted, at some sites, to future property owners providing that the nature of the contami-nation is understood and considered in a reclamation plan. Community grants for site clearing and cleanup are provided by state and federal governments and offer a reasonable approach to the redevelopment of industrial lands or for parks, recreation areas, and open spaces (Kelly and Becker 2000).

An example of such a cooperative agreement is observed in Casper, Wyoming, where a regional PGA-class golf course has been constructed on a portion of an old petroleum refining site. Cooperative agreements among government jurisdic-tions and private owners offered development incentives that led to not only the clean-up of the site, but intensive remediation and reclamation efforts. Certainly, the potential for each site must be evaluated according to scientific and engineer-ing information and the relative hazard it represents to development, but in many cases opportunities exist for innovative remediation and suitable low-intensity land use development.

Finally, the institutional structure for future land use planning should be based on a cooperative effort among local governments. The costs for planning, regulation, and development are also commonly shared by combining city and county agencies. A shared geographic information system and professional personnel are cost-effective and a necessary part of the rational planning process. Conditions have changed, and so too must the institutional response.

COLLABORATION: A NEW PARADIGM FOR LAND AND RESOURCE PLANNING

Change is also apparent in the way that people are now more willing to come together and work on common solutions that will benefit the entire community. People across the West have become increasingly sophisticated in their perception and awareness of natural resource issues and land use. Most land and resource issues are no longer viewed as single problems to be addressed in isolation. These days, land use is necessarily multidimensional, and resources are viewed as entangled in an indivisible spatial matrix, where overall sense of place has begun to command just as much attention as membership in some categorical user group. No longer can opposing sides hold fast to myopic viewpoints as the only means to achieve the desired ends. Taking an extreme position in the hopes of obtaining an acceptable compromise is no longer an effective strategy. There is finally a recognition that public lands and private lands are part and parcel of the same local ecosystem, that the interwoven web of environmental processes and biotic functioning does not, cannot, adhere to the boundaries circumscribed by an imposed artifice of legal tenure.

Often this new holistic perspective has targeted land and resource planning at the watershed scale, in places such as Idaho's Henry's Fork, where citizens have learned to get involved in decision-making structures by following the model of grassroots ecosystem management (Weber 2003). This is a local, decentralized approach, where human populations closest to the resources and resident within the total environment are recognized as having the greatest stake in how that environment is managed. There is a also a realization among people who have experienced successful solutions to land and resource problems that collaborative rather than confrontational resolution holds the best promise for addressing inevitable future issues among local participants.

CONCLUSION

Frederick Jackson Turner in his famous paper "The Significance of the Frontier in American History" concluded that "up to our own day American history has been to a large degree the colonization of the Great West" (Turner 1920, 1). Written in

1896, that statement summarized an epic story of the American experience. Despite what critical historiography has done to the Turner thesis, and rightly so, we might take that particular statement at face value. The settlement frontier of the nineteenth century presented opportunities for landownership, resource development, and economic and social advancement. The quest for these same opportunities continues to the present day. Increasingly, however, the attraction of the land is related more to scenic amenities and outdoor recreation opportunities than to traditional land settlement activities. The rapid advance of postmodern American settlement systems into the rural West presents a new set of challenges for managing land and resource use. The limited supply of water in the arid regions increasingly results in conflicts among traditional users, environmental systems, and new developments. The best land for traditional agricultural cropping or commercial timber production typically offers the most advantage for high-value residential or commercial development. Scenic environments attract the greatest demand for large-scale residential-recreational developments.

The changing geography of the New West that we have described in this book requires a concurrent development of social policies and institutions relevant to contemporary land use and development challenges. We assert that comprehensive, rational planning offers a locally representative, information-rich, organized approach to resolving potential land and resource conflicts. Today, the quest for individual opportunity needs to be balanced with the same cooperative public spirit that prevailed during the settlement of the West in an earlier era.

REFERENCES

Aberley, Doug, ed. *Futures by Design: The Practice of Ecological Planning*. Gabriola, BC: New Society Publishers, 1994.

Alexander, Ernest R. *Approaches to Planning: Introducing Current Planning Theories, Concepts and Issues*. New York: Gordon and Breach Science Publishers, 1986.

Brick, Philip, Donald Snow, and Sarah van de Wetering, eds. *Across the Great Divide. Explorations in Collaborative Conservation and the American West*. Washington, D.C.: Island Press, 2001.

Brunner, Richard D., Christine H. Colburn, Christina M. Cromley, Roberta A. Klein, and Elizabeth A. Olson. *Finding Common Ground: Governance and Natural Resources in the American West*. New Haven: Yale University Press, 2002.

Calthorpe, Peter, and William Fulton. *The Regional City: Planning for the End of Sprawl*. Washington, D.C.: Island Press, 2001.

Columbia River Gorge National Scenic Area Act (CGC). 1986. Public Law 99-663.

De Chira, Joseph, and Lee E. Koppelman. *Standards for Site Planning*. New York: McGraw Hill, 1984.

Dluhy, Milan, and Kan Chen. *Interdisciplinary Planning: A Perspective for the Future*. New Brunswick, N.J.: Rutgers, The Center for Urban Policy Research, 1986.

Hall, Kenneth B., Jr., and Gerald A. Porterfield. *Community By Design: New Urbanism for Suburbs and Small Communities*. New York: McGraw-Hill, 2001.

Huxhold, William E., and Allan G. Levinsohn. *Managing Geographic Information System Projects*. New York: Oxford University Press, 1995.

Kelly, Eric, and Barbara Becker. *Community Planning: An Introduction to the Comprehensive Plan*. Washington, D.C.: Island Press, 2000.

Land Conservation and Development Commission (LCDC). *Oregon Statewide Planning Goals and Guidelines*. Salem, Ore: LCDC, 2004.

Lapping, Mark B., Thomas L. Daniels, and John W. Keller. *Rural Planning and Development in the United States*. New York: Guilford Press, 1989.

Maguire, David J., Michael F. Goodchild, and David W. Rhind. *Geographical Information Systems: Principles and Applications*. New York: John Wiley & Sons, 1991.

Marsh, William M. *Environmental Analysis for Land Use and Site Planning*. New York: McGraw-Hill, 1978.

———. *Landscape Planning: Environmental Applications*, 4th ed. New York: John Wiley & Sons, 2005.

McHarg, Ian. *Design with Nature*. Garden City, N.J.: Natural History Press, 1969.

National Association of Regional Councils (NARC). 2004. <www.assocregionalcouncils.org>. [accessed December 2004]

Sheridan, Thomas E. Cows, Condos, and the Contested Commons: The Political Ecology of Ranching on the Arizona-Sonora Borderlands. *Human Organization* 60 (2001):141–152.

Simonds, John O. *Earthscape: A Manual of Environmental Planning*. New York: McGraw-Hill, 1978.

Steiner, Frederick. *The Living Landscape: An Ecological Approach to Landscape Planning*. New York: McGraw-Hill, 1991.

Tahoe Regional Planning Compact (TRPA). 1969. Public Law 96-551.

Theobald, David, and N. Thompson Hobbs. Collaborative Development of a Conservation Planning System: A Case Study of Summit County, Colorado. In *Rocky Mountain Futures*, edited by Jill Baron, pp. 255–268. Washington, D.C.: Island Press, 2002.

Todd, Kim W. *Site, Space and Structure*. New York: Van Nostrand Reinhold, 1985.

Tahoe Regional Planning Compact. Public Law 96-551, 1980.

Turner, Frederick Jackson. *The Frontier in American History.* New York: Henry Holt, 1920.

U.S. Bureau of the Census. Special Statistical Report. *National and State Population Estimates.* Washington, D.C.: U.S. Bureau of the Census, 1995.

Van der Ryn, Sim, and Peter Calthorpe. *Sustainable Communities: A New Design Synthesis for Cities, Suburbs, and Towns.* San Francisco: Sierra Club Books, 1986.

Weber, Edward P. *Bringing Society Back In: Grassroots Ecosystem Management, Accountability, and Sustainable Communities.* Cambridge: MIT Press, 2003.

Wheeler, Stephen M. *Planning for Sustainability: Creating Livable, Equitable, and Ecological Communities.* London: Routledge, 2004.

Appendix

The following text has been attributed to John Clarke, former county commissioner from Larimer County, Colorado, and is reprinted here from the Larimer County Planning Department's web site: www.co.larimer.co.us/planning/planning/ code_of_the_west/.

"THE CODE OF THE WEST"

The Code of the West was first chronicled by the famous western writer Zane Grey. The men and women who came to this part of the country during the westward expansion of the United States were bound by an unwritten code of conduct. The values of integrity and self-reliance guided their decisions, actions and interactions. In keeping with that spirit, we offer this information to help the citizens of Larimer County who wish to follow in the footsteps of those rugged individualists by living outside city limits

Introduction

It is important for you to know that life in the country is different from life in the city. County governments are not able to provide the same level of service that city governments provide. To that end, we are providing you with the following information to help you make an educated and informed decision to purchase rural land.

Access

The fact that you can drive to your property does not necessarily guarantee that you, your guests and emergency service vehicles can achieve that same level of access at all times. Please consider:

1.1—Emergency response times (sheriff, fire suppression, medical care, etc.) cannot be guaranteed. Under some extreme conditions, you may find that emergency response is extremely slow and expensive.

1.2—There can be problems with the legal aspects of access, especially if you gain access across property belonging to others. It is wise to obtain legal advice and understand the easements that may be necessary when these types of questions arise.

1.3—You can experience problems with the maintenance and cost of maintenance of your road. Larimer County maintains 1103 miles/1775 kilometers of roads, but many rural properties are served by private and public roads which are maintained by private road associations. There are even some county roads that are not maintained by the county—no grading or snow plowing. There are even some public roads that are not maintained by anyone! Make sure you know what type of maintenance to expect and who will provide that maintenance.

1.4—Extreme weather conditions can destroy roads. It is wise to determine whether or not your road was properly engineered and constructed.

1.5—Many large construction vehicles cannot navigate small, narrow roads. If you plan to build, it is prudent to check out construction access.

1.6—School buses travel only on maintained county roads that have been designated as school bus routes by the school district. You may need to drive your children to the nearest county road so they can get to school.

1.7—In extreme weather, even county maintained roads can become impassable. You may need a four wheel drive vehicle with chains for all four wheels to travel during those episodes, which could last for several days.

1.8—Natural disasters, especially floods, can destroy roads. Larimer County will repair and maintain county roads, however, subdivision roads are the responsibility of the landowners who use those roads. A dry creek bed can become a raging torrent and wash out roads, bridges, and culverts. Residents served by private roads and/or bridges have been hit with large bills for repairs and/or reconstruction after floods.

1.9—Unpaved roads generate dust. When traffic levels reach specific levels, Larimer County treats county system roads to suppress the dust, but dust is still a fact of life for most rural residents.

1.10—If your road is unpaved, it is highly unlikely that Larimer County will pave it in the foreseeable future. Check carefully with the County Road and Bridge Department when any statement is made by the seller of any property that indicates any unpaved roads will be paved!

1.11—Unpaved roads are not always smooth and are often slippery when they are wet. You will experience an increase in vehicle maintenance costs when you regularly travel on rural county roads.

1.12—Mail delivery is not available to all areas of the county. Ask the postmaster to describe the system for your area.

1.13—Newspaper delivery is similarly not always available to rural areas. Check with the newspaper of your choice before assuming you can get delivery.

1.14—Standard parcel and overnight package delivery can be a problem for those who live in the country. Confirm with the service providers as to your status.

1.15—It may be more expensive and time consuming to build a rural residence due to delivery fees and the time required for inspectors to reach your site.

Utility Services
Water, sewer, electric, telephone and other services may be unavailable or may not operate at urban standards. Repairs can often take much longer than in towns and cities. Please review your options from the non-exhaustive list below.

2.1—Telephone communications can be a problem, especially in the mountain areas of Larimer County. From time to time, the only phone service available has been a party line. If you have a private line, it may be difficult to obtain another line for fax or computer modem uses. Even cellular phones will not work in all areas.

2.2—If sewer service is available to your property, it may be expensive to hook into the system. It also may be expensive to maintain the system you use.

2.3—If sewer service is not available, you will need to use an approved septic system or other treatment process. The type of soil you have available for a leach field will be very important in determining the cost and function of your system. Have the system checked by a reliable sanitation firm and ask for assistance from the Larimer County Environmental Health Department.

2.4—If you have access to a supply of treated domestic water, the tap fees can be expensive. You may also find that your monthly cost of service can be costly when compared to municipal systems.

2.5—If you do not have access to a supply of treated domestic water, you will have to locate an alternative supply. The most common method is use of a water well.

Permits for wells are granted by the state engineer and the cost for drilling and pumping can be considerable. The quality and quantity of well water can vary considerably from location to location and from season to season. It is strongly advised that you research this issue very carefully.

2.6—Not all wells can be used for watering of landscaping and/or livestock. Permits from the state engineer may restrict water to use to that which is used inside of a home. If you have other needs, make certain that you have the proper approvals before you invest. It may also be difficult to find enough water to provide for your needs even if you can secure the proper permit.

2.7—Electric service is not available to every area of Larimer County. It is important to determine the proximity of electrical power. It can be very expensive to extend power lines to remote areas.

2.8—It may be necessary to cross property owned by others in order to extend electric service to your property in the most cost efficient manner. It is important to make sure that the proper easements are in place to allow lines to be built to your property.

2.9—Electric power may not be available in two phase and three phase service configurations. If you have special power requirements, it is important to know what level of service can be provided to your property.

2.10—If you are purchasing land with the plan to build at a future date, there is a possibility that electric lines (and other utilities) may not be large enough to accommodate you if others connect during the time you wait to build.

2.11—The cost of electric service is usually divided into a fee to hook into the system and then a monthly charge for energy consumed. It is important to know both costs before making a decision to purchase a specific piece of property.

2.12—Power outages can occur in outlying areas with more frequency than in more developed areas. A loss of electric power can also interrupt your supply of water from a well. You may also lose food in freezers or refrigerators and power outages can cause problems with computers as well. It is important to be able to survive for up to a week in severe cold with no utilities if you live in the country.

2.13—Trash removal can be much more expensive in a rural area than in a city. In some cases, your trash dumpster may be several miles from your home. It is illegal to create your own trash dump, even on your own land. It is good to know the cost for trash removal as you make the decision to move into the country. In some cases, your only option may be to haul your trash to the landfill yourself. Recycling is more difficult because pick-up is not available in most rural areas.

The Property

There are many issues that can affect your property. It is important to research these items before purchasing land.

3.1—Not all lots are buildable. The Larimer County Assessor has many parcels that are separate for the purpose of taxation that are not legal lots in the sense that a building permit will not be issued. You must check with the Larimer County Planning Department to know that a piece of land can be built on.

3.2—Easements may require you to allow construction of roads, power lines, water lines, sewer lines, etc. across your land. There may be easements that are not of record. Check these issues carefully.

3.3—Many property owners do not own the mineral rights under their property. Owners of mineral rights have the ability to change the surface characteristics in order to extract their minerals. It is very important to know what minerals may be located under the land and who owns them. Much of the rural land in Larimer County can be used for mining, however a special review by the county commissioners is usually required. Be aware that adjacent mining uses can expand and cause negative impacts.

3.4—You may be provided with a plat of your property, but unless the land has been surveyed and pins placed by a licensed surveyor, you cannot assume that the plat is accurate.

3.5—Fences that separate properties are often misaligned with the property lines. A survey of the land is the only way to confirm the location of your property lines.

3.6—Many subdivisions and planned unit developments have covenants that limit the use of the property. It is important to obtain a copy of the covenants (or confirm that there are none) and make sure that you can live with those rules. Also, a lack of covenants can cause problems between neighbors.

3.7—Homeowners associations (HOAs) are required to take care of common elements, roads, open space, etc. A dysfunctional homeowners association or poor covenants can cause problems for you and even involve you in expensive litigation.

3.8—Dues are almost always a requirement for those areas with a HOA. The bylaws of the HOA will tell you how the organization operates and how the dues are set.

3.9—The surrounding properties will probably not remain as they are indefinitely. You can check with the Larimer County Planning Division to find out how the properties are zoned and to see what future developments may be in the planning stages. The view from your property may change.

3.10—If you have a ditch running across your property there is a good possibility that the owners of the ditch have the right to come onto your property with heavy equipment to maintain the ditch.

3.11—Water rights that are sold with the property may not give you the right to use the water from any ditches crossing your land without coordinating with a neighbor who also uses the water. Other users may have senior rights to the water that can limit your use or require you to pay for the oversizing or other improving of the ditch.

3.12—It is important to make sure that any water rights you purchase with the land will provide enough water to maintain fruit trees, pastures, gardens or livestock.

3.13—The water flowing in irrigation ditches belongs to someone. You cannot assume that because the water flows across your property, you can use it.

3.14—Flowing water can be a hazard, especially to young children. Before you decide to locate your home near an active ditch, consider the possible danger to your family.

Mother Nature
Residents of the country usually experience more problems when the elements and earth turn unfriendly. Here are some thoughts for you to consider.

4.1—The physical characteristics of your property can be positive and negative. Trees are a wonderful environmental amenity, but can also involve your home in a forest fire. Building at the top of a forested draw should be considered as dangerous as building in a flash flood area. Defensible perimeters are very helpful in protecting buildings from forest fire and inversely can protect the forest from igniting if your house catches on fire. If you start a forest fire, you are responsible for paying for the cost of extinguishing that fire. For further information, you can contact the Larimer County Emergency Services Department.

4.2—Steep slopes can slide in unusually wet weather. Large rocks can also roll down steep slopes and present a great danger to people and property.

4.3—Expansive soils, such as Bentonite Clay (which is common in the foothills) can buckle concrete foundations and twist steel I-beams. You can know the soil conditions on your property if you have a soil test performed.

4.4—North facing slopes or canyons rarely see direct sunlight in the winter. There is a possibility that snow will accumulate and not melt throughout the winter.

4.5—The topography of the land can tell you where the water will go in the case of heavy precipitation. When property owners fill in ravines, they have found that the water that drained through that ravine now drains through their house.

4.6—A flash flood can occur, especially during the summer months, and turn a dry gully into a river. It is wise to take this possibility into consideration when building.

4.7—Spring run-off can cause a very small creek to become a major river. Many residents use sand bags to protect their homes. The county does not provide sandbags, equipment or people to protect private property from flooding.

4.8—Nature can provide you with some wonderful neighbors. Most, such as deer and eagles, are positive additions to the environment. However, even "harmless" animals like deer can cross the road unexpectedly and cause traffic accidents. Rural development encroaches on the traditional habitat of coyotes, bobcats, mountain lions, rattlesnakes, prairie dogs, bears, mosquitoes and other animals that can be dangerous and you need to know how to deal with them. In general, it is best to enjoy wildlife from a distance and know that if you do not handle your pets and trash properly, it could cause problems for you and the wildlife. The Colorado Department of Wildlife and the Larimer County Health Department are two good resources for information. They have many free publications to help educate you about living in the wild.

Agriculture

The people who tamed this wild land brought water to the barren, arid east slope of the Rockies through an ingenious system of water diversion. This water has allowed agriculture to become an important part of our environment. Owning rural land means knowing how to care for it. There are a few things you need to know:

5.1—Farmers often work around the clock, especially during planting and harvest time. Dairy operators sometimes milk without stopping and hay is often swathed or baled at night. It is possible that adjoining agriculture uses can disturb your peace and quiet.

5.2—Land preparation and other operations can cause dust, especially during windy and dry weather.

5.3—Farmers occasionally burn their ditches to keep them clean of debris, weeds and other obstructions. This burning creates smoke that you may find objectionable.

5.4—Chemicals (mainly fertilizers and herbicides) are often used in growing crops. You may be sensitive to these substances and many people actually have severe allergic reactions. Many of these chemicals are applied by airplanes that fly early in the morning.

5.5—Animals and their manure can cause objectionable odors. What else can we say?

5.6—Agriculture is an important business in Larimer County. If you choose to live among the farms and ranches of our rural countryside, do not expect county government to intervene in the normal day-to-day operations of your agri-business neighbors. In fact, Colorado has "Right to Farm" legislation that protects farmers and ranchers from nuisance and liability lawsuits. It enables them to continue producing food and fiber.

5.7—Colorado has an open range law. This means if you do not want cattle, sheep or other livestock on your property, it is your responsibility to fence them out. It is not the responsibility of the rancher to keep his/her livestock off your property.

5.8—Before buying land you should know if it has noxious weeds that may be expensive to control and you may be required to control. Some plants are poisonous to horses and other livestock.

5.9—Animals can be dangerous. Bulls, stallions, rams, boars, etc. can attack human beings. Children need to know that it is not safe to enter pens where animals are kept.

5.10—Much of Larimer County receives less than 15 inches (38 cm) of precipitation per year. As a result, we have a problem with overgrazing, and fugitive dust. Without irrigation, grass does not grow very well. There is a limit to the amount of grazing the land can handle. The Larimer County Cooperative Extension Office can help you with these issues.

In Conclusion

Even though you pay property taxes to the county, the amount of tax collected does not cover the cost of the services provided to rural residents. In general, those living in the cities subsidize the lifestyle of those who live in the country by making up the shortfall between the cost of services and the revenues received from rural dwellers.

This information is by no means exhaustive. There are other issues that you may encounter that we have overlooked and we encourage you to be vigilant in your duties to explore and examine those things that could cause your move to be less than you expect.

We have offered these comments in the sincere hope that it can help you enjoy your decision to reside in the country. It is not our intent to dissuade you, only inform you.

Index

About the Authors

Philip L. Jackson, Ph.D., is professor and program director of geography at the Department of Geosciences, Oregon State University. His specialty is land use, natural resources, and climatology.

Robert Kuhlken, Ph.D., is professor at the Department of Geography and Land Studies, Central Washington University. His specialty is land use and cultural geography.

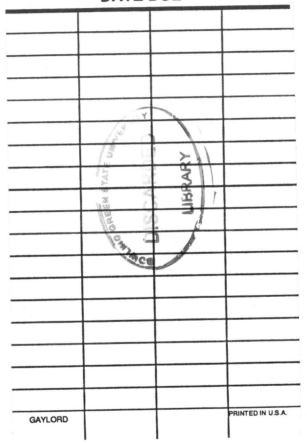